PASS the

CompTIA

Security+

Exam

SY0-501

Hazim Gaber, B.Sc. (ENG), CSSBB, PMP

2

Published By

HSM Press

HSMG Services & Consulting Inc.

34th Floor

10180 101 ST NW

Edmonton, AB T5J 3S4

Canada

Phone: 1-800-716-8955

www.hsmglobal.ca

books@hsmglobal.ca

Foreword

I am delighted to have the opportunity to help you improve your security skills and to obtain the prestigious & internationally-recognized Security+ designation.

This book has been organized to make it easier to absorb and understand the information. I have included practical examples where appropriate.

This is a work in progress. If you have any suggestions to improve this book, or if you see any errors, or if you need help, I would be grateful if you contacted me. My e-mail address is hazim@hsmservices.ca

Visit the Security+ Page at hsmpress.ca/comptia

Regards,

Hazim

March 2020

Table of Contents

Contents

Part A: Introduction

What is the CompTIA Security+?

CompTIA Security+ is an entry level credential for IT Professionals to identify issues and solve problems with computer network security.

CompTIA Security+ allows you to do the following

- Detect security threats
- Install and configure network components that protect critical systems & infrastructure
- Design security network architecture
- Install and configure identity and access systems
- Implement best practices for risk management and business continuity
- Install and configure public key cryptography infrastructure

You should have

- At least two years experience in IT administration and security
- Day-to-day knowledge of technical security information
- Broad knowledge of security threats
- Experience with computer networks

CompTIA overlaps with

- Networking certifications (Cisco CCNA for example)
- Virtualization certifications (VMWare)
- Storage certifications

What can you do with a CompTIA Security+ Certification?

- Security Engineer
- Systems Administrator
- Network Administrator
- Penetration Tester
- Security Consultant

Department of Defense

The US Department of Defense requires security staff and contractors to have active security certifications. That means that you won't be permitted to perform your job without an active certification, even if you have the relevant experience and skills. CompTIA Security+ is considered a valid DoD certification.

CompTIA is "vendor neutral"

According to CompTIA: "All CompTIA certification exams are vendor-neutral. This means each exam covers multiple technologies, without confining the candidate to any one platform. Vendor-neutrality is important because it ensures IT professionals can perform important job tasks in any technology environment. IT professionals with vendor-neutral certifications can consider multiple solutions in their approach to problem-solving, making them more flexible and adaptable than those with training in just one technology."

I decided when writing this book, to keep it vendor-neutral, but to use examples of popular technologies. It is important to understand the theory behind everything, but at the same time, when you are in the field, you will be required to use real software and technology. Sometimes we can't help ourselves. For example, "Group Policy" is one of the topics on the exam, but "Group Policy" is a Microsoft system. Group Policy can't be vendor-neutral.

CompTIA Security+ consists of one 90-minute exam

CompTIA Security+ SY0-501 has been updated in October 2017 by adding:

- Practical and hands on ability to identify real threats

It will probably be updated again in 2020 or 2021

How do I obtain the Security+ Certification?

You must pass the exam, SY0-501. The passing score is 750 (out of a possible score from 100 to 900). The exam is 90 minutes long and contains a maximum of 90 questions. The actual number of questions will depend on the difficulty. If you receive an exam with more difficult questions, there may be fewer questions.

About the Exam

- You can register online to take the exam. The online system will show you the dates and times that are available.

- You may be able to write the exam on a Saturday or Sunday, depending on the Prometric Test Center.
- You may reschedule the exam for free, if you do so at least 30 calendar days before the exam.
- You may reschedule the exam for USD$70, if you do so at least 2 calendar days before the exam.
- You may not reschedule the exam if there are less than 2 calendar days before the exam.
- If you do not show up to the exam or are more than 15 minutes late to the exam, you will not be allowed to write the exam, and will forfeit the entire fee.

- At the exam center, you are required to show a piece of government-issued photo ID.
- You will be required to empty your pockets and place the contents in a locker.
- If you are wearing eyeglasses, they will be inspected.
- You may be checked with a metal detector.
- You can only bring your photo ID and locker key into the exam room.
- The test center will provide you with scratch paper, a pencil, and a basic calculator.

- While you write the exam, you will be monitored via audio and video surveillance.
- Each exam is up to 90 multiple-choice questions, and you have 90 minutes to complete the exam.
- You can take a break at any time, but the time on the exam will continue to elapse.
- It goes without saying that cheating will not be tolerated!

- The questions are
    - Multiple-choice (single, and multiple responses)
    - Drag & Drop
    - Performance Based (you are provided with a scenario, which you must explore; you are required to correct the issue)

About this Book
- The Exam has 6 Main Topics
- We're going to cover each topic in order
- This is the best way because some readers have advanced knowledge and just need to brush up on specific topics, while other people are starting from the very beginning
- Sometimes that won't make sense because we are explaining an advanced concept before explaining a basic concept, but I will explain concepts as necessary
- Keep everything in the back of your mind; you might choose to go back and re-read a section

Sample Performance based Question

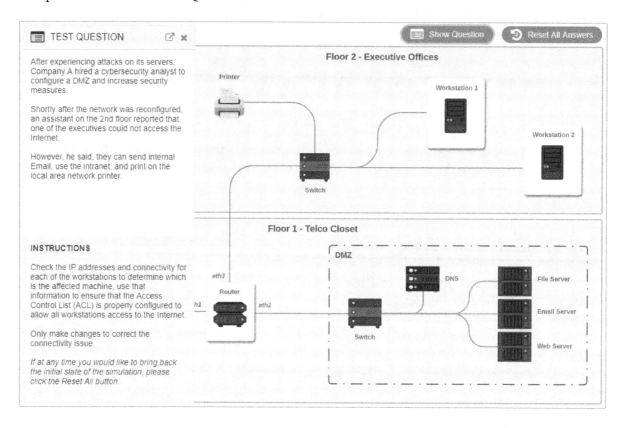

TEST QUESTION

After experiencing attacks on its servers, Company A hired a cybersecurity analyst to configure a DMZ and increase security measures.

Shortly after the network was reconfigured, an assistant on the 2nd floor reported that one of the executives could not access the Internet.

However, he said, they can send internal Email, use the intranet, and print on the local area network printer.

INSTRUCTIONS

Check the IP addresses and connectivity for each of the workstations to determine which is the affected machine, use that information to ensure that the Access Control List (ACL) is properly configured to allow all workstations access to the Internet.

Only make changes to correct the connectivity issue.

If at any time you would like to bring back the initial state of the simulation, please click the Reset All button.

Show Question   Reset All Answers

Floor 2 - Executive Offices

Printer

Workstation 1

Workstation 2

Switch

Floor 1 - Telco Closet

DMZ

eth3

Router

DNS

File Server

h1   eth2

Switch

Email Server

Web Server

Breakdown of SY0-501

Coverage Amount	Coverage Details

Coverage Amount

23%

Coverage Details

1.0 Network Concepts

- Explain the purpose and use of ports and protocols
- Explain devices, applications, protocols and services at their OSI layer
- Explain the concepts and characteristics of routing and switching

18%

2.0 Infrastructure

- Install and configure network components, both hardware and software-based, to support organizational security
- Given a scenario, use appropriate software tools to assess the security posture of an organization
- Given a scenario, troubleshoot common security issues
- Given a scenario, analyze and interpret output from security technologies
- Given a scenario, deploy mobile devices securely
- Given a scenario, implement secure protocols

17%

3.0 Network Operations

- Explain use cases and purposes for frameworks, best practices and secure configuration guides
- Given a scenario, implement secure network architecture
- Given a scenario, implement secure systems design
- Explain the importance of secure staging deployment concepts
- Explain the security implications of embedded systems

- Summarize secure application development and deployment concepts
- Summarize cloud and virtualization concepts
- Explain how resiliency and automation strategies reduce risk
- Explain the importance of physical security controls

20%

4.0 Network Security

- Compare and contrast identity and access management concepts
- Given a scenario, install and configure identity and access services
- Given a scenario, implement identity and access management controls
- Given a scenario, differentiate common account management practices

22%

5.0 Network Troubleshooting and Tools

- Explain the importance of policies, plans and procedures related to organizational security
- Summarize business impact analysis concepts
- Explain risk management processes and concepts
- Given a scenario, follow incident response procedures
- Summarize basic concepts of forensics
- Explain disaster recovery and continuity of operation concepts
- Compare and contrast various types of controls
- Given a scenario, carry out data security and privacy practices

Recommended Tools, Hardware & Software

Every job requires tools, and the Security+ is no different. You won't need the tools for your exam, but you will need them for your job.

I recommend

- Buy high quality tools that will last a long time. Cheap tools are more expensive in the long term. They break down and cause frustration.
- Ask for advice, read reddit reviews, read reviews on Amazon, watch YouTube videos, until you find the tools that are best for you. Ask me!

Recommended Tools, Supplies, & Equipment

Some of these are recommended by CompTIA and some are recommended by me!

Laptops & Smartphones

Apple Tablet/Smartphone
Android Tablet/Smartphone
Windows Tablet/Smartphone

Software

Some of the software may also be incorporated into hardware

Packet Sniffer
Protocol Analyzer
Terminal Emulation Software such as
PuTTy
Linux/Windows OS
Software Firewall
Software IDS/IPS
Network Mapper
Hypervisor Software
Virtual Network Environment
Wi-Fi Analyzer
Spectrum Analyzer
Network Monitoring Tools
DHCP Service
DNS Service
Knowledgebase / Ticket Management
Software such as AutoTask or Service Now
Expliotatin

Equipment

- Layer 2/3 Switch
- Router
- Firewall
- VPN Concentrator
- Wireless Access Point
- Laptop that supports virtualization
- Media Converter
- Configuration Terminal (with Telnet and SSH)
- VoIP System (including a phone)
- SOHO Router/Switch
- Surge Suppressor
- Power Distribution Unit (PDU)
- Uninterruptable Power Supply (UPS)
- Managed Switch
- Hub
- Access Point
- Server
- IDS/IPS
- DLP Appliance

Tools

- RJ-11/RJ-45 Crimper
- Cable tester
- Punchdown Tools with Cutting and Non-Cutting 110, 66, BIX, and Krone Blades
- Cable Stripper
- Coaxial Crimper
- Wire Cutter
- Tone Generator and Probe
- Fiber Termination Kit
- Optical Power Meter
- Butt Set
- Multimeter
- Power Supply Tester
- Screwdriver, Drill, or Screw Gun and Assorted Bits

Spare Parts

Optical and Copper Patch Panels
Punchdown Blocks – 66, 110, and BIX
NICs
Power Supplies
GBICs
SFPs
Patch Cables – cat5e, cat6, fiber
RJ-45 Connectors
RJ-45 Jacks
RJ-11 Connectors
Unshielded Twisted Pair Cable Spool or Box
Coaxial Cable Spool or Box
F-Connectors / BNC Connectors
Fiber Connectors
Antennas
Bluetooth Wireless Adapters
Console Cables and RS-232 to USB Serial Adapter
Rack Screws
Assorted Sheet Metal, Wood, & Drywall Screws
Velcro
Zip Ties
Grounding Cable and Lugs

Some Secret Tools

USB Rubbery Ducky
Wi-Fi Pineapple
Egotistical Giraffe

3DES	Triple Digital Encryption Standard
AAA	Authentication, Authorization, and Accounting
ABAC	Attribute-based Access Control
ACL	Access Control List
AES	Advanced Encryption Standard
AES256	Advanced Encryption Standard 256bit
AH	Authentication Header
ALE	Annualized Loss Expectancy
AP	Access Point
API	Application Programming Interface
APT	Advanced Persistent Threat
ARO	Annualized Rate of Occurrence
ARP	Address Resolution Protocol
ASLR	Address Space Layout Randomization
ASP	Application Service Provider
AUP	Acceptable Use Policy
AV	Antivirus
AV	Asset Value
BAC	Business Availability Center
BCP	Business Continuity Planning
BIA	Business Impact Analysis
BIOS	Basic Input/Output System
BPA	Business Partners Agreement
BPDU	Bridge Protocol Data Unit
BYOD	Bring Your Own Device
CA	Certificate Authority
CAC	Common Access Card
CAN	Controller Area Network
CAPTCHA	Completely Automated Public Turing Test to Tell Computers and Human Apart
CAR	Corrective Action Report
CBC	Cipher Block Chaining
CCMP	Counter-Mode/CBC-Mac Protocol
CCTV	Closed-Circuit Television
CER	Certificate
CER	Cross-Over Error Rate
CERT	Computer Emergency Response Team
CFB	Cipher Feedback
CHAP	Challenge Handshake Authentication Protocol

CIO	Chief Information Officer
CIRT	Computer Incident Response Team
CMS	Content Management System
COOP	Continuity of Operations Plan
COPE	Corporate Owned, Personally Enabled
CP	Contingency Planning
CRC	Cyclic Redundancy Check
RL	Certificate Revocation List
CSIRT	Computer Security Incident Response Team
CSO	Chief Security Officer
CSP	Cloud Service Provider
CSR	Certificate Signing Request
CSRF	Cross-Site Request Forgery
CSU	Channel Service Unit
CTM	Counter-Mode
CTO	Chief Technology Officer
CTR	Counter
CYOD	Choose Your Own Device
DAC	Discretionary Access Control
DBA	Database Administrator
DDoS	Distributed Denial of Service
DEP	Data Execution Prevention
DER	Distinguished Encoding Rules
DES	Digital Encryption Standard
DFIR	Digital Forensics and Investigation Response
DHCP	Dynamic Host Configuration Protocol
DHE	Data-Handling Electronics
DHE	Diffie-Hellman Ephemeral
DLL	Dynamic Link Library
DLP	Data Loss Prevention
DMZ	Demilitarized Zone
DNAT	Destination Network Address Translation
DNS	Domain Name Service (Server)
DoS	Denial of Service
DRP	Disaster Recovery Plan
DSA	Digital Signature Algorithm
DSL	Digital Subscriber Line
DSU	Data Service Unit
EAP	Extensible Authentication Protocol
ECB	Electronic Code Book
ECC	Elliptic Curve Cryptography

ECDHE	Elliptic Curve Diffie-Hellman Ephemeral
ECDSA	Elliptic Curve Digital Signature Algorithm
EFS	Encrypted File System
EMI	Electromagnetic Interference
EMP	Electro Magnetic Pulse
ERP	Enterprise Resource Planning
ESN	Electronic Serial Number
ESP	Encapsulated Security Payload
EF	Exposure Factor
FACL	File System Access Control List
FAR	False Acceptance Rate
FDE	Full Disk Encryption
FRR	False Rejection Rate
FTP	File Transfer Protocol
FTPS	Secured File Transfer Protocol
GCM	Galois Counter Mode
GPG	Gnu Privacy Guard
GPO	Group Policy Object
GPS	Global Positioning System
GPU	Graphic Processing Unit
GRE	Generic Routing Encapsulation
HA	High Availability
HDD	Hard Disk Drive
HIDS	Host-Based Intrusion Detection System
HIPS	Host-Based Intrusion Prevention System
HMAC	Hashed Message Authentication Code
HOTP	HMAC-based One-Time Password
HSM	Hardware Security Module
HTML	Hypertext Markup Language
HTTP	Hypertext Transfer Protocol
HTTPS	Hypertext Transfer Protocol over SSL/TLS
HVAC	Heating, Ventilation and Air Conditioning
IaaS	Infrastructure as a Service
ICMP	Internet Control Message Protocol
ICS	Industrial Control Systems
ID	Identification
IDEA	International Data Encryption Algorithm
IDF	Intermediate Distribution Frame
IdP	Identity Provider
IDS	Intrusion Detection System
IEEE	Institute of Electrical and Electronic Engineers

IIS	Internet Information System
IKE	Internet Key Exchange
IM	Instant Messaging
IMAP4	Internet Message Access Protocol V4
IoT	Internet of Things
IP	Internet Protocol
IPSec	Internet Protocol Security
IR	Incident Response
IR	Infrared
IRC	Internet Relay Chat
IRP	Incident Response Plan
ISA	Interconnection Security Agreement
ISP	Internet Service Provider
ISSO	Information Systems Security Officer
ITCP	IT Contingency Plan
IV	Initialization Vector
KDC	Key Distribution Center
KEK	Key Encryption Key
L2TP	Layer 2 Tunneling Protocol
LAN	Local Area Network
LDAP	Lightweight Directory Access Protocol
LEAP	Lightweight Extensible Authentication Protocol
MaaS	Monitoring as a Service
MAC	Mandatory Access Control
MAC	Media Access Control
MAC	Message Authentication Code
MAN	Metropolitan Area Network
MBR	Master Boot Record
MD5	Message Digest 5
MDF	Main Distribution Frame
MDM	Mobile Device Management
MFA	Multi-Factor Authentication
MFD	Multi-Function Device
MITM	Man-in-the-Middle
MMS	Multimedia Message Service
MOA	Memorandum of Agreement
MOU	Memorandum of Understanding
MPLS	Multi-Protocol Label Switching
MSCHAP	Microsoft Challenge Handshake Authentication Protocol

MTBF	Mean Time Between Failures
MTTF	Mean Time to Failure
MTTR	Mean Time to Recover or Mean Time to Repair
MTU	Maximum Transmission Unit
NAC	Network Access Control
NAT	Network Address Translation
NDA	Non-Disclosure Agreement
NFC	Near Field Communication
NGAC	Next Generation Access Control
NIDS	Network-Based Intrusion Detection System
NIPS	Network-Based Intrusion Prevention System
NIST	National Institute of Standards & Technology
NTFS	New Technology File System
NTLM	New Technology LAN Manager
NTP	Network Time Protocol
OAUTH	Open Authorization
OCSP	Online Certificate Status Protocol
OID	Object Identifier
OS	Operating System
OTA	Over The Air
OVAL	Open Vulnerability Assessment Language
P12	PKCS #12
P2P	Peer to Peer
PaaS	Platform as a Service
PAC	Proxy Auto Configuration
PAM	Pluggable Authentication Modules
PAP	Password Authentication Protocol
PAT	Port Address Translation
PBKDF	Password-Based Key Derivation Function 2
PBX	Private Branch Exchange
PCAP	Packet Capture
PEAP	Protected Extensible Authentication Protocol
PED	Personal Electronic Device
PEM	Privacy-Enhanced Electronic Mail
PFS	Perfect Forward Secrecy
PFX	Personal Exchange Format
PGP	Pretty Good Privacy
PHI	Personal Health Information
PII	Personally Identifiable Information
PIV	Personal Identity Verification
PKI	Public Key Infrastructure

POODLE	Padding Oracle on Downgrade Legacy Encryption
POP	Post Office Protocol
POTS	Plain Old Telephone System
PPP	Point-to-Point Protocol
PPTP	Point-to-Point Tunneling Protocol
PSK	Pre-Shared Key
PTZ	Pan-Tilt-Zoom
RA	Recovery Agent
RA	Registration Authority
RAD	Rapid Application Development
RADIUS	Remote Authentication Dial-In User Server
RAID	Redundant Array of Inexpensive Disks
RAS	Remote Access Server
RAT	Remote Access Trojan
RBAC	Role-Based Access Control
RBAC	Rule-Based Access Control
RC4	Rivest Cipher Version 4
RDP	Remote Desktop Protocol
RFID	Radio Frequency Identifier
RIPEMD	RACE Integrity Primitives Evaluation Message Digest
ROI	Return on Investment
RMF	Risk Management Framework
RPO	Recovery Point Objective
RSA	Rivest, Shamir, & Adleman
RTHB	Remotely Triggered Black Hole
RTO	Recovery Time Objective
RTOS	Real-Time Operating System
RTP	Real-Time Transport Protocol
S/MIME	Secure/Multipurpose Internet Mail Extensions
SaaS	Software as a Service
SAML	Security Assertion Markup Language
SAN	Storage Area Network
SAN	Subject Alternative Name
SCADA	System Control and Data Acquisition
SCAP	Security Content Automation Protocol
SCEP	Simple Certificate Enrollment Protocol
SCP	Secure Copy
SCSI	Small Computer System Interface
SDK	Software Development Kit

SDLC	Software Development Life Cycle
SDLM	Software Development Life Cycle Methodology
SDN	Software Defined Network
SED	Self-Encrypting Drive
SHE	Structured Exception Handler
SFTP	Secured File Transfer Protocol
SHA	Secure Hashing Algorithm
SHTTP	Secure Hypertext Transfer Protocol
SIEM	Security Information and Event Management
SIM	Subscriber Identity Module
SLA	Service Level Agreement
SLE	Single Loss Expectancy
SMB	Server Message Block
SMS	Short Message Service
SMTP	Simple Mail Transfer Protocol
SMTPS	Simple Mail Transfer Protocol Secure
SNMP	Simple Network Management Protocol
SOAP	Simple Object Access Protocol
SoC	System on a Chip
SPF	Sender Policy Framework
SPIM	SPAM over Internet Messaging
SPoE	Single Point of Failure
SQL	Structured Query Language
SRTP	Secure Real-Time Protocol
SSD	Solid State Drive
SSH	Secure Shell
SSID	Service Set Identifier
SSL	Secure Sockets Layer
SSO	Single Sign-On
STP	Shielded Twisted Pair
TACAS+	Terminal Access Controller Access Control System Plus
TCP/IP	Transmission Control Protocol/Internet Protocol
TGT	Ticket Granting Ticket
TKIP	Temporal Key Integrity Protocol
TLS	Transport Layer Security
TOTP	Time-Based One-Time Password
TPM	Trusted Platform Module
TSIG	Transaction Signature
UAT	User Acceptance Testing

UAV	Unmanned Aerial Vehicle
UDP	User Datagram Protocol
UEFI	Unified Extensible Framework Interface
UPS	Unterruptable Power Supply
URI	Uniform Resource Identifier
URL	Universal Resource Locator
USB	Universal Serial Bus
USB OTG	USB On The Go
UTM	Unified Threat Management
UTP	Unshielded Twisted Pair
VDE	Virtual Desktop Environment
VDI	Virtual Desktop Infrastructure
VLAN	Virtual Local Area Network
VLSM	Variable Length Subnet Masking
VM	Virtual Machine
VoIP	Voice Over IP
VPN	Virtual Private Network
VTC	Video Teleconferencing
WAF	Web Application Firewall
WAP	Wireless Access Point
WEP	Wired Equivalent Privacy
WIDS	Wireless Intrusion Detection System
WIPS	Wireless Intrusion Prevention System
WORM	Wire Once Read Many
WPA	Wi-Fi Protected Access
WPA2	Wi-Fi Protected Access 2
WPS	Wi-Fi Protected Setup
WTLS	Wireless TLS
XML	Extensible Markup Language
XOR	Exclusive Or
XSRF	Cross-Site Request Forgery
XSS	Cross-Site Scripting

Part B: SY0-501 1.0 Threats, Attacks and Vulnerabilities

1.1 Given a scenario, analyse indicators of compromise and determine the type of malware

- *Viruses*
- *Crypto-malware*
- *Ransomware*
- *Worm*
- *Trojan*
- *Rootkit*
- *Keylogger*
- *Adware*
- *Spyware*
- *Bots*
- *RAT*
- *Logic Bomb*
- *Backdoor*

What is malware? Malware is a type of application that has an illegitimate intent. There are many types of malware and they can overlap significantly.

Let's be clear. When people think of malware, they think of Windows computer viruses. But in reality, there are many forms of malware that can infect Apple computers, Apple iPhones, and Android smartphones. And there are many forms of malware that infect surveillance cameras, routers, medical devices, and industrial control equipment. If a device contains some kind of "computer" – a component that calculates something or makes decision – then there is ALWAYS a possibility that it could become infected. And if there is a possibility, then somebody out there will find a way.

I don't want to sound pessimistic, but

- Practically every computer has a security flaw or backdoor
- There are many individuals and organizations who do nothing but look for ways to attack computers, either for fun or for profit

Once a system (computer) is infected it should be

- Disconnected from any network (ethernet, Wi-Fi, etc.)
- Reimaged (reload the operating system, applications, and data from a clean back up). Some infections affect the system firmware and can only be cleaned with a hardware replacement.

Viruses

A **virus** is an unauthorized program that causes undesired activity. A virus is not a standalone program, but instead it latches on to another legitimate program. When the legitimate program runs, so does the virus.

Viruses typically infect executable programs such as programs with extensions of .exe. Viruses can also infect documents, such as Microsoft Word documents or Microsoft Excel spreadsheets. These are known as macro viruses. Current versions of Microsoft Office disable macros by default (a user can open a Microsoft Office document file without allowing the macro to execute).

Viruses can enter automatically through backdoors. A user could inadvertently introduce a virus by clicking on attachments or downloading files from the internet.

The damage that a virus does is called the **payload**. Viruses can cause a wide range of effects from being simply a nuisance to deleting files. Viruses that infect industrial control systems can cause millions of dollars in damage. Viruses that infect medical equipment can put lives at risk.

A virus can be detected and prevented using an **antivirus program**. An antivirus program has two methods of detecting viruses

- **Definitions**: A definition is a specific "fingerprint" of the virus. An antivirus program may contain hundreds of thousands of virus definitions. It scans each new file introduced into the computer against the definitions. If the attributes of a file match a definition, then the antivirus program knows that it has located a virus (and knows which virus it has located).

  To develop the antivirus definitions, the antivirus software manufacturer must first obtain copies of the virus and create the definition. That means that some computers have already been infected with the virus by the time the definition has been created. Thus, definitions do not provide complete protection against viruses.

  A **polymorphic virus** is one that attempts to change its code. Each time the virus runs, the code changes slightly, but the damage that it causes remains the same. A polymorphic virus attempts to hide from antivirus definitions.

- **Heuristics**. A heuristic is a type of artificial intelligence. It allows the antivirus program to determine whether a specific program is legitimate or not, based on its behavior. For example, a program that attempts to modify critical system files is likely not legitimate.

  The latest generation antivirus programs share data with the cloud. For example, Norton Antivirus automatically collects data regarding suspicious applications from users. This data is sent to a response center for further analysis. Norton Antivirus then updates all user programs with the results. By sharing data with the cloud, antivirus programs are able to detect viruses faster.

The most famous computer viruses have been

- ILOVEYOU. Released in 2000, ILOVEYOU was transmitted via e-mail with a subject line of "I love you". It overwrote system files and personal files, before spreading through e-mail. It caused $15 billion in damage.
- MyDoom. Similar, to ILOVEYOU, MyDoom spread via e-mail in 2004. It is estimated that 25% of all e-mails sent in 2004 were infected with MyDoom. It caused $38 billion in damage.
- Stuxnet. Stuxnet is a special kind of virus because it infected the firmware of a USB drive. The firmware of a USB drive is not typically accessible to the computer or to an antivirus program – it's considered "read only" memory and allows the USB drive to read/write data from/to the computer.

The Stuxnet virus contained a second virus inside of it. When the USB drive was inserted into a PLC (an industrial control system), the second virus infected the PLC. Stuxnet only infected Siemens S7 PLCs.

Stuxnet was used to infect industrial control systems that were "air gapped" (not connected to the internet or to any network).

Stuxnet was unusual because
  - It took advantage of multiple zero-day exploits (security holes that are unknown to the software manufacturers). A zero-day exploit is considered valuable to a virus manufacturer/hacker, and to use several in the same virus is highly unusual. Zero-day exploits are quickly patched by manufacturers once discovered and can't be reused. A zero-day exploit could be worth up to a million dollars. To use several million dollars worth of zero-day exploits in a virus that brings the creator no financial reward is highly unusual.
  - It limited its infection to only specific types of computers and PLCs. Most virus manufacturers do not want to limit the damage that they cause.
  - It is estimated that Stuxnet took between three man-years and fifteen man-years to prepare. Development of Stuxnet required advanced knowledge of the Windows operating system, USB firmware, and Siemens PLCs.

Crypto-malware

Crypto-malware and **ransomware** are closely related. Crypto-malware is a type of virus or malicious program that encrypts data on a computer.

The malware can be introduced through e-mail or downloaded files. The malware usually encrypts user documents, videos, photos, and music. It does not usually encrypt system files.

The distribution of crypto-malware is usually automated, although people or organizations can be specifically targeted. It should be noted that after the crypto-malware has infected the computer, then the author is able to view the contents of the computer. At that point, he can make an assessment as to how high of a ransom to charge. For example, if an ordinary person was targeted, the ransom might be low, but if a hospital was targeted, then the ransom might be high.

After infection, the computer operates as normal, but the user is provided with a message that their files have been encrypted. The malware usually instructs the user to pay a ransom to unlock the files. The ransom must typically be paid in bitcoin.

There are two types of crypto-malware

- Crypto-malware that pretend to encrypt the files. They change the file extension to something random, but do not encrypt the file. When the extension is changed back to the original, the files revert to normal. These forms of crypto-malware are extremely rare.
- Crypto-malware that encrypt the files. After the files are encrypted, the key is sent to a central server. The user receives the decryption key after paying the ransom. Some forms of crypto-malware do not provide the option to decrypt the files, either because they are misconfigured or because the intention is to prevent a user from accessing his files.

Ransomware

Ransomware is an extension of crypto-malware, in that it instructs the user to pay a ransom in exchange for unlocking the files.

Typically, the user is instructed to visit a TOR website, where they are provided further instructions. TOR websites are generally able to hide their location, although law enforcement agencies have developed methods to identify them. The user is instructed to pay the ransom with cryptocurrency (untraceable currency) such as bitcoin.

In most cases, the hackers provide the victim with the tool to decrypt their files upon receipt of payment. In some cases, the hackers do not.

The ransom amounts have ranged from the equivalent of $500 to $20,000 depending on the person or organization that was affected. Many organizations pay the ransom and don't publicly admit that they have been hacked.

How to prevent ransomware

- Proper user education to teach users how to identify potential ransomware delivered via e-mail, and to not open unusual attachments.
- Block e-mail attachments that contain macro-enabled Microsoft Word and Excel documents.
- Regularly install Windows operating system security updates

How to defeat ransomware once infected

- Attempt to restore data from backup or from the Volume Shadow Copy. This only works if the organization has backed up their data, and only the data that was backed up can be restored. This is not effective against newer versions of ransomware, which delete the Volume Shadow Copy.
- Attempt to decrypt the ransomware. Police forces in the EU have been able to provide victims with assistance in decrypting some forms of ransomware. Some versions of ransomware use weak encryption that can be broken through brute force or other techniques.
- Pay the ransom. In earlier cases, it was almost certain that the hackers would automatically (or manually) provide the decryption key upon payment of the ransom. In more recent cases, this is not guaranteed because there are many copycat ransomware viruses created by people with very little knowledge or infrastructure. Ransomware developers have franchised their operation to "script kiddies" who are simply distributing the ransomware and collecting payments. There are also versions of ransomware that have been put out by nation-states to cause political disruption; this type of malware only destroys data but is disguised as ransomware.

Notable infections

- In 2019, Jackson County, Georgia paid $400,000 to remove ransomware from their computers.
- University of Calgary paid $20,000 to decrypt computers infected by ransomware in 2017. The FBI later charged two people in Iran with spreading the virus, which infected computers at health care providers and other organizations.

Notable ransomware

- CryptoLocker was transmitted over e-mail as a ZIP file. Inside the e-mail was an executable disguised as a PDF. The decryption key was sent to a remote server. A victim could pay a ransom and receive a decryption key automatically. The creators of CrytoLocker made an estimated $27 million. In 2014, security firm FireEye was able to obtain the database of decryption keys, allowing victims to decrypt their files for free.
- WannaCry took advantage of a zero-day exploit in the Windows Server Message Block. WannaCry infected computers that had not patched the Windows Server Message Block vulnerability. The average ransom amount was $600. Over 200,000 computers were infected, with losses estimated at over $4 billion.
- Unlike other forms of ransomware, Petya encrypted the master boot record of a Windows computer. This caused the entire computer hard drive to be encrypted. Another version, known as NotPetya was targeted towards Ukrainian government entities and critical infrastructure. NotPetya quickly spread to other computers worldwide and could not be decrypted. It is believed that NotPetya was created by the Russian government.

Worm

The difference between a **worm** and a virus is that the worm replicates by itself, whereas the virus must attach itself to a legitimate file. The virus only runs when the legitimate file runs.

Worms can generally spread over a network from computer to computer, by themselves. They take advantage of security holes.

Examples of worms

- SQL Slammer took advantage of a buffer overflow bug in Microsoft SQL Server. The worm would randomly generate IP addresses and then send itself to those IP addresses. If the IP addresses belonged to computers that were running an unpatched version of SQL Server, then the worm would be successful in infecting them. The worm caused many internet routers to crash, and reboot. Each time the routers rebooted, they would resend routing updates to each other, which would cause internet traffic congestion. SQL Slammer was exceptional in that it fit inside a single data packet.

Trojan

A **trojan** is a legitimate program that hides an illegitimate program. A user must install the trojan and/or give it permission before it can take effect. Trojan is named after the Trojan horse.

Trojans can hide in many programs including toolbars, screensavers, games, and other applications.

Examples of Trojans

- FinFisher (FinSpy), which is developed by Lench IT Solutions plc. This trojan is used to infect Windows computers and all brands of phones. It travels through e-mail, links, and security flaws in popular programs. Many antivirus programs are unable to detect it.

  FinFisher is sold to law enforcement agencies and dictatorships, some of which are accused of numerous human rights violations.

Rootkit

A **rootkit** provides unauthorized administrative level access to a computer by changing its operating system and attempting to bypass its security functions.

There are five types of rootkits

- **Firmware**. A firmware rootkit hides inside the device firmware (such as the BIOS, video card controller, router, network card, or hard drive controller). The device firmware is not typically scanned by (and is out of reach of) antivirus programs. While manufacturers such as HP have introduced BIOS integrity features that check for changes to the BIOS firmware, rootkits can infect other components such as the graphics card or hard drive.

- **Virtual**. A virtual rootkit is also known as a hypervisor rootkit. It operates between the processor and the operating system. It intercepts calls made by the operating system, like a "man-in-the-middle" attack. The result is that the processor believes that it is talking to the operating system and the operating system believes that it is taking to the processor, but, both are talking to the rootkit. The rootkit sends everything it learns to a central server.

- **Kernel**. A kernel rootkit runs on a computer with the highest privileges (the same privileges as the operating system) by replacing parts of the operating system core and device drivers. A kernel rootkit can't be detected by an antivirus program because the rootkit is acting like part of the legitimate operating system.

- **Library**. A library level rootkit replaces legitimate operating system DLLs with fake ones. A library is a set of code/functions that an application can reference (a software developer will include different DLLs with their application so that they don't have to rewrite thousands of lines of code). When an application references code in an infected DLL, the rootkit will also run.

- **Application Level**. An application level rootkit replaces application files with fake versions. The application may need to run at an elevated level in order to cause damage.

Examples of rootkits

- LoJack. LoJack is a legitimate rootkit that comes preinstalled in the BIOS of some laptops. If the laptop is lost or stolen and later connected to the internet, LoJack will report the location of the laptop to a server. LoJack is designed to remain on the laptop even if its hard disk drive is erased or replaced.

- Sony BMG. In 2005, Sony installed a rootkit known as XCP (Extended Copy Protection) on music CD's that it released. When users attempted to play the CD's through their computer, the rootkit created security vulnerabilities. The intention of the rootkit was to prevent people from copying music off the CD's, but the rootkit created security holes and hid in the background.

Sony was forced to recall all unsold music CDs and faced multiple class-action lawsuits.

Keylogger

A **keylogger** records each key that a user presses. It may also take screenshots, activate the webcam, or activate the microphone without the knowledge or consent of the user.

The keylogger reports all data back to a central source or records the data on the computer for further retrieval. Data may be sent via

- Email
- FTP
- Wireless/Bluetooth to a nearby receiver

A keylogger may have legitimate purposes if installed by an employer or law enforcement agency. Some antivirus programs will detect keyloggers created by law enforcement and some will deliberately ignore them.

A keylogger may be used to invade the privacy of another person (stalking) or it may be used for financial gain (the logged data is analysed to obtain online banking passwords, e-mail passwords, etc.).

The keylogger may be introduced into a system through another type of malware such as a virus or trojan.

Whether the keylogger can be detected by an antivirus program depends on where it runs. Keyloggers that run in the operating system kernel or through a hypervisor may be undetectable.

Keyloggers can also be hardware-based

- Keyboard keylogger device (USB device that sits between the keyboard cable and the computer). A keyboard's circuitry can be covertly modified to include a keylogger.
- Wireless keyboard sniffer (device that can intercept signals between a wireless keyboard and the dongle; this device functions when the connection is not encrypted or where the encryption method can be easily broken)

How to prevent keyloggers

- It is difficult, if not impossible to detect a hardware based keylogger, especially one that is embedded into the device circuitry. Keeping computer hardware physically secure is the best defense. In addition, the use of multi-factor authentication methods can keep accounts secure even when the usernames and passwords are compromised.
- Most software-based keyloggers are detectable by antivirus programs. Some software-based keyloggers that take advantage of zero-day exploits or that operate on the firmware, kernel, or hypervisor level cannot be detected.

Adware

Adware is software that shows advertisements. The advertisements may appear as pop-ups, videos, or audio. Adware may be included in legitimate software programs such as games, music applications, or other applications. Typically, adware is bundled with low-quality applications. The advertisements are also of low quality as most legitimate advertisers do not want to be associated with this type of exploitation.

Adware can also be installed without the user's consent when introduced as part of a computer virus or trojan.

Adware can hijack legitimate website advertisements. When a user visits a legitimate website, the adware swaps advertisements placed by the website owner with advertisements sold by the adware publisher. Thus, the revenue from the advertisements is diverted to the adware publisher without the knowledge of the user or website owner.

It may be difficult or impossible to remove adware. Adware may spy on a user's activity or browsing history. The adware publisher may sell this data to market research firms or use it to show the user more relevant advertising.

It is illegal to install or distribute adware without the consent of the user. In addition, the user must have an opportunity to remove the adware. There is no specific anti-adware law, but Section 5 of the Federal Trade Commission Act prohibits "unfair or deceptive acts". The Federal Trade Commission (FTC) is empowered to commence civil actions against publishers who distribute adware.

Spyware

Spyware is software that spies on a user's activity. Spyware can include keyloggers but can also include components that take screenshots or videos, activate the webcam or microphone, and/or copy files.

The distribution of spyware can be prosecuted under the Computer Fraud & Abuse Act, as further discussed in this book. It can be further prosecuted under harassment and stalking laws if the behavior amounts to such.

Bots

A **bot** is a computer that is under the control of another program or user. A bot is not a form of malware, but malware can be used to take control of a computer.

A group of bots is known as a botnet. A malicious botnet operator will distribute viruses that infect computers and take control of them. Each of these computers becomes a bot, and together they are a botnet. The botnet can remain dormant when not in use. The operator will then license or sell the capacity of the botnet to other criminals for use in attacks.

Bots are typically used for Distributed Denial of Service Attacks, and bitcoin mining.

Recently, hackers have been infecting IP cameras and routers and adding them to their botnets.

Examples of bots

- Mirai. Most web-accessible routers and IP cameras come preconfigured with default usernames and passwords. Most home users of routers and IP cameras neglect to change the default usernames/passwords (in some cases, it is impossible to change the default username/password).

  Mirai scanned IP addresses at random and located web-accessible routers and IP cameras. It then attempted to log in using default usernames/passwords. Once successful, it infected the devices. Once infected, the devices are added to the botnet and used to launch attacks.

RAT

A **RAT** (**Remote Access Trojan**) allows a hacker to gain remote access to a system. A RAT can be introduced through a virus or trojan.

There are many legitimate remote access programs, including TeamViewer, Bomgar, and LogMeIn. These programs typically do not hide their existence or operation to the legitimate user, but they can be hijacked by malicious users.

Logic Bomb

A **logic bomb** is a program that is installed by a legitimate user. The logic bomb appears to be legitimate. The logic bomb remains dormant until activated by a specific date/time or event. In Windows, the logic bomb can be programmed to activate in the Event Scheduler.

The logic bomb can steal data, delete data, or cause other harmful actions. Logic bombs are commonly installed by disgruntled system administrators. After the system administrator is fired or quits, the logic bomb activates and damages the company's systems.

Backdoor

A **backdoor** is a method for accessing a system illegitimately. A backdoor could be a remote access trojan, remote software, or a hard-coded username/password in an application. While a backdoor could be a legitimate tool implemented by a software developer, once discovered, system security would be greatly compromised.

The government has advocated implementing backdoors in encryption technologies that only they can access. This is always a terrible idea because a backdoor can be exploited by an unauthorized third party. A technology that is advertised as being secure should always be secure from everybody.

Laws Relevant to Malware

In the United States, all distribution of malware falls under the **Computer Fraud & Abuse Act** (18 U.S. Code § 1030). This broad law covers most forms of computer abuse.

Specifically, section (5) states that whoever "knowingly causes the transmission of a program, information, code, or command, and as a result of such conduct, intentionally causes damage without authorization, to a protected computer; "can be punished by imprisonment for up to ten years.

Note that the term "protected computer" is defined as

- any computer that is used by a financial institution of the United States,
- any computer that is used by the United States government, or
- a computer "which is used in or affecting interstate or foreign commerce or communication, including a computer located outside the United States that is used in a manner that affects interstate or foreign commerce or communication of the United States;

The federal government's jurisdiction is limited to matters that affect financial institutions, the federal government, or interstate/foreign commerce. The federal government does not have jurisdiction over crimes that occur within a single state (unless they involve a federal subject matter).

But note the following:

- Due to the nature of the internet, some data will almost always travel between different states, even if the hacker and the victim are in the same state. Thus, most computer crimes fall under federal jurisdiction and can be prosecuted by the federal government.
- In addition, Courts have held that provided the computer is "connected to the internet", then it falls under the definition of "interstate or foreign commerce", even if there was no proof that the Defendant used the computer to access the internet or used the internet to access the computer.
- State and local governments typically don't have the resources or experience to investigate/prosecute complex computer crimes and will refer such cases to the FBI.
- An "air gapped" computer (one that is not connected to the internet, such as a control system for a power plant or industrial facility) can fall under the jurisdiction of the CFAA provided that it affects "interstate or foreign commerce".

The Defendant must

- Access the computer "without authorization"; or
  - Most courts have held that authorization is valid until it is revoked by the issuing party
  - A few courts have held that authorization could be considered invalid when the Defendant accesses the computer in a manner contrary to the interests of the authorizing party

- "Exceed authorized access"
  - The authorizing party has prohibited the Defendant from accessing the computer for a specific purpose
  - The authorizing party did not expressly prohibit the Defendant from accessing the computer, but the Defendant acted contrary to the authorizing party's interests

In general, Courts have drawn a distinction between accessing a computer without authorization (applies to outsiders) and exceeding authorized access (applies to insiders).

18 U.S.C. § 1030(a)(2) applies to keyloggers and other forms of spyware, if the Defendant

- Intentionally accesses a computer without authorization; and
  - Access must be intentional
- Obtains "information" from "any protected computer"
  - Information can be obtained even if the Defendant did not copy or download a file

18 U.S.C. § 1030(a)(5) applies to acts that damage a computer system or information

It is a felony to damage a computer system or information if

- A loss of $5000 or more results
- The medical care of a person is modified
- Physical injury is caused
- Public health or safety is affected
- Systems used by the government for justice or national security are affected; or
- Ten or more computers are damaged within a one-year period

Damage can occur

- When the act impairs the integrity of the data (such as when the data is deleted or changed)
- When the act affects the availability of the data (such as in a denial of service attack that brings a website offline)
- When the victim must investigate to determine if the data bas been damaged (even if it is determined later that no files have been changed)

The loss amount can include

- Cost to any victim
- Cost of investigating the security breach
- Cost of restoring the data and/or repairing the systems
- Lost revenue

1.2 Compare and contrast types of attacks

- *Social Engineering*
  - *Phishing*
  - *Spear Phishing*
  - *Whaling*
  - *Vishing*
  - *Tailgaiting*
  - *Impersonation*
  - *Dumpster Diving*
  - *Shoulder Surfing*
  - *Hoax*
  - *Watering Hole Attack*
  - *Principles (Reasons for Effectiveness)*
    - *Authority*
    - *Intimidation*
    - *Consensus*
    - *Scarcity*
    - *Familiarity*
    - *Trust*
    - *Urgency*
  - *Application/Service Attacks*
    - *DoS*
    - *DDoS*
    - *Man-in-the-Middle*
    - *Buffer Overflow*
    - *Injection*
    - *Cross-Site Scripting*
    - *Cross-Site Request Forgery*
    - *Privilege Escalation*
    - *ARP Poisoning*
    - *Amplification*
    - *DNS Poisoning*
    - *Domain Hijacking*
    - *Main-in-the-Browser*
    - *Zero Day*
    - *Replay*
    - *Pass the Hash*
    - *Hijacking and Related Attacks*
      - *Clickjacking*

- - - *Session Hijacking*
    - *URL Hijacking*
    - *Typo Squatting*
  - *Driver Manipulation*
    - *Shimming*
    - *Refactoring*
  - *MAC Spoofing*
  - *IP Spoofing*
- *Wireless Attacks*
  - *Replay*
  - *IV*
  - *Evil Twin*
  - *Rogue AP*
  - *Jamming*
  - *WPS*
  - *Bluejacking*
  - *Bluesnarfing*
  - *RFID*
  - *NFC*
  - *Disassociation*
- *Cryptographic Attacks*
  - *Birthday*
  - *Known Plain Text/Cipher Text*
  - *Rainbow Tables*
  - *Dictionary*
  - *Brute Force*
    - *Online vs Offline*
  - *Collision*
  - *Downgrade*
  - *Replay*
  - *Weak Implementations*

Social Engineering

Social engineering is the attempt to use psychological methods to manipulate individuals into providing confidential information or access to systems.

Unlike malware, social engineering relies on human emotion
- Wanting to be liked
- Fear
- Wanting to help
- Intimidation
- Familiarity
- Hostility

A good book on social engineering is *Social Engineering: The Art of Human Hacking* by Christopher Hadnagy.

Phishing

Phishing is the attempt to obtain sensitive data by pretending to be a trusted entity. Phishing usually occurs through e-mail or telephone. Phishing is usually sent as a mass e-mail to thousands or millions of people.

Typically, a user will receive an e-mail asking them to sign in to their bank account or other account (PayPal, eBay, Amazon). The e-mail is fake, and the website that the e-mail leads to is fake (but appears to be real).

Typical phishing e-mails will say
- Your account has been compromised and you must log in to correct the issue
- Your account will be suspended if you don't log in
- You have received a large payment (Interac eTransfer) and you must log in to accept the money

The hacker may register a domain that looks like the legitimate one. For example, the user may register www.paypa1.com instead of www.paypal.com. Or the hacker may register a domain that is completely unrelated to the original website and attach a subdomain that looks like the legitimate site. For example, the hacker registers fakewebsite.com and attaches the "www.paypal" subdomain to it, making www.paypal.com.fakewebsite.com. The users will see the first part of the URL "www.paypal.com" and think they are on a legitimate site, even though the user's browser went to fakewebsite.com.

Update Required!!

Recently, there's been activity in your PayPal account that seems unusual compared to your normal account activities. Please log in to PayPal to confirm your identity.

This is part of our security process and helps ensure that PayPal continue to be safer way to buy online. Often all we need is a bit more information. While your account is limited, some options in your account won't be available.
How to remove my limitation?
You can resolve your limitation by following these simple steps:

- **Log in here.**

- Provide the information needed. The sooner your provide the information we need, the sooner we can resolve the situation.

"If this message sent as Junk or Spam, its just an error by our new system, please click at Not Junk or Not Spam"

Sincerely,

PayPal

How do we prevent phishing?
- Proper user education to identify suspicious e-mails.
  - Knowledge that legitimate e-mails from banks and other sites will contain the user's full name while phishing e-mails will not (unless the sender has access to the user's data)
  - Phishing e-mails and/or websites may (but not always) contain poor grammar or spelling
  - Phishing websites will not contain the correct URL. Users should always check that they have visited the correct URL.
- Automated systems that detect and filter phishing e-mails. These systems are built into most web browsers and e-mail systems and verify that the e-mails originated from legitimate sources and that the websites are legitimate.

Spear Phishing

Spear Phishing is like phishing, but it targets specific groups or people. The more precise the targeting, the higher the response rate.

A normal phishing attack could target millions of users. For example,

- A hacker could send a fake e-mail appearing to be from Bank of America to 1,000,000 e-mail addresses
- From those 1,000,000 addresses, only 250,000 might work
- The SPAM filter would block 200,000 from those 250,000
- From the 50,000 only 10,000 might have accounts at Bank of America
- 80% of those users might be smart enough to detect the phishing scam, in which case only 2,000 people respond
- The attack is shut down early on, and many users are unable to respond, so the hackers only collect data from 500 users
- The success rate is about 0.005%. Although it is low, the return on investment might be high. It may cost the hackers a few hundred dollars out the e-mail, but they might be able to collect at least $100 from each user (for a total of $50,000).

In spear phishing, the hackers identify specific customers of Bank of America for example. They may use a list stolen from the bank. The hackers customize the e-mail to include the name and other personally identifying information of each recipient. As a result, the SPAM filter will be less likely to identify the e-mail as SPAM, and the user will be more likely to respond.

Whaling

Whaling is like Phishing, but targets high-value individuals such as celebrities, CEOs or other executives. Whaling is specifically targeted to the high-value individual. Whaling takes more effort to execute, but the response rate is higher, and the amount of money stolen from each user is higher. Many high-net worth individuals have access to credit cards with high limits.

Another scheme involves a scammer visiting a store such as Best Buy and attempting to illegally purchase expensive electronics in the name of a celebrity on credit. The scammer disappears with the electronics and the store is never paid. The store should have verified that the buyer legitimately represents the celebrity.

How do we prevent whaling?
- Proper user education
- 100% identity verification of the person who is seeking information.
- A high-net worth individual should understand that he is at much higher risk of exploitation either through fraud or extortion schemes. This person should employ people who specialize in detecting and preventing these threats.

Vishing

Vishing is like Phishing but uses the telephone (VoIP) network. The thieves will place phone calls that appear to come from legitimate entities such as the IRS, a bank, or a credit card company. The thieves will attempt to obtain sensitive data such as credit card numbers or bank account numbers.

Common features
- The scammer will threaten the victim with legal action or arrest if they do not comply
- The scammer will ask the victim to purchase gift cards from a store and send them the numbers
- The scammer will speak with a foreign accent or bad grammar

How to Prevent?
- If a user receives a telephone call from somebody who is seeking sensitive information, they should
    - Verify that the number is in fact legitimate
    - Hang up and call the number back (as caller IDs can be spoofed)
    - Verify that the caller will require the information (for example a bank will never ask a client for his/her PIN)
    - Provide the required information through the legitimate online website of the purported requester (such as IRS.gov)

Tailgaiting

Tailgaiting is an attempt to obtain unauthorized access to a physical facility.

Many offices, industrial facilities, and data centers are controlled via electronic proximity card and/or biometric locks. When a legitimate user unlocks an entrance with their access card and/or biometric lock, an intruder can follow them into the building. Tailgaiting works because

- A person might hold the door open for a person who is walking behind him (doing otherwise might be considered rude)
- A person might not wait to verify that the door closed and locked behind him, and another person might follow him. The door lock might not work properly, in which case the door does not fully close.

How to prevent

- Proper user education to enforce the use of access cards and prohibit tailgating. Users should know that not holding the door is not considered rude.

- Install a security guard at each entrance or monitor entrances with security cameras
- In more extreme cases, installation of man trap doors might be necessary. A man trap door allows only one person to enter at a time. The man trap door contains cameras with artificial intelligence to detect the number of people inside and permits entry to only one individual at a time.

Impersonation

Impersonation is acting like another person. The thief will pretend to be a person known to the victim (or employed in a position known to the victim), and steal information from the victim through trickery.

Impersonation can occur via e-mail, telephone, or in person.

The type of impersonation
- IT help desk person (the thief acts like a member of the IT help desk and calls the victim asking for access to the computer or access to some information that the victim possesses)
- Manager/CEO (the thief acts like a member of senior management and uses their position of authority to obtain information)
- Co-Worker (the thief acts like a co-worker, and uses their friendship to obtain information)
- Government Official/Law Enforcement (the thief acts like a member of law enforcement and uses threats or intimidation to obtain information)
- Contractor/Janitor (the thief acts like a contractor and obtains unauthorized access to the building and then steals information)

The thief will normally have obtained information that the victim will know (information about a project, co-worker, manager, etc.). By name-dropping and information-dropping, the thief will appear legitimate to the victim.

How to prevent
- Proper user education.
- Ensure that a user verifies the ID of each person they interact with (if not known personally) before providing any information. The company should foster a culture where verifying the identity of another employee (even that of a senior manager) is encouraged and not considered rude.
- 100% identification verification of each contractor requiring access to the building or to the customer's system.

Dumpster Diving

Dumpster Diving involves searching the garbage of a target. Individuals frequently throw out documents, USB drives, computer hard drives, and other items containing sensitive information.

Dumpster Diving is not necessarily illegal because items are considered public property/abandoned once put in the trash. Police and private investigators also use Dumpster Diving to collect evidence. If the dumpster is located on private property, it may be considered trespassing.

A company that is suspects it is being spied on might consider filling the dumpster with fake documents or with USB drives that are full of malware. This could serve to trick the enemy or identify them.

Dumpster Diving can occur within an office. For example, an office worker put sensitive papers into a trash can in his office during the day. These are later collected and stolen by a contracted janitor in the evening.

How to prevent
- Shred all sensitive documents before disposing of them. Use a cross-cut shredder. Vertical shreds can be put back together.
- There are multiple directives for shredding sensitive documents and computer storage components including DoD 5220.22. The type of shredding (the size of the shreds) depends on the sensitivity of the information; the more sensitive the information, the smaller the shreds.
- Require all employees to maintain a clean desk. All sensitive documents must be locked before the employee leaves for the day.

Shoulder Surfing

Shoulder Surfing is when a thief looks over the shoulder of a victim. Shoulder surfing can occur at a computer or at an ATM. The thief may watch the screen or the keyboard.

Shoulder surfing happens at offices, in airports, and on public transportation.

How to prevent
- Install shields at ATMs and debit/credit card terminals
- Install privacy screens on computers/laptops.
- If using a laptop on an airplane or other public place, the user should avoid doing anything sensitive and/or be wary of his/her neighbors/surroundings.

Hoax

A **hoax** is a fake threat. A user might respond to the hoax in a way that weakens security. A hoax might take the form of a

- Death of an important person
- Impending attack/war
- Adverse weather/tornado
- Potential security threat

Watering Hole Attack

In a **watering hole attack**, a thief plants a form of malware on a frequently visited website. The users visit the website and download the malware.

A watering hole attack typically takes advantage of a zero-day exploit. It allows malware to download in the background without any indication to the user.

How to prevent
- Proper antivirus can prevent many watering hole attacks
- Website operators should ensure that their servers and code are up to date
- Watering hole attacks that take advantage of zero-day exploits cannot be prevented

Principles (Reasons for Effectiveness)

Why do social engineering attempts work? There are many reasons.

- **Authority**
    - The person on the other end of the phone call/in person acts with authority. People are afraid to challenge those who appear to be in a position of authority (such as members of senior management).
    - Authority can be established by confidence, tone of voice, clothing, and/or uniforms.
    - People are afraid to challenge authority because of perceived negative consequences (getting fired)
    - The consequences do not have to be explicitly stated by the thief. They can be implied, or the user might simply assume what they are based on the alleged authority.
    - Social engineering authority attacks can be prevented by enforcing policy against all users, regardless of their position. The company must create a culture where verifying the identity of another person is encouraged, regardless of that person's position.
    - For example, the thief could pretend to be a member of senior management and convince the victim that she could lose her job if she does not comply. The thief could demand that the victim provide him with corporate financial information, or wire money to a third party.

- **Intimidation**
    - Intimidation uses the threat or idea of negative consequences if the person fails to comply.
    - The thief does not have to make any direct threats, but instead may cause the victim to believe that negative consequences will occur (or the victim may assume that negative consequences will occur if they fail to comply).
    - For example, the thief could pretend to be a police officer and convince the victim that she will be arrested if she does not comply. The thief demands that the victim disclose sensitive data relevant to an investigation.

- **Consensus**
    - Consensus involves a group-decision.
    - If a social engineer is unable to convince a specific person to perform an action, he could attempt to convince others in that person's social circle. Those other people could convince the victim to proceed.
    - For example, the thief could convince the victim that her co-workers completed the same action.

- **Scarcity**
    - Scarcity means that something is unavailable or in limited supply.
    - If the victim values something that is scarce, they may forgo normal procedures and fall into the trap to obtain that item.
    - For example, the victim wants a rare (sold out) toy at Christmas time. The thief convinces her that he can supply the toy if she provides him with her credit card/banking information (which he uses fraudulently). The victim never receives the toy.

- **Familiarity**
    - The victim feels familiar with the situation and proceeds because nothing seems out of place.
    - The thief can convince the victim to focus on ideas that are familiar, by dropping names, projects, or other tasks into the conversation.
    - Although the victim does not know the thief, she is led to believe that he is a legitimate co-worker.

- **Trust**
    - The victim trusts the thief and proceeds with their own free will.
    - The victim believes that the person they are talking to or the site that they have visited is legitimate.
    - The thief may take time to build this trust, especially with a high-value target. The greater the victim trusts the thief, the more the victim will be willing to do.

- **Urgency**
    - Urgency is like scarcity
    - Urgency builds on the idea that there is a limited time to act.
    - People hate losing money more than they hate not making money.
    - For example, the victim could be told that money is about to be withdrawn from their bank account and they only have a few minutes to stop it (by providing their banking information to the thief). Normally, the victim would take their time to check that the person they are speaking with is legitimate but bypasses these risk controls because of the urgency.

DoS

DoS is **Denial of Service**. There are millions of web servers operating on the internet (which host websites). If a hacker wants to bring down a web server, the hacker would flood that server with massive amounts of traffic. The web server would then be unable to respond to legitimate traffic, and ordinary users would be unable to visit the website. This is known as denial of service. Services other than websites exist on the internet (credit card processing, databases, etc.), and all are vulnerable to DoS.

There are many types of DoS attacks
- **SYN flooding**. When a user wants to connect to a web server, a three-way handshake (SYN, SYN/ACK, ACK) process occurs between the two computers.
  - The user sends a SYN message to the server; the server responds with a SYN/ACK message to the user, and the user responds with an ACK message to the server
  - In SYN flooding, the hacker imitates a legitimate user and sends more SYN requests than the web server can handle. The web server responds with the SYN/ACK response, but the hacker does not complete the third part by sending the SYN.
  - The server keeps a connection open waiting for an ACK message that never arrives. The server can only keep a limited number of connections open. If all of them are waiting for ACK messages that will never arrive, then the server won't be able to establish connections with legitimate users

- **Fragmenting**. When data travels over the internet, the sending computer breaks it down into pieces known as packets. The packets may take different routes to reach their destination. The receiving computer puts the packets back together. The data in each packet should not overlap.
  - In a fragmenting attack, the hacker send data to the server, but puts overlapping data into each packet
  - The server attempts to put the data back together but can't. If the operating system isn't equipped to recognize this attack and discard the bad packets, then it will crash.

How to prevent Denial of Service
- Most DoS attacks are preventable now. Why?
- A hacker will not have enough bandwidth to bring down a large web service. Major websites such as Google, Facebook, eBay, etc. use distributed server farms consisting of millions of servers, with redundant pathways to the internet. A hacker will not have enough capacity to overload their systems.
- Most enterprise systems contain firewalls that can easily detect and block DoS attacks. If a substantial amount of illegitimate traffic appears to be originating from a single source, it can simply be turned off.
- Web server software should be updated so that

- For a small monthly fee, services such as CloudFlare offer large-scale cloud-based firewalls to protect smaller websites from DoS attacks (which they normally could not afford).
- A company should never be a victim to the same attack twice. After the first attack, they must investigate and rewrite their systems so that it never happens again. The most common types of attacks are well documented, and systems are available to prevent them.

DDoS

Distributed Denial of Service was invented after DoS stopped working (due to improvements in internet infrastructure).

With **DDoS,** a hacker infects thousands (or hundreds of thousands) of computers (or other IP devices such as cameras) and uses all of them to send traffic to a web server that he wants to crash (remember botnets?). These computers are known as bots. Since the traffic appears legitimate (and is in fact originating from hundreds of thousands of different sources, in different geographic locations, different internet service providers, and different computer types), it is difficult to filter or prevent.

The botnet operator will continue to acquire additional bots, to grow his botnet. The operator will lease his network of bots to a person or organization that wants to bring down a website (for revenge, competition, or other reasons).

How to prevent
- Services such as CloudFlare use large scale cloud-based firewalls to mitigate DDoS attacks. They set up a server farm with a large amount of bandwidth that can be "donated" to a website facing a DDoS attack. CloudFlare's bandwidth can accept the DDoS attack.
- Users should use antivirus and firewall programs to prevent their computers from becoming infected and turned into bots.
- Manufacturers of IP cameras and wireless routers should put in the effort to make their devices more secure (so that they do not become infected and used in DDoS attacks).

Man-in-the-Middle

In a **Man-in-the-Middle attack**, a hacker inserts himself between the sender and recipient of an electronic communication. Keep in mind that more than 60% of internet traffic is machine generated (one computer talking to another with no human interaction).

Consider that Alice and Bob are two hypothetical internet users having an encrypted conversation. They could be two humans, or it could be that Alice is an online banking user and Bob is the bank. The purpose of the communication is irrelevant. Consider that the hacker, Eve, wants to spy on them.

Alice and Bob's messages pass through a central server. Depending on Alice and Bob's geographical locations, the messages may pass through many servers, routers, switches, fiber optic cables, and copper lines. The internet is fragmented, and different parts are owned by different companies. If Alice is in New York and Bob is in Los Angeles, the traffic must pass through many states, and many internet service providers.

- If the traffic between Alice and Bob is unencrypted, and Eve can obtain access to one of the servers, routers, switches, or physical connections, then Eve can spy on the conversation.

- If the traffic is unencrypted, but Alice does not have access to one of the servers in the connection, Eve could trick Alice into sending messages addressed to Bob to her instead (by corrupting/modifying Alice's address book). Eve would do the same to Bob. In Alice's address book, Eve replaces Bob's address with her own. In Bob's address book, Alice replaces Alice's address with her own. Alice sends messages to Eve thinking she is sending them to Bob, and Bob sends messages to Eve thinking he is sending them to Alice. Now Eve can read Alice's messages and forward them to Bob. Eve can also read Bob's messages and forward them to Alice. Neither Alice nor Bob is aware that Eve is reading their communications.

- If the communication is encrypted and uses public key cryptography (such as Apple iMessage), a man-in-the-middle attack is more difficult. Users encrypt messages with public keys (which they obtain from a central directory). If Alice wants to send a message to Bob, she obtains Bob's public key from Apple, encrypts the message, and sends it to Bob. Bob uses his private key (which only he knows) to decrypt the message. If Eve can intercept the message, she could perform a man-in-the-middle attack
  - We will discuss public key cryptography in more depth later, but in general consider this
    - A private key can only decrypt a message. A user keeps his private key secret.

- The user generates a public key from his private key. He gives the public key to everybody who wants to send him a message. The public key can only encrypt a message.
  - Eve generates her own public and private keys
  - She hacks into the central directory and changes Bob's public key to her own
  - Alice decides to send a message to Bob. She checks the directory for Bob's public key, and receives what she thinks is Bob's public key (but is in fact Eve's public key)
  - Alice sends the message to Eve (thinking she is sending it to Bob)
  - Eve decrypts the message, reads it, and then encrypts it with Bob's public key
  - Eve sends the message to Bob
  - Bob receives the message, thinking it came from Alice and decrypts it with his own private key
  - Eve does the same thing with Alice's public key so that she can intercept messages that Bob is sending to Alice

How to prevent

- The best way to prevent a man-in-the-middle attack is to encrypt all communications with a reliable encryption algorithm (one that uses a long enough key length and is generated through open-source methods)
- Second, ensure the integrity of the public key. Do not trust "key directories" such as Apple iMessage for obtaining public keys, especially for sensitive communications. Apple controls all the public keys in iMessage and a rogue operator could inject their own public keys, creating the man-in-the-middle attack illustrated above. The best way to ensure the integrity of the public key is to personally distribute it to the person that you want to communicate with.

Buffer Overflow

A **buffer overflow** is one of the most common types of attacks.

What is a **buffer**? The buffer is kind of like a lineup at airport security. The flow of passengers is not steady. When there are more passengers than security guards, a long lineup develops. If the airport doesn't have enough room to hold all the passengers, they might have to wait outside.

The buffer is the same. Consider a web server or other computing device. Information is coming in over a wire. Sometimes the information is coming in quickly, and sometimes it is coming in slowly. The server must take each piece of data and process it somewhere. When the levels of traffic are high, the server can't process all of it in real time. Thus, all data first enters a buffer, where it lines up to be processed. The server takes data from the buffer at a steady rate.

- For example, the traffic ranges from 0.5GB/s to 2GB/s
- The server can process data at 1GB/s
- If the traffic is 1GB/s or less, the server can process the traffic in real time. The traffic passes through the buffer but doesn't spend any time there.
- If the traffic is more than 1GB/s, the server can't process the traffic in real time. The buffer starts to fill up.

The buffer has limited capacity. If the buffer fills up, then it should reject additional data. For example, if the buffer has a capacity of 10GB, and data comes in at a rate of 2GB/s, but the computer can only process 1GB/s, then after 10 seconds, the buffer will be full.

The buffer may be designed to hold specific sizes of data. For example, a buffer may be designed to store IP addresses. Recall that an IP address is 12 digits. If a hacker sends a piece of data that is larger than what the buffer expects, a buffer overflow results. For example, if the IP address is 12 digits, and the hacker sends 14 digits, a buffer overflow could result.

In 2014, a major exploit known as Heartbleed caused security vulnerabilities across millions of websites, including Facebook, Google, and Revenue Canada. How did it work?
- Websites encrypt their data with an algorithm known as SSL
- A developer created an app called OpenSSL, which makes it easy for web developers to implement SSL in their website, using minimal code
- Millions of websites, including millions of the worlds largest websites used the OpenSSL app
- When a user visits a website, a connection is created. The user's computer and the web server keep the connection open for as long as necessary (but for no longer than necessary). To preserve resources, the server closes the connection when it is no longer required. It checks if the user is still present through a method known as a "heartbeat", which is the

electronic equivalent of asking the user "are you there?" ever minute. If the user says "yes", the connection stays open. If the user doesn't reply, the server closes the connection.

- o Every minute, the user's computer sends a small random amount of data to the web server. The user's computer sends the web server the length of the data as well.
- o For example, the user's computer might send "sdkjfasfjksdlfskldflskdf" length:24
- o The web server sends the data back. Thus, the web server and the user's computer know that both are still online and agree to keep the connection active.
- o In fact, the server stores the data in a buffer and gives it an address (the address is the spot where the data starts). To return the data to the user, the server locates the data at that address, and counts the number of spaces based on the length it was provided. If the data's address starts at position 40 in the buffer, then the server will start reading at position and count another 23 position. Thus, the server will return the data from position 40 to position 63.
- o A hacker found out that OpenSSL didn't verify the accuracy the length that the user's computer provided.
- o Thus, a hacker could send a small amount of data such as "aaa" and a large length such as length:4523
- o The server would store "aaa" in memory and then send back 4523 bits of data, starting with "aaa". If aaa started at position 40, the server would reply with the data from position 40 to position 4562. What kind of data is stored in the other positions? Anything is possible.
- o If the hacker repeated these steps, eventually he would receive most of the contents of the server's memory, which could include encryption keys and private banking information.
- o This bug could have been easily prevented with a few lines of code to verify the length of the data.
- o Once discovered, it was quickly patched. But hackers had been using the security hole to steal data undetected for over two years.

How to prevent

- Proper code and error handling in programs. The buffer overflow happens because the computer receives data in an unexpected format and doesn't know what to do. Buffer overflows can be prevented by writing good code that checks for errors and refuses to accept data that does not meet the required format. A program shouldn't crash when it receives invalid data; it should simply reject it.
  - o The correct data has an expected format (length, character type, contents, format, etc.)
  - o In pseudocode, write an "if" statement. If the data doesn't match the expected format, then reject the data.

Injection

Injection takes the form of SQL injection, XML injection, or LDAP injection.

Most websites are "database driven". That is, the front end of the website (the code, the photos, and the videos) are static/dynamic web pages and files, but data (usernames, passwords, comments, video views, etc.) are stored in databases. The most common database format is SQL (available in MS SQL and MySQL).

Consider a standard form on a website (such as a registration form). When a user fills out the form and presses the submit button, the data from the form goes to a script (some computer code). The script processes the data and enters it into a database.

A database is like a giant Microsoft Excel spreadsheet.
- It consists of one or more tables.
- Each table has a unique name
- Each table has one or more columns
- Each column must have a unique name and must specify the type of data that can be stored inside it (for example, text, numbers, integers, etc.)
- Each row in a table is known as a record
- We can speak to the database through a database language. Each database has its own unique language. For example, we can speak to a MySQL database through the MySQL language. We can tell the database to create a new table, delete a table, add columns to a table, add data to a table, retrieve data from a table, search for data, etc.. There are entire books written about MySQL.

Consider a user named Bob Jones, who registers on our website by filling out a form with three fields: First Name, Last Name, and Username. We previously created a database table to hold all our user data. We called this table "username_table".

Bob filled out the following information
- First Name: Bob
- Last Name: Jones
- Username: bjones

Bob's data goes to a script, which generates an SQL statement as follows (this would insert the data 'Bob', 'Jones', 'bjones' as a new line in the table). The semi-colon indicates the end of the line.

INSERT INTO username_table VALUES ('Bob', 'Jones', 'bjones');

If Bob was sneaky, he could enter *'bjones'); DROP TABLE username_table;'* as his username. Drop Table is a command that tells the SQL database to delete the table.

Bob wouldn't know exactly the name of the table or the format of the script (because he wouldn't know what kind of database we are using), but he could make a few guesses (or he could discover the name of the table through an error message on the site). On a side note, a database (or database server) should never talk directly to a user or be exposed to the internet – it should only communicate with a web server.

This results in the following SQL statement

INSERT INTO username_table VALUES ('Bob', 'Jones', "bjones'); DROP TABLE username_table;

The first half of the statement inserts the data as normal. But the second half (*DROP TABLE username_table;*) deletes the entire username table! SQL injection attacks are easily preventable with the right code.

How to prevent
- Use prepared statements when working with SQL
- Sanitize the data (do not allow users to enter special characters unless necessary). This should be enforced both on the client side and on the server side (malicious users can defeat client-side error handling). Do not accept invalid data.
    - Why bother with client-side error handling if the server can prevent everything? Client-side error handling enhances the user experience, for legitimate users. Client-side error handling also reduces the load on the server.
- Turn off verbose mode/error outputs in your code. If there is a bug in the code, or if the application encounters an error, many web languages (such as PHP or ASP) will print the error directly in the web browser. These errors can contain exact file directories and SQL database information, which would be exposed to all website visitors.

Cross-Site Scripting (XSS)

In **cross-site scripting**, a user includes script as part of their input in a web form or link. There are three types

- Non-persistent XSS attack, where the script is executed by the web server immediately and sent back to the browser
  - For example, a hacker sends a user a link to a legitimate online banking website, but the link includes some code that executes (through the website) in the user's browser. The script copies the user's login credentials and sends them to the hacker.
- Persistent XSS attack, where the script is stored by the web server and executed against others
  - For example, a hacker posts a YouTube comment and includes some HTML (which includes links and photographs to an ecommerce site). The HTML executes in each visitor's web browser, and all visitors see the comment (including the links and photographs). This is unlikely to happen on YouTube because data is sanitized, but it is certainly possible on other websites.
- DOM-based XSS attack, where the script is executed by the browser

How to prevent
- Proper input validation in web forms both on the web browser side and on the server side
- Remove or filter all script characters from web forms, including "<", ";", and "|"
- Use anti-XSS libraries such as ANTIXSS
- Use Content Security Policy in the website

Cross-Site Request Forgery

In **Cross-Site Request Forgery**, a user is authenticated on a website, and while authenticated, a second website hijacks the session and executes an unauthorized action on the first website.

For example, a user is logged in to Bank of America's online banking site and has transferred money to his mother. The user is still authenticated by the bank's website, which will not require him to reauthenticate for subsequent transactions. If the user visits a malicious website, that website could send data to the bank's website and place a money transfer without the user's knowledge.

A successful cross-site attack requires the hacker to guess the contents of the website's form (the online banking form field names), including secret authentication keys. If the hacker had previously visited the online bank site and viewed its source code, obtaining the form field names would be trivial. The authentication keys may change for every session.

How to prevent
- Proper website coding including tokenization (such as Synchronizer Token Pattern, Cookie-to-Header Token) to randomly generate authentication tokens
- Use of Same-Origin Policy. Same-Origin Policy allows a web browser to execute scripts from one web page on a second webpage only if both pages originated from the same server (same domain name).
  - http://www.example.com/page1.html and http://www.example.com/page2.html will be compatible
  - http://www.example.com/page1.html and http://www.something.com/page2.html will NOT be compatible
- Browser extensions such as RequestPolicy or uMatrix can prevent Cross-Site Request Forgery attacks.
- Use multi-factor authentication where possible.
- Access sensitive sites through an "incognito" web browser window. Log out of sensitive browser windows when complete.

Privilege Escalation

Privilege Escalation is where a hacker attempts to obtain higher credentials. In a system, there may be "guest", 'user", and "admin" privileges. There many be different levels of admin privileges. If a hacker obtains access to the system as a guest, he could use it to obtain higher level privileges by snooping around.

Some programs, services, or processes may run under elevated/admin privileges. If there is a security hole in one of these applications, a hacker could take advantage of it to execute code that runs under the same privilege as the original application.

For example, the Cisco VPN application must be able to regularly update itself. Doing so requires admin privileges. Therefore, the Cisco VPN application runs under admin privileges, even on a standard user's account. If there was a security vulnerability in the Cisco VPN application, a hacker could log in as a guest or regular user and trick the Cisco VPN application into executing a malicious program under the same admin privileges that it has.

How to prevent
- Implement User Account Control on Windows, or scripts in UNIX
- Regularly update applications and regularly install operating system updates
- Do not allow any applications with admin privileges to run under guest accounts

ARP Poisoning

ARP is **Address Resolution Protocol**. Every network device has a unique MAC address, set from the factory. A MAC address is kind of like a serial number. When a device connects to a network, it announces its MAC address.

Every device is assigned (or should be assigned) a unique IP address. On a LAN (Local Area Network), devices communicate by addressing data to the each other's MAC addresses. A device will not address a communication to another device's IP address unless they are on different networks.

If the sender knows the recipient device's IP address, but not it's MAC address, it uses ARP to discover the MAC address. It does so by flooding the network with a request for the MAC address. Since the device doesn't know who it is looking for, every device on the network receives the request. It sends the electronic equivalent of a "hey if this is your IP address, reply with your MAC". The device in question replies with its MAC address.

The opposite is also possible. A device can flood the network with a request for an IP address when the MAC address is known. This is known as reverse ARP or RARP.

Each network device stores common MAC addresses and their corresponding IP addresses in a table known as the ARP table, so that it doesn't have to look them up each time it needs to send data (too many ARP lookups can overload the network).

There is no authentication mechanism for the ARP table. Each device simply adds/updates the ARP table when data is received. A device will update the ARP table with new data even if it did not create an ARP request. There is no way to check if a device has lied about its MAC address.

ARP Poisoning is when a hacker sends wrong data to corrupt the ARP table.
- Let's say our office has a printer with an IP address of 10.10.1.1 and a MAC address of AB:CD:EF:12:34:56
- Bob wants to print some sensitive documents. His computer knows that the printer's IP address is 10.10.1.1 but doesn't know its MAC address. It sends out an ARP request to 10.10.1.1, and the printer responds with AB:CD:EF:12:34:56
- Bob's computer stores this data in its ARP table
- Bob's computer sends documents to be printed to AB:CD:EF:12:34:56
- A hacker comes along and plugs a laptop into an open ethernet port in Bob's office. The hacker's laptop has an IP address of 10.10.1.2 and a MAC address of AA:BB:CC:11:22:33
- The hacker sends out an ARP message saying that 10.10.1.1 belongs to AA:BB:CC:11:22:33, the hacker's computer
- Bob's computer sends all printed documents to the hacker's computer instead of the printer

- The hacker can forward Bob's documents to the printer, so that they print correctly, and Bob doesn't suspect that his documents have been stolen

How to prevent
- Obviously, the hacker should never have been able to plug his laptop into an open ethernet port in Bob's office.
    - Somebody should have noticed that there was an intruder and called the police
    - An open ethernet port should never be patched into a switch
    - The hacker's laptop should never have been permitted to access the network, even if the port was open
- Use ARP spoofing detection software. The software can perform cross-checking of ARP entries against a DHCP server or switch, which has accurate information.
- Critical system components should have static ARP entries that cannot be changed. This could require a substantial amount of maintenance for hosts that are DHCP.

Amplification

Amplification is when the effects of an attack is magnified. An attacker can do so by creating a loop in the attack mechanism. One example is in a DDoS attack.

DNS Poisoning

DNS Poisoning is like ARP Poisoning.

What is **DNS**? Recall that every computer on the internet has a unique IP address. That means, every website's server has a unique IP address. Humans are not good at remembering IP addresses. If you had to remember and type in the IP address for every website you visited, the internet would not be very useful. Instead, you type in a domain name, such as google.com.

The DNS (Domain Name System) knows what every domain name is, and what its corresponding IP address is. When you type in a Domain Name, your computer queries the DNS to find the correct IP address for that website's server.

Who operates DNS
- There are many online public DNS servers such as Google DNS (8.8.8.8 and 8.8.4.4). These provide records for publicly-available websites.
- Many ISPs operate DNS servers for their own customers. These provide records for publicly-available websites and are only accessible to their own customers. For example, Comcast might operate a DNS for their own customers. A customer can choose to bypass Comcast's DNS and use Google's DNS.
- Many companies operate their own DNS servers for their own offices. These provide DNS for internal systems and internal websites and may also provide DNS for publicly-available websites. A public DNS would not be able to provide a DNS record for an internal device.
- Each Windows machine operates its own DNS to keep track of the most recently visited websites.

An authoritative DNS server (or nameserver) holds the original records for the website in question. Different DNS servers can be authoritative for different websites. A recursive (non-authoritative) DNS server is one that requests DNS data from the authoritative DNS server.
- For example, AWS Route 53 DNS Servers are authoritative for amazon.com because they hold amazon.com's original DNS records
- If a user queries the AWS server, he will receive an authoritative answer about the location of the amazon.com servers
- After querying the AWS DNS server, DNS servers at the user's ISP and office cache the DNS data. Now, DNS servers closer to the user know the IP address of amazon.com
- The user (or other users) can go back to these servers to perform DNS lookups, but the answer will be non-authoritative.

In DNS Poisoning, a hacker corrupts the DNS records. The hack can take place at the top-level DNS servers, at the ISP level, at the office level, or at the computer level. The corrupted DNS can force a user to visit a fake server.

- For example, Bank of America is located at IP address 11.11.11.11
- A hacker sets up a server at 9.9.9.9 and then corrupts the DNS server to point users to Bank of America's website at 9.9.9.9. The users' computers visit the website at 9.9.9.9 thinking they are accessing a legitimate Bank of America server.

How to prevent

- Use an authoritative DNS server. An authoritative DNS server is one that provides original DNS data. An authoritative DNS server can be hacked, but it is less likely.
- The US government is working on a program known as Domain Name System Security Extensions. This program will distribute digital signatures with DNS data, ensuring its authenticity.

Domain Hijacking

Each domain name must be registered at an accredited registrar. Each domain name must be renewed yearly. Registrars are licensed by **ICANN (Internet Corporation for Assigned Names & Numbers)**. The registrars control the original data regarding the owner of the domain name and the original name servers. The name servers tell visitors which DNS servers to check with when looking up domain name information.

A domain name owner can edit or update their domain name data by logging in to a web-based control panel at their registrar. A domain name owner can transfer a domain name from one registrar to another.

Domain Hijacking is the act of stealing another person's domain name. The thief could do so by

- Hacking in to the registrar's website and transferring the name to another registrar. The original owner would have difficulty retrieving control over the domain name.
- Hacking in to the registrar's website and forwarding the domain name to a server controlled by the hacker. Visitors would then be directed to the wrong server. The hacker could place advertisements, malware, or phishing schemes on the server.
- In both cases, the thief would likely obtain the owner's password via social engineering or a phishing scam.

How to prevent

- Register the domain name with a large registrar that takes security seriously
- Lock the domain name at the registrar so that it cannot be transferred to another registrar
- Choose a difficult password and use multi-factor authentication where possible

Man-in-the-Browser

In the **Man-in-the-Browser attack**, a piece of malware infects the user's computer and intercepts web browser activity. The malware must be designed to recognize specific behaviors such as online banking, PayPal, eBay, or ecommerce sites.

For example, malware is installed on a user's computer. The user logs in to Amazon and makes a purchase, but the malware changes the shipping address to one belonging to the thief. The package is then routed to the thief instead of the victim.

Zeus was a popular piece of man-in-the-browser malware. It was transmitted through e-mail. Hackers used Zeus to capture online banking passwords, logged in to those online bank accounts, and made monetary transfers to their own accounts. To avoid getting caught, the hackers created bank accounts under fake names. They hired mules to withdraw the cash from ATMs and ship it to the hackers' European destinations. The losses exceeded $70 million. After an extensive FBI investigation, over 100 people were arrested and charged with bank fraud and money laundering.

How to prevent
- It is difficult to detect Zeus and other Man-in-the-Browser applications even with antivirus programs. Nevertheless, good antivirus programs are necessary.
- Use multi-factor authentication for online banking websites. Even if the username/password is compromised, the hacker won't be able to gain access to the account.
- Set limits on the amount of money that can be transferred through online banking, and regularly monitor all accounts for suspicious transactions.

Zero Day

A **Zero Day attack** is one that uses a Zero Day exploit. A Zero Day exploit is a vulnerability in a software program or system that has just been discovered; therefore, there is no patch. Day Zero is the day that the exploit is first discovered by the public.

A hacker might discover a zero-day vulnerability and use it to exploit systems for days, weeks, or even years before it is detected. Hackers sell zero-day exploits to other hackers and to government agencies. Some intelligence agencies purchase and store zero-day exploits until they need to use one to attack a high-value target. Once the public discovers the zero-day exploit, the software manufacturers and antivirus companies will work to patch it, usually in a matter of days.

The Zero Day vulnerability is not a form of malware. It is simply a backdoor that a hacker can use to insert some form of malware, which could include a Man-in-the-Browser or DDoS.

Replay

A **replay attack** is when a hacker captures part of an electronic communication and retransmits it. For example, if a user transferred money via online banking, the hacker could capture the transmission instructions and resend them to the bank later. The bank would transfer the money twice.

How to prevent
- Encrypt all communications with strong algorithms
- Require all communications to expire after a short period of time
- Even with encryption, a hacker could steal the encrypted communication and resend it (without knowing the contents). To prevent, use a cryptographic nonce (a unique randomly generated number) in each communication, such as a session ID. If the recipient receives two messages with the same nonce, it will reject the second one.

Pass the Hash

It is bad security practice to store user passwords in plain text. Most websites and applications store user passwords as hashes. A hash is a one-way cryptographic function (a hash can be created from the password, but the password cannot be created from the hash).

When a user signs up at a website, the website hashes the user's password and stores the hash. When the user attempts to log in, the website hashes the password entered by the user. The website compares the hash of the password entered with the hash of the password stored by the website. If they match, the user is authenticated.

Websites use store passwords as hashes so that even if the hash database was compromised, the user passwords would not be. Hash algorithms are complicated and will be discussed in more detail.

With **Pass the Hash**, a hacker can capture the hash that was used in the authentication or registration process. The hacker then injects the hash into a website or Windows process to gain access to the computer, without ever knowing the password.

How to prevent
- Secure applications so that they do not accept hashes directly from users
- Use session keys during communication

Hijacking and Related Attacks

There are many forms of hijacking, where a hacker takes over a user's experience after he has logged in. Hijacking can be simple or complicated. Hijacking attempts include

- **Clickjacking**. In clickjacking, a user visits a website and clicks on something different from what he expected. A hacker could inject code to create transparent overlays on a website. Or a hacker could modify the code.
  - One popular clickjacking method involves advertisements.

    Many website owners' partner with Google AdSense. Google AdSense provides each owner with a code containing their account number. The website owner places the code in any spot where they would like advertising to appear. When the website loads, the code queries Google's servers and inserts an advertisement. Google handles all advertising sales. When visitors click on the ads, revenue is generated (Google and the website owner split the revenue).

    A hacker can sign up for Google AdSense and swap the website owner's code with their own code. This does not happen at the server level, but instead at the web browser level (the user's computer is infected with malware that detects AdSense advertisements and swaps the code). When the user clicks on the advertisement, the hacker's AdSense account is credited, and the website owner is deprived of the revenue without ever realizing it.

- **Session Hijacking**. In a session hijacking, the user has an existing TCP/IP session with a server. The hacker hijacks the session and continues to communicate with the server (pretending to be the user).

- **URL Hijacking**. In a URL hijacking, the hacker edits a browser URL. The original domain name might stay the same, but the hacker could modify a portion of the URL after the domain.
  - For example, the hacker could modify the URL to redirect the victim to a different website or to execute a script on the existing website.

- **Typo Squatting**. In Typo Squatting, a hacker purchases domain names that are like popular domain names.
  - For example, the hacker purchases gooogle.com (which is similar to google.com). The hacker points gooogle.com to their own server, where they serve malicious content (advertisements, viruses, phishing scams, etc.) A visitor who accidentally types in gooogle.com visits the wrong website and his computer is infected or he is tricked into giving up sensitive information.

How to prevent

- Brand owners can register domain names that are common misspellings of their own names. Brand owners with trademarks can litigate against hackers who are typo squatting against their names without any legitimate purpose.

- Users should verify carefully that they are entering in the correct URLs and that no malicious content has been added.

The **Anticybersquatting Consumer Protection Act** prohibits the registration of a domain name that is a trademark (or confusingly similar to a trademark) if the registration was made in bad faith. A person injured by the registration may bring action in federal court.

15 USC § 8131 prohibits the registration of a domain name that is a person's name without that person's consent, if the registration was made for profit.

The act does not prohibit freedom of speech; thus, a user may register a domain name that is critical of an organization or brand that includes that organization's trademark.

Truth in Domain Names Act makes it a federal crime to register a domain if the domain is used to trick visitors into viewing obscenities. John Zuccarini was the first person charged under the act.

Driver Manipulation

A **driver** is a piece of software that allows an operating system to communicate with a piece of hardware. Hackers can manipulate drivers in two ways

- **Shimming**. Shimming places source code between the driver and the operating system. Shimming is useful because it allows a driver developer to create one version of a driver for multiple versions of an operating system. The developer then adds a "shim" – a small piece of code – so that the driver can work with multiple operating systems. Each operating system receives a different shim. Hackers can insert malicious code into the driver shims.
- **Refactoring**. Refactoring allows the internal code to change without modifying its external functionality. Refactoring is useful because it allows developers to optimize their code, allowing it to operate faster. A hacker can insert malicious code into a refactored driver.

How to prevent
- Only install drivers that are digitally signed. The digital signature verifies that the driver's source code is authentic. By default, newer versions of Windows will not accept unsigned drivers (and disabling this feature requires a reboot of the computer).

MAC Spoofing

Recall that each network device is manufactured with a unique, unmodifiable (in theory) MAC address. On a LAN, one security measure to prevent rogue devices is to only allow traffic between trusted MAC addresses. If an intruder attempts to connect a new device to the network, it will not be permitted to communicate.

If a hacker learns the MAC address of a legitimate network device, he can change his device's MAC address and gain access to the network (and to the traffic originally directed to the legitimate device).

How to prevent
- Require additional user authentication before allowing a device to access the network
- Use port security on switches. A switch can remember which MAC address sent traffic on which port. If the switch detects the same MAC address on a different port, it can either shut down the port or alert an administrator of the discrepancy.

IP Spoofing

Recall that each network device is assigned a unique IP address. Two network devices can communicate over a WAN or public network if they know each other's IP addresses. A hacker can intercept their communication by changing his machine's IP address to match that of one of the devices. This method takes special skill and control/modification of network routers, because

- Most network devices/computers will detect the IP address conflict.
- The device whose IP address is spoofed will not receive any traffic because it is being intercepted by the hacker's computer. The hacker's computer would pretend to be the legitimate computer and carry on the communication.
- To remain undetected, the hacker will have to intercept the IP traffic through the router and then forward it to the legitimate recipient.

A broadcast IP address is a special type of IP address that exists in every network. The broadcast address allows a device to send a single message to all the IP addresses on that network. One type of broadcast message is known as an "echo". Devices receiving the "echo" message reply to the sending device.

In a Smurf Attack, the hacker forges the "from" portion of the echo message so that it appears to have come from another system. The device whose address appears in the "from" portion will receive all the replies. Depending on the size of the network, and the number of echo messages sent, that device could receive hundreds or thousands of replies.

In any TCP/IP communication, data is broken into fragments known as packets. The sender numbers each packet in order (1, 2, 3, etc.), but the increment is not necessarily one (it could be any random integer). The hacker must be able to guess the correct sequence number and increment when creating spoofed packets. A hacker can do so by intercepting enough packets and analyzing their sequence numbers.

How to prevent

- Encrypt all traffic. An IP spoofing attempt will not allow a hacker to read encrypted traffic.
- Set firewalls to drop traffic that originates from outside the network but appears to come from inside the network (could indicate that the address has been spoofed).

Wireless Attacks

There are many types of wireless attacks.

- **Replay**. In a Replay attack, the hacker intercepts and repeats data (as discussed previously). It is much easier to collect wireless data undetected because the data travels through the air and not a wire.

- **IV**. IV is also known as Initialization Vector. When a client connects to an access point, the access point generates an IV to randomize the encryption key used in the connection. The IV is originally sent to the client in plain text (unencrypted). If a hacker detects the IV, then he can use it to guess the encryption key and decrypt all further communication between the client and the access point.

- **Evil Twin**. A wireless client will connect to the access point that has the highest signal (typically the one that is nearest to the client). In an Evil Twin attack, the hacker deploys a wireless access point with the same SSIDs as the legitimate access points, but with a higher signal strength. Clients that are preconfigured to connect to the SSIDs will connect to the evil twin.

  The evil twin attack can be prevented by authenticating all wireless connections through certificates. The client should be required to verify the identity of the network that it is connecting to. A rogue access point will not be able to prove its identity.

- **Rogue AP**. A Rogue AP is an evil twin that forwards traffic to the main network. The Rogue AP allows a hacker to act as a man-in-the-middle and intercept all traffic.

  Preventing Rogue APS can be done by
  - Using access points that detect Rogue APs (Cisco Aironet APs have optional Rogue AP detection modules)
  - Using MAC address filtering on the network to prevent unauthorized devices from connecting

- **Jamming**. Wireless Access Points operate on a specific band of the electromagnetic frequency spectrum (2.4 GHz and 5 GHz). A hacker can flood the air with useless signals in the same frequency. If these signals are more powerful than those put out by the access point, they will prevent legitimate users from connecting. Signal jamming has applications in other types of networks (cell phone jamming, radar jamming).

- **WPS**. WPS, or Wireless Protected Setup, was a feature that allowed devices to connect to a wireless network without having to enter a security key. It was designed for cheaper devices such as printers (that often didn't have a keypad/touchscreen interface to enter the key). A user could connect their printer to the network by pressing the "WPS" button on their access point and then waiting for it to pair with their wireless device. WPS exchanges an 8-digit code with the wireless device, which can be easily detected through brute force.

- **Bluejacking**. In Bluejacking, a hacker sends an unsolicited message to another person's cellular telephone over Bluetooth. Bluejacking can be prevented by setting the device to undiscoverable or by prohibiting devices from automatically pairing.

- **Bluesnarfing**. In Bluesnarfing, a hacker copies data off a victim's phone over Bluetooth. Each Bluetooth device has a unique 48-bit name. In older versions of Bluetooth, the hacker could guess the device name through brute force.

- **RFID**. RFID or Radio Frequency Identification tags are used to track inventory, keys, and equipment. They are used in large warehouses and smaller retail stores. They are also used to provide access control. RFID tags take two forms: active (contains a battery and broadcasts a signal) and passive (does not contain a battery, and is activated when it is near an antenna). A hacker could target the
    - Communication between the RFID tag and its antenna (intercept an unencrypted or weakly encrypted communication)
    - The RFID reader (by posing as a fake RFID card)
    - The RFID tags (by posing as a fake RFID reader)

- **NFC**. NFC or Near Field Communication is a technology that allows smartphones to communicate with each other and with other devices. The most common type of NFC technology allows users to engage in debit/credit card transactions via their smartphones. A user registers a payment card with an application on the phone and then passes their phone over a credit card terminal to complete the payment.

  A hacker could steal NFC data from a smartphone if he was able to get close enough. NFC attacks can be prevented by turning NFC off. Only turn NFC on when you are ready to use it.

- **Disassociation**. In a disassociation attack, a hacker forces a client to disassociate from an access point. A hacker can force a client to disassociate from an access point by sending a "disassociation" message to the client.
    - The disassociation message is a standard message that an access point could sent to a client to disconnect it
    - It contains the MAC address of the client and the SSID of the access point

- If a hacker intercepts communication between the client and the access point, he could learn the MAC address of the client, and then create a fake disassociation message
- The hacker must send these messages to the client constantly, or it will try to reconnect

Cryptographic Attacks

In **cryptography** the data is encrypted. Hackers try to decrypt it. There are many ways, but all cryptographic attacks can be prevented. Some of the attacks include

- **Birthday.** Consider a set of values (not necessarily unique values), k. In any set k, the possibility that at least two values are identical is $1.25k^{1/2}$. If we have a set of two values, then the possibility that they are identical is $1.25(2)^{1/2} = 1.75\%$. As the set grows, the possibility that two entries will be identical also grows. This idea came from the fact that in a room of 30 people, there is at least a 50% chance that two of them share a birthday.

- **Known Plain Text/Cipher Text.** If the hacker can intercept a portion of the plain text communication and the corresponding portion of the cipher, he can use cryptanalysis to decrypt the algorithm. The hacker does not require the entire communication, only a portion. Good encryption algorithms can mitigate this threat because they use large keys.

- **Rainbow Tables.** Recall that it is bad security practice to store passwords in plain text. Passwords are typically hashed, and the hash is stored (the hash is not reversible).

  But a hacker could generate a dictionary of passwords (common and uncommon) and calculate the corresponding hash for each one. This dictionary is known as a rainbow table. The hacker could then steal a hash and look up the corresponding password for each one.

  Rainbow tables are readily available on the internet for passwords up to eight characters (every possible combination!) and rainbow tables of even longer passwords can be computed.

  To prevent the use of rainbow table attacks, modern password hash functions incorporate a 'salt'. The salt is a random set of characters appended to the end of each password before the hash is calculated. The hash and the salt are stored in plain text. If the hash database is compromised, the hacker would have to regenerate each rainbow table incorporating the salt into every password to make any sense of it. This would be practically impossible.

- **Dictionary.** A Dictionary attack uses a list of predetermined passwords and brute force to guess the password. The dictionary could consist of common words in the English language, especially common passwords such as "password", "12345678", and "abcd".

  A hacker could create a custom dictionary based on the user account that he is trying to hack into. For example, the dictionary could be customized to include the names of the user's children, pets, vehicles, etc..

Many organizations force users to choose complex passwords. Password complexity could include

- o Not reusing the same password
- o Including upper case letters, lower case letters, numbers, and special characters
- o Ensuring that the password meets a minimum length
- o Not using a person's name, address, or username in the password

Yet, it is still possible to create a custom dictionary based on the password complexity requirements. For example, if the user's password was 'donkey', then a complicated password might be 'D0nkey!'. Users tend to substitute @ for a, 0 for o, 1 for l, and so forth in a predictable manner.

A dictionary attack can be prevented by limiting the amount of password attempts a user has before his account is locked out. Of course, the dictionary attack could occur offline, or the hacker may have a way to bypass the incorrect password attempt count.

- **Brute Force**. A brute force attack is like a dictionary attack, except that the system attempts every password combination possible (based on the character set), starting from the letter a and working its way up until the password is guessed. For example, the system will guess the password 'sdfsfgdgsdfsdfd', and then the next password would be 'sdfsfgdgsdfsdf*e*'

The length of time for a brute force attack to be successful depends on the computing power available (how many passwords can be attempted every second) and the length of the password (how many passwords need to be attempted).

An online brute force attack is when the brute force occurs against a live computer. For example, consider Active Directory, a Microsoft system that stores user accounts on a central server. When a user attempts to log in to an Active Directory-based computer, the computer validates the login credentials with the server. On a successful login, the computer caches the correct credentials on the local computer. If the computer is later offline (or off the local network), the user can still log in (the computer validates the login with the cached credentials).

- o In an online attack, the hacker would brute force the computer's login while it is connected to the Active Directory server. This attack would likely be unsuccessful because the server would notice the incorrect logins and disable the account.
- o In an offline attack, the hacker would brute force the computer's login while it is not connected to the Active Directory server. This attack may or may not be successful depending on the length and complexity of the password.

How to prevent

o   Offline attacks can't be prevented. Where possible, secure equipment so that it is not stolen. Stolen equipment is more susceptible to offline attacks.
o   Enforce stronger password requirements (including special characters, numbers, upper/lower case letters).
o   Enforce a timer that delays the entry of passwords. This can be accomplished at the software or hardware level, by hashing the password multiple times.
o   Offline data can be encrypted with a strong algorithm that takes several seconds to validate the password. This would be a minor inconvenience to a user entering an incorrect password, but would substantially slow down a brute force attack.

Collision

Recall that a **hash function** cannot be reversed. Part of the reason is that multiple input values can result in the same hash. Consider that a hash has a specific length (for example 48 characters) and character set (only letters and numbers), but that passwords could have an unlimited length and a much wider character set.

Mathematically speaking, the set of hashes is finite, but the set of passwords is infinite. If we divide the number of passwords by the number of hashes, we still have an infinite number of passwords for every hash.

Therefore, it is possible to locate two different passwords that result in the same hash value. This is known as a **collision** and will be discussed in further detail later.

Downgrade

When two parties choose to communicate, they must first agree on the **encryption algorithm** that they will use. The parties should choose secure algorithms. If one party uses outdated technology, it may only support a weaker form of the encryption algorithm. It would then ask the other party to use the same, weaker form of encryption.

A hacker could take advantage of the **downgrade** feature by requesting that another party communicate with it via a weaker form of encryption. The hacker would then break the weaker form of encryption.

One tool that takes advantage of this system is known as a **StingRay**. It is used to intercept communications between cell phones and cell phone towers. Cell phones use a form of encryption known as A5/1. Communication between the cell phone and the tower is encrypted via A5/1. Some older cell towers use a weaker form of encryption known as A5/2, which can be easily broken.

The StingRay acts like a fake cell phone tower. The cell phone connects to the StingRay instead of the tower. The StingRay forces the cell phone to use a weaker form of encryption known as A5/2. The StingRay then obtains encrypted data from the cell phone and decrypts it to obtain the A5/2 encryption key. With the encryption key, the StingRay can then decrypt all cellular communications (voice and SMS).

How to prevent
- Enforce strong forms of encryption without exception
- Use end-to-end encryption applications on cell phones. Do not send sensitive data via SMS or MMS. Use a VoIP app with end-to-end encryption when placing a phone call.

Replay

In a **replay attack**, a hacker collects data and resends it. The data must still be relevant for the attack to work. For example, if a user places an order with a credit card, the hacker can intercept the transaction and place it again.

How to prevent
- Include cryptographic tokens in communications, which serve to prevent the replay attack

Weak Implementations

A **weak implementation** is when a developer installs a cryptographic algorithm that is weak, even when a stronger algorithm is available. For example, many websites continue to use weaker forms of SSL encryption even when stronger forms of encryption such as TLS are available.

How to prevent
- Third parties, such as developers of web browsers, should enforce stronger encryption standards, and block websites/applications that choose to continue using weak algorithms

Laws Relevant to Social Engineering

As mentioned previously, the Computer Fraud and Abuse Act applies to most forms of unauthorized access to a computer system.

In the cases of fraud over the telephone, in person, or over a computer (e-mail, social media, text, etc.), 18 USC § 1343 – Wire Fraud – applies. Note the three conditions that the Defendant must have

- Obtained money or something of value
- Done so by false or fraudulent pretences
- Used the 'wires' in a way that affected interstate or foreign commerce

State laws of fraud, larceny, or theft may apply when interstate or foreign commerce is not affected. But most fraudulent schemes occur over the internet and/or on a large scale, making the federal law apply.

Note that the StingRay is used by many law enforcement agencies to track and intercept cellular telephone traffic.

The use of the StingRay by law enforcement is legal and a warrant is not required.

- Note that phone taps take two forms
  - Wiretap. In a wiretap, the law enforcement agency obtains a warrant from a federal judge, which permits them to listen to the contents of a phone call (or multiple phone calls) initiated by a specific phone number or multiple numbers.
  - Pen Register. In a pen register, the law enforcement agency obtains a subpoena (not necessarily from a judge), which permits them to record the phone numbers dialed by a specific phone number. They may also record the duration of the calls and the times that they were placed (but not the actual contents of the calls).
- The manufacturer of the StingRay claims that the device does not intercept actual voice conversations; therefore, the StingRay's use is not the same as a phone wiretap, but instead a pen register.
- The Department of Justice determined that they do not require a search warrant before using a StingRay, but they do require their agents to obtain warrants unless compelling circumstances exist (evidence would be destroyed prior to obtaining the warrant). By obtaining the warrant, they reduce the risk of legal challenges against the evidence.
- Some federal courts have ruled that the use of a StingRay requires a warrant.
- The states of Virginia, Washington, California, Minnesota, and Utah have passed laws requiring law enforcement to obtain warrants prior to using StingRays.

1.3 Explain threat actor types and attributes

- *Types of actors*
    - *Script Kiddies*
    - *Hactivist*
    - *Organized Crime*
    - *Nation states/APT*
    - *Insiders*
    - *Competitors*
- *Attributes of Actors*
    - *Internal/External*
    - *Level of Sophistication*
    - *Resources/Funding*
    - *Intent/Motivation*
- *Use of Open-Source Intelligence*

Types of actors

Many different organizations and individuals choose to perform malicious attacks. The type of actor is defined by what they stand to gain more than their nationality or age.

Script kiddies

A **script kiddie** is a relatively unsophisticated hacker. A script kiddie may download or purchase malware deployment tools and deploy them. Note that many developers of malware make it available on the internet for others to use.

A script kiddie may be caught quickly after they go on a website such as reddit or 4chan to brag, or if they do not take measures to mask their online identity.

Script kiddies perform a clear majority of the attacks, but not necessarily the most damage.

Hactivist

A **hactivist** is more advanced than a script kiddie. A hacktivist can write scripts, and hacktivists may work together to advance a specific political or social purpose. For example, an environmental or animal rights activist may hack into an oil company and erase their data.

Organized Crime

Organized crime involves criminal organizations that hack for a financial motivation. Due to the substantial return on investment, organized criminal organizations can afford to invest in employees with advanced hacking skills and high-end technology. These organizations can also afford to engage in schemes that take a long time to pay off.

A criminal organization can participate in a scheme on behalf of another organization (for example a nation-state may pay a criminal organization to steal data from a country or business).

Criminal organizations cover their tracks by using cryptocurrency and the dark web.

Some of the activities that organized criminals engage in

- Ransomware
- Denial of Service
- SPAM
- Identity Theft
- Credit Card Fraud
- Sale of Illegal Products/Services on the Dark Web

Nation states/APT

A **nation state** is a government agency that engages in hacking. Nation state intelligence agencies purchase and store millions of dollars worth of zero-day vulnerabilities, which they use against high value targets.

A nation state will engage in attacks for

- National security purposes
- Political purposes
- Intellectual property theft that is then provided to companies within the country
- Cyber attacks against business competitors in other countries

Attacks by nation states may cost millions of dollars to develop and may take years of planning. The attacks may be performed by intelligence agencies or subcontracted to third parties (or to companies that are state-run/state-affiliated).

The use of cyber warfare is increasingly popular, and all countries are engaging in it.

APT is known as an **Advanced Persistent Threat**. A major strategy in intellectual property theft is to slowly steal secrets from a competitor's systems without being caught, over a period of several years. This is accomplished by installing a backdoor into the system or possibly by bribing system administrators to provide access (or to ignore the backdoor).

In 2013, Ji Li Huang, and Xiao Guang Qi, both citizens of China, pled guilty for attempting to steal trade secrets from the Pittsburgh Corning Corporation, which produces FOAMGLAS® insulation. How did they do it?

- They placed an advertisement in a Kansas City newspaper that was near Corning's manufacturing plant. They used the advertisement to recruit an experienced employee of Corning's plant.
- The two Defendants asked the Defendant to provide them with trade secrets belonging to his employer. They offered him $100,000 in cash. They also offered him the opportunity to move to China and set up an insulation manufacturing plant there.
- The two Defendants were also spotted attempting to access the Corning plant, without authorization.
- The Corning employee notified his employer, who notified the FBI
- The FBI set up a sting operation at a nearby hotel. The employee met with the Defendants at the hotel and provided them with fake documents. When the money was exchanged, the two Defendants were arrested.

Companies that are vulnerable to foreign actors include those with employees who are

- Loyal to a foreign government
- In financial distress

- Have a large ego and can be easily manipulated. A smart employee, like a scientist or engineer, may have a timid personality and few social connections. It is easy to take him to a bar or restaurant and sweet talk him. Then he will give up all the company secrets. People like to talk, and people like to brag about their accomplishments.

How to detect

- Employees who are sponsored by a foreign government to study or work in the United States may collect data and trade secrets
- Employees who are requesting information about subject matters that are unrelated to their job description
- Employees who are stealing sensitive data
- Employees who are bringing recording devices to work without authorization
- Employees who frequently travel to their home country on short trips. A person visiting their family is likely to make longer, less frequent trips.
- Employees who appear to have more money than they should

How to prevent

- Perform background checks, including credit checks on all employees and contractors
- Store proprietary information securely
- Implement a document control system that tracks each time a document is viewed, printed, or modified, and by whom. Set the system to alert the administrator when anomalies are discovered.
- Provide a method for allowing employees to anonymously report suspicious behavior, and fully investigate each report
- Screen employees against foreign risk.
- Prohibit employees from bringing recording devices and external storage devices (such as USB drives) to work

Insiders

An **insider** is a person who is inside the organization. This person may be a contractor or an employee. The insider may be motivated by

- Financial purposes. For example, stealing data to provide to a business competitor.
- Political purposes. For example, stealing government secrets to provide to a foreign country (in exchange for a financial or political reward).
- Personal reasons. The employee may be upset with the way that the company treats him or the way that the company conducts itself in the community.

An insider may cooperate with an attacker on the outside. The insider may weaken security protocols at his organization and/or ignore an attack placed by an outsider.

It is difficult to detect and/or prevent attacks placed by insiders because most of their behavior may appear legitimate and because they already have access and knowledge of the organization.

Two famous insiders who leaked data were Edward Snowden and Chelsea Manning. Snowden was a contractor for a US government agency, who leaked thousands of classified documents. Manning was a member of the military. Neither of them was motivated by financial purposes, but instead were dissatisfied with the conduct of their organizations.

How to prevent

- The type of security protocols required depend on the sensitivity of the information that the employee has access to
- It is important to conduct background checks on current and future employees and on contractors
- More severe methods include
    - Implement security protocols including document controls that monitor when files are accessed/printed/modified
    - Search all employees when they leave the building
    - Prohibit personal electronic devices
    - Provide multiple people with access to security system checking (and enforce vacations and job rotations)
- It is important to note that most of the information leaves the building through the brains of the employees, and there is currently no way to prevent people with good memories from taking information out of the organization.

Competitors

A **competitor** is an individual or organization that is in the same market or industry as the victim. The competitor may try to steal intellectual property, trade secrets, or business strategies. The competitor may also try to sabotage operations. For example, a competitor may attempt to hack into a piece of industrial equipment and attempt to destroy it.

The competitor may be in the same town, a different state, or a different country.

Attributes of Actors

We can classify actors by their attributes

- **Internal/External.** Internal actors are those within the company. Internal actors may have less resources, but they have access to the systems (many times they have admin level access). External actors require additional steps to access the system.
- **Level of Sophistication.** The level of sophistication is low with script kiddies and higher with nation states. Many attacks can be performed at low levels because of unpatched vulnerabilities or negligent security practices.
- **Resources/Funding.** Nation states and criminal organizations have better access to funding.
- **Intent/Motivation.** Organized crime and competitors have specific financial goals. Script kiddies just want bragging rights.

Use of Open-Source Intelligence

It is important for security professionals to share information about threats. For example, Las Vegas casinos all share information about individuals who pose a threat to their gambling operations.

Some locations where a security professional can find information include

- Industry organizations/lobby groups
- Government agencies (some government agencies are the source of security threats)
- Other companies in the same industry (even competitors)
- Internet blogs such as Stack Exchange

1.4 Explain penetration testing concepts

- *Active Reconnaissance*
- *Passive Reconnaissance*
- *Pivot*
- *Initial Exploitation*
- *Persistence*
- *Escalation of Privilege*
- *Black Box*
- *White Box*
- *Gray Box*
- *Penetration Testing vs Vulnerability Scanning*

A **penetration test** is when an outside person is hired to find security risks in an organization. Some organizations give the penetration tester permission to attack any system and discover all possible security holes because they want to make their systems better. Others limit the penetration tester's scope because they do not want to admit to their customers, employees, shareholders, or themselves that there are security flaws in their systems.

A penetration test does not have to be electronic in nature. It can be as simple as an unauthorized person walking into a building and stealing papers from a filing cabinet.

To properly perform a penetration test, the tester must know

- The common attack methods employed by hackers
- The type of information and resources that a hacker would like to steal (intellectual property, financial information, etc.)

The tester should obtain written approval from the highest levels of the organization before proceeding with the penetration test. Many of the actions performed by the tester could be considered crimes (trespassing, unauthorized access to a computer system, theft, fraud, etc.). If the tester is caught in the act, local staff may report him to the police.

Active Reconnaissance

In **active reconnaissance testing**, the tester uses methods that can be detected. These methods are more intrusive but allow deeper access. In addition, if the active reconnaissance is not detected, then it is clear that the enterprise does not have intrusion detection systems or does not monitor them.

Passive Reconnaissance

In passive reconnaissance testing, the tester uses methods that do not allow detection. They do so through user interviews, phishing attempts, internet searches, and use of wireless packet sniffers such as Wireshark. Passive reconnaissance methods cannot be detected.

Pivot

A **pivot** is when a tester infiltrates part of a network and uses it to attack a second part of the network. For example, a tester is unable to access the file server from outside the network. But the tester can infiltrate a user's computer, and then uses the user's computer to access the file server.

Initial Exploitation

The **initial exploitation** is the first attack that the tester completes. It is not necessarily the goal of the tester. It is to demonstrate how an attacker would enter a system. Consider this example

- An attacker would like to steal files from a file server
- The attacker first sends a phishing e-mail to an employee at the company
- The employee clicks on the link and allows the attacker to access his computer
- The attacker then uses the employee's computer to connect to the file server and steal the files

The initial exploitation is the phishing e-mail sent to the employee, but the actual goal is to take the files from the server.

Persistence

Persistence is placing an element (a backdoor) inside the network or system that does not go away. A back door could be created through a security hole, a piece of malware, or a user account. A back door could also be known as an Advanced Persistent Threat. Persistence is mainly used to steal data in the long term.

Escalation of Privilege

As discussed earlier, **Escalation of Privilege** is when Lower-level account is used to obtain higher privileges. Sometimes a process will run with administrative privileges but contains a security hole. Once the tester has infiltrated the system at a low level, he can take advantage of root processes to obtain additional privileges.

Black Box

A **Black Box test** is when the tester has no knowledge of the inner workings of the system. The tester interacts with the system just like a normal (or malicious) user, attempting different inputs to damage or infiltrate the system. A Black Box test simulates the normal operation of the application or system but does not detect all vulnerabilities.

White Box

A **White Box test** is when the tester has full knowledge of the inner workings of the system. The tester attempts to penetrate any item that he believes is weak. A white box tester will understand how data flows through the application and will be able to take advantage of all the different routes.

Gray Box

A **Gray Box test** is when the tester has some knowledge of the inner workings of the system. The tester interacts with the system just like a normal user but can also eliminate areas that are a waste of time to test. A Gray Box test can be the most efficient form of testing because all possible attack points are tested.

Penetration Testing vs Vulnerability Scanning

Vulnerability Scanning is the process of looking for security holes in a system. For example, a network administrator could use a port sniffer to detect open ports on a server or router.

- The system should be scanned on a regular basis. Due to software updates, configuration changes, and zero-day exploits, an administrator must never assume that a secure system will stay secure.

- Sometimes it's not possible to patch a hole in a system because the patch would reduce the system's functionality. In those cases, the administrator must add layers of security between the system and the public. These layers of security could include firewalls or monitoring.

  Imagine having an open patio on a house. An intruder could walk up to the patio and steal a chair. But taking the patio away (or locking up the chairs) would reduce the functionality of the patio. A better solution would be to install a fence, alarm, or surveillance cameras.

  Consider having a file server that is accessible to users inside and outside the network (necessary for remote/travelling employees). The file server is a security risk but disabling file sharing would reduce its functionality. The solution then is to
  - Use Windows authentication to permit/deny access to the file server (and/or to specific files/folders)
  - Install a VPN between the network and the outside world so that users working remotely must access the server through a VPN

- Some scenarios
  - A security hole in a Windows server operating system is discovered, and no patch is available for several weeks. The options are
    - Shut down the server until the patch is available. No users will be able to access the server.
    - Protect the server with a firewall (internal to the network)
  - A security hole is discovered in the firmware of a piece of industrial equipment at a factory, and the manufacturer of the equipment went out of business. The options are
    - Shut down production and attempt to repair the equipment. This will be expensive and may not even be possible.
    - Replace the equipment. It may take a long time to source replacement equipment that is compatible with the existing system.
    - Protect the equipment with a firewall or VLAN so that users are unable to access it. Threats can come from inside the network.

- In an organization, most actions undergo cost-benefit analysis. The organization must determine if the benefit from the security outweighs its cost (reduction of functionality).

1.5 Explain vulnerability scanning concepts

- *Passive Test Security Controls*
- *Identify Vulnerability*
- *Identify Lack of Security Controls*
- *Identify Common Misconfigurations*
- *Intrusive vs. Non-Intrusive*
- *Credentialed vs Non-Credentialed*
- *False Positive*

Passive Test Security Controls

In a **passive test**, the vulnerability scan checks the systems for security holes. It does not check actual security controls. For example, the vulnerability scan may detect open ports on a server (inside the network), which are not accessible outside the network due to the presence of a firewall.

A passive test will not identify vulnerabilities that are already protected by security controls. That means that the vulnerabilities can be exploited if the security controls are damaged or removed.

A vulnerability test looks for specific, pre-defined vulnerabilities, which could include

- Open ports on a server or other device
- Improperly configured access control lists on firewalls
- Network switch ports with no security
- Unused network switch ports that aren't shut down
- Port forwarding on a router
- Weak/default passwords on network equipment
- Servers with unpatched operating systems

Vulnerability tests aren't necessarily "creative". They do simulate initial actions taken by hackers to compromise systems (the initial exploits), but do not necessarily simulate all the steps a hacker would take.

Identify Vulnerability

After performing the vulnerability scan, the tools/administrator must be prepared to report the actual vulnerabilities detected. Only by reporting them can they be repaired.

Vulnerability reports can be automatically generated or manually created.

Reports can take many different formats depending on the quantity and type of data being collected and depending on the reader of the report (IT Department, Security Consultant, CEO, etc.) – know your audience! If the report is used to justify the cost of patching identified vulnerabilities, it may include a cost-benefit analysis or a discussion about the threat posed by each vulnerability.

The report may contain a large amount of sensitive data, but an organization may choose to make parts of the report public to promote transparency.

Identify Lack of Security Controls

The vulnerability test should identify exploits that are not protected by security controls. Security controls could include

- Firewalls
- MAC address filtering
- Strong passwords and automatic lockout/expiry of user accounts
- VLANs

Identify Common Misconfigurations

The vulnerability test should identify common misconfigurations of common equipment. These could include

- Firewalls
- Switches
- Routers
- Servers
- Computers
- VoIP Phones
- Surveillance cameras

Intrusive vs. Non-Intrusive

An intrusive vulnerability scan

- Makes changes to system components
- Is more disruptive to the operations of the organization (since systems may be reconfigured)

A non-intrusive vulnerability scan

- Does not make changes to system components
- Is less disruptive to the operations of the organization

Credentialed vs Non-Credentialed

A credentialed vulnerability scan

- Allows the scan tools to be configured with an authorized username/password
- Provides deeper access into the system (including into resources that are not normally accessible with a hacking tool)
- Is more disruptive to the operations of the organization (since systems may be reconfigured)
- May not accurately simulate the behavior of a hacker who does not have credentials to log in to the system, or may accurately simulate the behavior of a hacker who has obtained compromised credentials

A non-credentialed vulnerability scan

- Does not allow the scan tools to be configured with an authorized username/password
- Provide lower access into the system
- Is less disruptive to the operations of the organization
- May more accurately simulate the behavior of a hacker who does not have credentials to log in to the system

False Positive

A **False Positive** is when the vulnerability scan indicates the presence of a vulnerability that does not exist. The repair or patching of a false positive can be expensive.

A **False Negative** is when a vulnerability exists, but the scan does not detect it. False Negatives dangerous because they are not detected. It is not possible to know how many vulnerabilities exist that have not been detected.

1.6 Explain the impact associated with types of vulnerabilities

- *Race Conditions*
- *Vulnerabilities due to*
    - *End-of-Life Systems*
    - *Embedded Systems*
    - *Lack of Vendor Support*
- *Improper Input Handling*
- *Improper Error Handling*
- *Misconfiguration/Weak Configuration*
- *Default Configuration*
- *Resource Exhaustion*
- *Untrained Users*
- *Improperly Configured Accounts*
- *Vulnerable Business Processes*
- *Weak Cipher Suites and Implementations*
- *Memory/Buffer Vulnerability*
    - *Memory Leak*
    - *Integer Overflow*
    - *Buffer Overflow*
    - *Pointer Dereference*
    - *DLL Injection*
- *System Sprawl/Undocumented Assets*
- *Architecture/Design Weakness*
- *New Threats/Zero Day*
- *Improper Certificate and Key Management*

Race Conditions

A **race condition** is a programming error caused when multiple inputs or algorithms do not occur in the same order. In a typical computer program, the order of operations is that

- Inputs are collected
- The program performs operations on the inputs, in a specific order
- The program outputs the result

More complicated programs may take inputs from different sources or perform the operations in a different order than was intended, especially if some operations are slower than others. This can occur with multi-threaded programs and with asynchronous code (such as AJAX), where the program does multiple things at the same time.

AJAX is a web programming language that allows web pages to update without being refreshed. AJAX allows a web page to maintain a connection to the server and reload data when necessary. If the page itself needs to perform an operation on data that has not been received, errors can result.

Normal programming errors are typically "all or none". Either the error occurs, or it doesn't. Race condition errors may occur randomly or provide random results, depending on the timing of the other inputs or operations. This makes it more difficult to detect race condition errors.

Errors can be prevented by

- Providing valid references in the code
- Ensure that multi-threaded applications sync their threads
- Provide kernel locks
- With respect to AJAX, disable the asynchronous mode for algorithms that do not require it.

Vulnerabilities due to End-of-Life Systems, Embedded Systems, and Lack of Vendor Support

End-of-Life Systems

- An **end-of-life system** is one that has reached the end of its useful life (at least according to the manufacturer)
- The owner or user may still wish to continue using the system
    - The organization may not have an alternative system that can provide the same functionality, especially if it is a system that runs proprietary software
    - The organization may not have the financial resources or technical expertise to upgrade the system
    - The organization and/or users may be resistant to change
- The end-of-life is typically announced well in advance by the manufacturer (or can be predicted)
- The manufacturer will stop providing updates to the systems that have reached their end of life, and may stop looking for security holes that affect end-of-life systems
- Manufacturers of drivers, hardware, and software will also stop making devices and programs compatible with the old systems
- For example, end-of-life for the Windows XP operating system was on April 8, 2014, almost 12 years after it was released. Microsoft stopped providing support to most Windows XP users several years prior, but some organizations maintained extended maintenance contracts. On April 8, 2014, several alternatives were available including Windows 7, Windows 8, and Windows 10. Some organizations continue to use Windows XP.
- How to reduce risks with end-of-life systems
    - Understand that all systems have a finite life and plan for it. Record the date that end-of-life will occur and develop a migration plan prior to that date. The migration plan should include technical resources, a schedule, and a budget, and should be approved by management.
    - If it is not possible to migrate a system prior to the end of life, attempt to obtain the source code and retain developers who can modify it. This is a highly expensive option, and it is not usually possible to obtain the source code.
    - End-of-life systems that operate industrial equipment (and do not require modifications) should be air gapped (not accessible on a network) and full (bare metal) back ups should be made. In the event of a hardware or software failure, the system can be restored from back up.
    - Stockpile hardware and replacement parts for systems that are no longer manufactured. Extensively test software on replacement hardware (older software may not run on newer hardware).

Embedded Systems

144

- An **embedded system** is a system that is inside another system.
- Embedded systems can include the software that operates a vehicle, refrigerator, or industrial control system.
- The software may be contained on a Read Only Memory chip that cannot be modified. It may not be possible to detect or patch security vulnerabilities on the embedded system without remanufacturing the device.
- In addition, the software on the embedded system may be proprietary.
- How to prevent
  - Thoroughly research the manufacturer's reputation and expertise before purchasing any equipment
  - Attempt to locate products that use open source firmware and that can be updated
  - Develop a mitigation strategy such as a stockpile of replacement products from another vendor

Lack of Vendor Support

A manufacturer may not offer support for their product because

- The product has reached the end of its life
- The manufacturer has ceased operations
- The manufacturer has poor customer service and/or does not provide support without an expensive maintenance contract, which the client refuses to pay for (or cannot afford)
- The product's warranty has expired or has been invalidated (due to misuse, improper use, use with incompatible equipment, etc.)
- The customer purchased the product from an unauthorized source and the manufacturer refuses to support it
- The manufacturer no longer has the expertise to support the product or the manufacturer purchased the product from a white-label vendor (and the white-label vendor refuses to provide support)

Improper Input Handling

Consider that any computer program or application has three components

- **The input**
    - The input could be any kind of data
    - The input could be a file, a piece of text, a photograph, a phone number, or data collected from a sensor
    - A program can collect one or more inputs
    - A program can collect inputs by prompting users or automatically by querying other computers or programs
    - The input is collected from the user's computer (this is known as the 'client side') and sent to the server (this is known as the 'server side')
- **The algorithm**
    - The algorithm is what the program does to the input
    - For example, the program might take a phone number and enter it into a database, or take an e-mail address and send an automatic e-mail, or take a photograph and sharpen it
- **The output**
    - The output is the result of the program
    - The output can be provided to the user, e-mailed, stored in a database, stored in a file, etc.

Every language is different, but in general, computer programs do not like "special characters", such as commas, quotation marks, and especially semicolons. These special characters are used by programming languages to indicate the end of a line or the end of a piece of data. When inputted by users, they can trick the program into ending prematurely or receiving incorrect data.

The software should check to make sure that inputs are valid

- The software should check on the 'client side' and prompt the user to correct the input if it is in the wrong format. Checking on the client side is user friendly and takes up less resources from the server.
- The software should also check on the 'server side' because some users are sneaky and will attempt to bypass the error handling that is running on their own computer and send invalid data directly to the server.

How to prevent

- Escape special characters. Users may enter semicolons, or other special characters that the software does not understand. It is easy to "escape" special characters so that the program can understand them as input and not as part of its own code.
- Escaping special characters also prevents attacks such as cross-site scripting and cross-site request forgery.

- Use prepared statements to prevent SQL injection attacks.
- Users may enter data in the wrong format. Scripts exist to detect if the user has entered a valid e-mail address (name@domain.com), a valid phone number ((XXX)-(XXX-XXXX)) or a valid address/postal code. Improper data can be a waste of time for the person inputting data and for the person collecting it.

Improper Error Handling

Despite the best coding and testing, every computer program and web application will run into errors. Errors are common with agile code development, where new versions of the application are released each week, and with applications that are updated live.

When a program runs into an error, it should

- Record the update in a log that is accessible only to the developer/manager. The logs can be reviewed to detect and correct the sources of the error.

The program should not send the result of the error to the user. Errors could contain portions of the source code, SQL scripts, and file locations. A malicious user can use the errors to further exploit the system.

Misconfiguration/Weak Configuration

There are many ways that a system could be misconfigured

- Applications/Processes that consume too many system resources
- Use of default user accounts/passwords
- Lack of software updates
- Improper security rules (such as no firewall, open ports, no VLANs, etc.)

Default Configuration

The **default configuration** is the configuration that ships from the factory. The default configuration is not necessarily secure and may contain weak/no usernames/passwords. Sometimes it is not possible to change the default configuration or some of its components.

Some manufacturers create systems that are secure by default and will force users to choose secure credentials before allowing the system to operate.

Resource Exhaustion

Resource Exhaustion is where a system no longer has resources to operate. Some of the resources that a system requires

- **Memory**. Every system needs memory to run its applications. When the system does not have adequate memory, it slows down. It stores data in a page file. If the program does not have adequate garbage collection (release memory that is no longer in use), it could run out of memory quickly. For example, a hacker could create additional processes that occupy the system's memory and overload it, slowing it down or preventing it from completing other tasks. This could cause the system to shut down other running processes.

- **Hard Drive Space**. Every system needs hard drive space. Programs generate logs and other files that continue to fill up the space, and errors result when the hard drive is full. For example, hacker could cause the system to run out of hard drive space by uploading files (if the application allows it) or running processes that generate logs. When programs are no longer able to save to disk, they may crash.

- **Network Capacity**. Every system needs network capacity to communicate with the outside world and with other hosts on the network. For example, a hacker could launch a DDoS attack against a system that causes it to stop communicating.

Untrained Users

Untrained users and users who are computer-illiterate can cause damage to different systems. Ways in which users can cause damage

- Users are vulnerable to phishing scams and solicitations
- Users download and install malware onto their own computers and onto servers (or allow malware to spread across the network)
- Users misconfigure applications and systems without realizing it
- Users unplug power and network cables from switches, routers, and computers and then insert them into the wrong ports when the internet isn't working for them

Some users are well-educated (engineers, CEOs, etc.) and even highly-technical, but may be untrained with more complicated systems (such as routers and storage appliances).

How to prevent

- Proper user education
- Automatic scripts to set up computers
- Do not provide users with administrative credentials regardless of their position in the organization
- Keep network equipment secured

Improperly Configured Accounts

There are many types of accounts, and all accounts should be properly configured.

- Accounts to access network hardware/embedded devices. In many cases, the account credentials are embedded into the firmware and cannot be modified.

- On high end hardware such as Cisco Routers and Cisco Switches, there is an option to log in with a local account (stored on the device) or a server (such as RADIUS or TACAS server). It is better to use a server, where accessible. The default username and password should be changed, and/or local accounts should be disabled. Disabling the local account may not be practical if there is a network error and connectivity to the RADIUS or TACAS server is down (in which case only the local account can be used to log in).

  A person can reset the password on a Cisco device if that person has physical access to it. Therefore, network equipment should always be kept physically secure.

- On a large network, there may be hundreds or thousands of user accounts. There are generally two types of user accounts.
    - **Local Accounts**. A local account's credentials are stored on a local computer and allow access to only that computer. A local account may be an administrative account or a user account.

      The default local admin account should be changed or disabled. When the Windows operating system is not encrypted, it is always possible to enable the local admin account and/or reset its password by using a USB tool (such as Hirens Boot CD).

      If it is necessary to use a local administrative account, ensure that the BitLocker is enabled. In a large organization, the admin login and password should be randomized (don't use the same credentials for every computer).

      A user can use a local administrative account to crack the password for a domain account (and possibly for a domain administrative account).
        - If a Windows service is running under a domain account, then the password is stored on the computer in a reversible hash format.
        - Recall from earlier that it is good security practice to hash passwords and that it is possible to exploit a login by directly inputting the hash into a system. Windows passwords are hashed, but it is possible to obtain the hash of a domain account that had logged in to the computer and then to use the hash to authenticate again.
    - **Active Directory Accounts**. An Active Directory account's credentials are stored on a server. An Active Directory account can provide access to any computer that is

on the same domain. Active Directory accounts can provide more granular control, including

- Specific settings that a user is permitted to modify on a computer
- Access to specific printers and scanners
- Access to different shared folders and files
- Access to wireless networks
- Integration with, and access to, other applications such as SAP, Payroll, CRM, etc.
- Active Directory Groups
  - When there are many Active Directory accounts, it is difficult to manage each one separately.
  - An administrator will instead create groups. Each group has its own set of policies and parameters.
  - Groups can be based on what role or position a user plays in the organization (for example, the HR group provides access to the personnel files, and the Marketing group provides access to the Marketing Materials Folder).
  - A user can belong to one or more groups.
  - In a large organization, there may be hundreds or thousands of groups.
  - Security risks can result when a user belongs to the wrong group or when the group's policies are not properly configured. In those cases, the user may be provided with access to resources that he is not entitled to.

Vulnerable Business Processes

A **vulnerable business process** is a procedure in an organization that can be exploited. Vulnerable business processes can be found in any department but are most likely to be attacked when they involve money or proprietary data. Areas where processes can be exploited include

- Payroll
- Receiving invoices & paying vendors
- Recording and storing sensitive data
- Manufacturing processes

It is important to test all business processes, especially when they are automated. Companies automate common/frequent processes to reduce labor costs and errors. But automated processes can be exploited.

Weak Cipher Suites and Implementations

Data in transit (and in storage) should be encrypted with a strong algorithm.

Think of the algorithm like a lock on a door. There are many types of locks. Some locks can be easily broken or picked, and some locks are secure. Just like a lock on a door, every algorithm requires a key to operate. If every door had the same lock and the same key, then the algorithm wouldn't be secure against other people who had access to the key. With a computer algorithm, the key is a long, randomly-generated, number. A number so long it wouldn't fit on this page. The key to a good algorithm is the ability to randomly generate long numbers. The longer the key, the harder it is to crack.

There are three main ways to develop/implement encryption algorithms that are guaranteed to fail

- Developing a cryptographic algorithm or writing an implementation of an algorithm. It takes years to develop, test, and trust cryptographic algorithms, and even then, many cryptographic algorithms are regularly exploited. No organization has the technical capability to develop their own cryptographic algorithm.

  Cryptographic algorithms use complicated math. Cryptographic algorithms are supposed to rely on random numbers, but computers are not capable of truly generating random numbers. Instead, algorithms contain random number generators (code that attempts to generate numbers as randomly as possible).

  The random number generation can be frequently exploited in an algorithm. These exploits are not usually detectable until the algorithm has been in use for many years and patterns in the encrypted data emerge. At that point, the algorithm is known to be flawed and all the data encrypted by it becomes exploitable.

  Keep in mind that hackers (and government agencies) intercept and store encrypted data, waiting for a time when the algorithm becomes exploitable.

- Using a proprietary algorithm. A proprietary algorithm is one whose inner workings are kept a secret. The proprietary algorithms must not be used because it is never possible to understand whether it is functioning properly or not. In addition, the manufacturer of the proprietary algorithm may have inserted a backdoor that is undetectable.

- Using a weak algorithm. A weak algorithm is one that was previously accepted but is no longer considered secure.

  As computing power increases, it becomes possible to crack algorithms with keys of longer and longer lengths. Algorithms that were once considered uncrackable are now easily

156

exploitable.

Eventually (due to advances in computing power), every form of encryption used today will be cracked, and the data that was encrypted will be exploited. In theory, many of the forms of encryption in use today won't be cracked for at least 100 years, at which point, the data protected by them will be considered useless.

A strong algorithm can be implemented weakly. For example, the algorithm could be incorporated into a software program that does not randomly generate keys or that uses the same keys over and over. Each person who uses the software program encrypts their data with the same key.

How to prevent?

- One should assume that all encrypted data (and unencrypted data) in transit is being intercepted and stored forever.
- Select an algorithm that is well known to be secure and open-source.
- Ensure that the implementation of the algorithm is also secure and open-source.
- The longer the key, the harder it is to crack the data encrypted by the algorithm. At the same time, the longer the key, the longer it takes to encrypt the data. It is important to select a key length that balances those two concerns. Think about how much time it will take a hacker to decrypt the data (1 year, 10 years, 100 years?) and whether the data will still have value at that time.

Memory/Buffer Vulnerability

Memory Leaks and Buffer Vulnerabilities are caused by programming errors. There are several types

- **Memory Leak.** Every computer program occupies computer memory when it is running. The amount of memory depends on the size of the program and the type of data that it needs to store.

  Each portion of memory has a unique address. The program can call the memory and ask for data contained at a specific address (if that portion of the memory is assigned to it). For security reasons, a program should not be able to access memory assigned to a different program or to the operating system.

  Once a program is done with a portion of the memory, it should release it. This is known as "garbage collection". Some languages have an automatic garbage collection (a programmer doesn't have to worry about writing extra lines of code to reserve and release portions of memory)

For example, if a photograph is opened in Adobe Photoshop, that photograph is stored in the memory. If a website is opened in Google Chrome, that website is stored in the memory. The website shouldn't be able to access the photograph. If the website is closed or the photograph is closed, the portion of the memory where it resided should be released.

If the memory is not released, then eventually the memory becomes full of abandoned data from programs that might not even be running. When the computer runs out of memory, it starts to slow down or crash. The memory leaks are resolved when the computer reboots, but some computers and servers cannot be rebooted because they are in use by many people.

- **Integer Overflow.** An integer overflow is when a program attempts to store a value that is too large.

  Consider that in a programming language, there are many forms of inputs known as variables. In some programming languages, the programmer must "declare" the variable and its type before attempting to store data in it.

  The most common types of variables are
  - **String**. A string is a variable that can contain any type of character and can have a length of up to 256 characters.
  - **Integer**. An integer is a type of variable that can contain a whole number such as 1, 3, -1000, 45. An integer cannot contain a decimal.
  - **Single/Double**. A single/double is a type of variable that can contain a decimal.

  Depending on the type of language, the result of attempting to store a decimal value in an integer variable could be that the program crashes, nothing is stored, or a value such as '99999999' (or whatever the maximum value for that variable is) is stored.

- **Buffer Overflow.** A buffer is a place where input is stored prior to being accepted by the program. A hacker can overload the buffer by sending data that is larger than expected. For example, if phone numbers are ten digits long and a buffer is designed to hold phone numbers, a hacker could exploit it by sending data that is eleven digits long.

  A buffer saves data to memory. Prior to accepting the data, the buffer should check that it is the correct length. If it is too long, the buffer should reject the data. Without error handling, the buffer might attempt to store all the data in memory, which could overwrite other portions of the program or sensitive data.

- **Pointer Dereference.** Some programming languages use pointers.
  - As mentioned previously, all programming languages use variables to store data.

- When a programmer wants to use the value stored by the variable, the programmer references the variable. The data stored in the variable is stored in the memory, but the exact location is abstract and not relevant to the programmer.
- In some languages, the pointer is a variable that points to a specific address in the memory where the data is stored.
- The pointer is asking the computer to return the data stored at a specific address. The data may or may not be the correct data.

A pointer dereference is the act of obtaining the data stored by the pointer. The dereference can cause data leaks if the programming is sloppy and the wrong data is returned.

- **DLL Injection.** A DLL or Dynamic Link Library is a set of codes stored separately from the program. Many developers use DLLs so that they do not have to rewrite lines of code to perform common functions (such as figure out what time it is, read a file, write to a file, etc.).

A hacker can modify a DLL to perform malicious tasks and then insert it in a place where a good DLL was. The program will run the malicious DLL and execute the tasks placed by the hacker.

System Sprawl/Undocumented Assets

System Sprawl is when the computer system grows, and nobody knows what anybody has.

One company started out small and then merged with a larger company. During the merger, they connected all their hardware together. Eventually, the company grew bigger and acquired over 100 smaller companies. Each time, they took the hardware (computers, servers, switches, and routers) and connected them together. Eventually, nobody knew what equipment they had or how it worked. They couldn't keep track of the warranty repair, and when something broke, there was no procedure for fixing it.

Why is system sprawl bad?

- There is no consistency with respect to the brand or model of equipment in use. The organization may have equipment from dozens or hundreds of different vendors. It is difficult to maintain equipment from the different vendors or to obtain discounts.
- The organization is not aware of the age of the assets. There is no procedure to refresh the assets when they reach a certain age. When assets break down, there is no procedure to repair or replace them.
- The organization is not able to take advantage of warranty repairs associated with the assets.
- The organization may have unsecure hardware that hackers can exploit. The organization is not aware of the status of any asset (whether it is patched, secured, etc.).
- When it is time for an upgrade, the organization will not be aware of what systems should be upgraded. Replacing key pieces of equipment could cause the whole system to fail if nobody is aware of how things are connected or how they work together.

How to prevent

- Use an asset tracking program to track every piece of computer hardware purchased. The program can be integrated into SCCM or Active Directory so that the organization can keep track of
    - The exact location of each asset
    - Its manufacturer, serial number, model number, and warranty status
    - What it is connected to
    - The type of software installed, its configuration, and the status of any software updates
    - The user that it is assigned to
- Use an asset tracking program to track every device. Ensure that newly purchased devices are entered into the program.
- Give each device a unique hostname that identifies the type of device, its location, and its role
- Physically label each device

160

- Create network diagrams that show where devices are physically installed (physical diagrams) and how their ports are connected (logical diagrams)

Architecture/Design Weakness

Proper network design and architecture is important to keep data secure. Ways in which a network may be insecure

- Not enough VLANs or segmentation between different types of devices
- Port forwarding enabled without VPNs
- No encryption between devices
- No ACLs in place on switches or routers

New Threats/Zero Day

As mentioned previously, a **zero day** is a threat that has just been discovered and for which there is no patch. Once the zero-day threat is known to the public, the manufacturer will attempt to patch it (if the manufacturer still exists).

A zero-day threat can be discovered and exploited by a hacker days, weeks, or even years prior to the threat being known to the public. That means that the threat can be exploited for years before the public is made aware.

How can an organization protect themselves against threats that they don't even know exist? They can't. But an organization can use multiple layers of security to mitigate the risk associated with a zero-day threat, such as

- Applying patches to servers
- Strong passwords on servers and encryption
- Firewalls between servers and the internet
- VLANs and ACLs

Improper Certificate and Key Management

A **certificate** validates the identity of a third party or device. Certificates and encryption algorithms operate with Public Keys (which are known to the public) and Private Keys (which are only known by the holder.

If a **Private Key** is disclosed to another individual, intercepted communications could be decrypted by unauthorized persons.

Part C: SY0-501 2.0 Technologies and Tools

2.1 Install and configure network components, both hardware and software-based, to support organizational security

- *Firewall*
  - *ACL*
  - *Application-Based vs Network-Based*
  - *Stateful vs Stateless*
  - *Implicit Deny*
- *VPN Concentrator*
  - *Remote Access vs. Site-to-Site*
  - *IPSec*
    - *Tunnel Mode*
    - *Transport Mode*
    - *AH*
    - *ESP*
  - *Split Tunnel vs. Full Tunnel*
  - *TLS*
  - *Always-On VPN*
- *NIPS/NIDS*
  - *Signature-Based*
  - *Heuristic/Behavioral*
  - *Anomaly*
  - *Inline vs Passive*
  - *In-Band vs Out-of-Band*
  - *Rules*
  - *Analytics*
    - *False Positive*
    - *False Negative*
- *Router*
  - *ACLs*
  - *Antispoofing*
- *Switch*
  - *Port Security*
  - *Layer 2 vs Layer 3*
  - *Loop Prevention*
  - *Flood Guard*
- *Proxy*

- o Forward and Reverse Proxy
- o Transparent
- o Application/Multipurpose
- Load Balancer
  - o Scheduling
    - o Affinity
    - o Round-Robin
  - o Active-Passive
  - o Active-Active
  - o Virtual IPs
- Access Point
  - o SSID
  - o MAC Filtering
  - o Signal Strength
  - o Band Selection/Width
  - o Antenna Types and Placement
  - o Fat vs Thin
  - o Controller-Based vs Standalone
- SIEM
  - o Aggregation
  - o Correlation
  - o Automated Alerting and Triggers
  - o Time Synchronization
  - o Event Deduplication
  - o Logs/WORM
- DLP
  - o USB Blocking
  - o Cloud-Based
  - o Email
- NAC
  - o Dissolvable vs Permanent
  - o Host Health Checks
  - o Agent vs. Agentless
- Mail Gateway
  - o SPAM Filter
  - o DLP
  - o Encryption
- Bridge
- SSL/TLS Accelerators
- SSL Decryptors

- *Media Gateway*
- *Hardware Security Module*

Physical Security

Before discussing any network component's logical/digital security, it is important to understand how to configure the device.

Most devices allow configuration through a serial or USB console cable. A device can also be configured remotely. Configuration is typically password protected. Typically, there can be three passwords

- A basic login (most administrators don't activate the basic login, allows user to view basic data about the device)
- An enable password (allows more advanced settings, including the ability to view the configuration)
- A Configuration Terminal password (allows configuration changes)

The passwords can be set locally, or the device can be configured to connect to a RADIUS authentication server, which allows users to authenticate through Active Directory or similar protocols. If the "local" passwords are not enabled and there is no internet connection, a local user will not be able to log in to the device.

On most network devices, a user can reset the password by rebooting the device and holding down a mode or reset button. Some devices can be set to prevent the reset mechanism from functioning, which could be good or bad

- If the reset mechanism is enabled, and an intruder gains physical access to the device, he could reset the password and then read the configuration.
- If the reset mechanism is disabled, and the password is lost, the configuration cannot be updated.

Firewall

A **firewall** monitors and filters traffic on a network.

A firewall sits between the internet (WAN) and the local network (LAN). A firewall could also sit between different segments of a LAN. For example, a firewall could sit between a group of servers and the remainder of the network.

A firewall could be hardware based or software based. A firewall could be a component of a larger network device such as a router. In a large organization where a great deal of traffic passes through the network, a large, hardware-based firewall must be installed. Firewalls are rated based on the volume of traffic that they can handle. Of course, more complicated configurations can reduce the amount of traffic that a firewall can handle.

Common firewall brands include
- Sonicwall
- Cisco ASA (Adaptive Security Appliance)
- Fortigate
- Cisco Meraki

Configuration of a firewall may be
- Through a console (requiring special commands)
- Through a web-based GUI or software-based GUI
- Automatically through the cloud, which is useful for organizations that deploy dozens, hundreds, or thousands of devices

An organization may select a firewall brand based on their existing network infrastructure. For example, if the customer uses Cisco switches and routers in their network, they may choose to install Cisco ASA firewalls as well.

There are four components to a firewall configuration

- **ACL or Access Control List**. The Access Control List is a set of rules for what traffic is permitted to pass and what traffic is not permitted. There are many types of rules, based on
  - **Source IP address**. Where is the traffic coming from? The source IP address could be on the LAN or on the WAN. It could be a specific IP address or a range of addresses.

- **Destination IP address**. Where is the traffic going? The destination IP address could be on the LAN or on the WAN. It could be a specific IP address or a range of addresses.
- **Source Port Number**. What is the port number of the source traffic? The source port could be on the LAN or on the WAN. It could be a specific port or a range of ports.
- **Destination Port Number**. What is the port number of the destination traffic? The destination port could be on the LAN or on the WAN. It could be a specific port or a range of ports.
- **Username**. Access Control Lists can be user-based. Permissions can be granted or denied to specific users based on their needs in the organization. For example, guests can be permitted to access only the internet and not resources such as remote desktop or SQL servers.
- Rules can be specific or could combine a combination of parameters
  - For example, a rule could say 'Allow traffic from 10.1.1.1, port 5 to the range of IPs 192.168.3.0 to 192.168.3.255'. All traffic received from 10.1.1.1 port 5 will be permitted to access destinations in the range of 192.168.3.0 to 192.168.3.255. Traffic from other source IP addresses and/or ports will be rejected. Traffic from 10.1.1.1 to destinations outside of 192.168.3.0 and 192.168.3.255 will be rejected.
  - Always Allow. An Always Allow rule allows all traffic matching a rule. For example, "always allow traffic from the source IP 10.1.1.1". All traffic from 10.1.1.1 will be permitted regardless of the port number or destination.
  - Always Deny. An Always Deny rule denies all traffic matching a rule. For example, "always deny traffic from the source IP 10.1.1.1". All traffic from 10.1.1.1 will be denied regardless of the port number or destination.
- Order of Operations
  - A firewall could have dozens or thousands of rules. The rules are ranked in order of priority.
  - When the firewall receives a piece of traffic, it starts checking the rules in order until it finds one that matches the traffic's source and destination. It then applies that rule to the traffic.
  - The firewall will only apply one rule to a piece of traffic. Once that rule is applied, the firewall stops checking additional rules.
  - It is important to put the rules in order. When a firewall receives a piece of traffic that does not match any rules, it will either allow or reject the traffic based on its configuration.
  - Many firewalls are preconfigured with two default rules
    - Always allow traffic with a source inside the network (LAN)

- Always reject traffic with a source outside the network (WAN)
  - The two default rules should be put at the bottom of the list.
    - The first rule (allowing all traffic from inside the LAN) is dangerous because users cannot be trusted to access only safe resources on the internet. It should be modified (broken down) into two rules.
      - Always allow traffic with a
        - Source inside the network (LAN)
        - Destination outside the network (WAN)
        - Limited to specific ports outside the network (port 80, port 443, port 3306, etc.). The specific ports should be based on resources that users need to access.
      - Always deny traffic
        - Source inside the network (LAN)
        - Destination outside the network (WAN)
        - This rule applies second; any traffic not matching the previous rule will be denied

- **Application-Based vs Network-Based**
  - An application-based firewall will analyse traffic on a deeper level than a network-based firewall
  - The network-based firewall looks at traffic source and destination IP addresses, but the application-based firewall also looks at its contents
  - The application-based firewall does not look at the packets themselves but what is inside and forwards the data to the applications that require them.
  - An analogy is a person who is screening mail. A network-based firewall would look at the to and from addresses on the envelope before deciding whether to forward the mail. An application-based firewall would open each envelope and look at the contents.
  - Application-based firewalls can slow down traffic because they are analyzing the contents of each packet.

- **Stateful vs Stateless**
  - Consider that almost all traffic on the internet is two-way traffic. When a user downloads a file from the internet, that file download is two-way. The sender's computer is sending the file, one piece at a time (in packets). Each time the user's computer receives a packet, it acknowledges receipt. This is known as a connection.
  - Each connection is originated by only one party. In this case, the person who downloaded the file originated the connection.

- A stateless firewall applies rules based only on the source and destination IP addresses and ports of the packets., but a stateful firewall will identify which party originated the connection (whether that party was inside the network or outside), and then block or allow it based on the source. A packet that is normally permitted or denied by an ACL may be denied or permitted by a stateful firewall.
- A stateful firewall requires additional hardware to process the decision making.

- **Implicit Deny**
  - As mentioned previously, a firewall lists its rules in order and applies the first rule that matches the traffic
  - If the traffic does not match any rule, the firewall should deny it
  - This is known as "implicit deny"
  - The last rule in the list should be to deny all traffic

Cloud-Based Firewalls

Newer firewalls such as Fortigates and Cisco Meraki MX Series routers connect to the cloud. The cloud allows them to

- Automatically receive firmware updates
- Automatically download and update their configuration (and allow an administrator to configure multiple devices at the same time)
- Share threat intelligence data, even across organizations. For example, if a firewall detects a threat, it can upload the data to the cloud, where it is shared by many firewalls across the organization.

VPN Concentrator

A **VPN** is a **Virtual Private Network**. It allows a remote user (working from home, a hotel, a hotspot, etc.) to connect to a corporate network through a tunnel. Essentially, the traffic from the user's computer is packaged and sent through a tunnel to the corporate network. If the user accesses a website, that request is sent to the corporate network. The corporate network sends the traffic to the website. It takes the traffic that it received from the website and sends it back to the user through the VPN. Therefore, traffic received from the user appears to be coming from the corporate network, regardless of the user's location.

A VPN "tricks" the user's computer into thinking that it is on the corporate network so that the user can access resources such as internal applications, shared drives, and printers.

A VPN concentrator is a device that collects and manages VPN connections from multiple users and passes their traffic to the LAN. It could be hardware-based or software-based. The VPN concentrator functionality can be incorporated into another network device such as a router.

VPN functionality is incorporated into devices such as
- Cisco Routers
- Cisco ASAs
- Fortigates
- Sonicwall
- Cisco Meraki Routers

Remote users can use software to establish VPNs (such as Windows VPN or Cisco AnyConnect) or can install hardware-based VPN appliances such as Meraki Z3.

Features of the VPN concentrator include

- **Remote Access vs. Site-to-Site**. A Remote Access VPN allows users to connect back to a corporate network, typically through their computer. A Site-to-Site VPN allows two offices to connect to each other and pretend like they are part of the same physical network. A Site-to-Site VPN typically applies to the site's router and not to individual devices on the network.
  - o The performance on a VPN is affected by the quality of the user's internet connection, by the quality of the corporate network's internet connection, by the number of active users, and by the type of resources being accessed.
  - o When there are multiple sites that need to be connected, a site-to-site VPN should be replaced by a WAN

- **IPSec**. IPSec is a set of protocols that allow hosts to exchange packets securely. IPSec has several modes of operation, including
  - **Tunnel Mode**. The Tunnel Mode encrypts the source, destination, and contents of every packet. Essentially, it establishes a secure tunnel between two network devices where data can travel securely. The devices that are establishing the tunnel are not necessarily the devices that are creating the traffic. For example, a router is sending traffic on behalf of a server inside the network. An outsider will not be able to examine the source, destination, or contents of any traffic.

  - **Transport Mode**. The Transport Mode only encrypts the contents of the packet. It does not encrypt the source or destination. An outsider will be able to examine the source and destination. Transport Mode is established by the two network devices who are communicating, and not by the routers on the edges of the network.

  - **SA**. An SA, or Security Association is an algorithm and key that are used to encrypt traffic in an IPSec tunnel. Each direction of communication requires a separate SA. Therefore, most IPSec tunnels will require two SAs.

  - There are four methods of connecting a tunnel. Consider that two computers (each inside a separate network and behind a router) would like to communicate securely across the internet. How can an IPSec tunnel be established?
    - **Machine-to-Machine**. Two computers (or smartphones) establish a tunnel and communicate. This is not practical because each computer will expend a substantial amount of computing power encrypting and decrypting the IPSec traffic.
    - **Router-to-Router**. It is assumed that the connection between the computer and the router (on the internal network) is secure. The routers establish an IPSec tunnel. The computers no longer encrypt traffic between themselves and the routers. The routers encrypt all traffic between themselves.
    - **Machine-to-Machine and Router-to-Router**. This combines the previous two scenarios. Each machine establishes an IPSec tunnel with the router on its network, and the routers establish an IPSec tunnel between themselves.
    - **Remote User**. A remote user connects to a router through an IPSec tunnel, and then establishes a secondary IPSec tunnel to connect to a device deeper in the network.

  - **Tunnel Mode Encryption**. The tunnel mode is the method for encrypting the traffic. Consider that two routers have created an IPSec tunnel and that behind each router is a computer that wants to communicate. What is the order of operations?
    - The computer generates some data and places it in a packet.

- The computer puts the address of the remote computer in the header of the packet (or the address of the network that it is sending it to, when the network employs NAT – more on this later).
- The computer sends the packet to the router
- The router encrypts this packet, including the headers
- The router encapsulates this packet inside a larger packet and adds the recipient's router address to the header
- The router sends the packet to the destination router
- The destination router removes the outer header, decrypts the packet, and forwards it to the computer inside its network
- Neither computer is aware of the existence of the IPSec tunnel
    o Tunnel encryption works through the following security protocols
- **AH**. Authentication Header. When AH is used, the original IP header (created by the computer that generated the data) is visible to outsiders, but the contents are protected. AH protects the integrity of the data. That is, the recipient can be sure that the sender listed on the packet is in fact the true sender.
- **ESP**. Encapsulating Security Payload. ESP encrypts the contents of the data, but it does not guarantee integrity.
- It is recommended to use both AH and ESP, thereby providing privacy and integrity.
    o **IPSec algorithms**
- IPSec is a framework for exchanging data, but the contents of the framework vary from vendor to vendor and network to network. Just like there can be many different models of vehicles on a road, all following the same traffic rules, there can be many different types of algorithms to exchange data within a tunnel.
- Many different encryption algorithms can be used. This flexibility allows an algorithm to be replaced when it is discovered to be weak.
- Methods include
    • Diffie-Hellman key exchange with public key signing
    • MD5 and SHA-1 hashing algorithms to ensure data integrity
    o **IPv4 vs IPv6**. IPSec is integrated into all IPv6 packets by default, but not IPv4 packets. When IPv4 was designed, security was not a primary consideration. As the internet grew, the design of IPv6 required security to be integrated into all communications. A device can use IPv6 and not activate the IPSec feature however.

- **Split Tunnel vs. Full Tunnel**
    o In a Full Tunnel VPN, all traffic is routed through the VPN, but in a Split Tunnel VPN, only specific traffic is routed through the VPN.

o The advantage of a split tunnel is that it reduces bottlenecks. Consider a corporate user working from home. The user needs to access network resources such as a shared drive and corporate finance applications. This traffic must go over the VPN. The user is also watching YouTube videos. There is no reason to route YouTube videos over the corporate network (requiring encryption on both sides). YouTube traffic can travel over the user's home internet connection.

- **TLS**. In addition to providing internet security, Transport Layer Security is an alternative to IPSec VPN. A TLS VPN is useful when the network uses NAT.

- **Always-On VPN**. An Always-On VPN is just like it sounds. It is a VPN that is always on. Typically, an Always-On VPN is part of a hardware appliance, but it could also be software-based. When the VPN detects an active internet connection, it automatically attempts to re-establish the VPN.

  For security purposes, an Always-On VPN can block traffic from travelling over the internet when the VPN is not running. This would prevent a user from inadvertently disclosing his true location.

NIPS/NIDS

A **NIPS** is a **Network-Based Intrusion Prevention System**, and a **NIDS** is a **Network-Based Intrusion Detection System**.

A NIDS can only detect unauthorized access, but a NIPS can detect and react to the unauthorized access.

NIPS and NIDS have the following characteristics:
- Signature-Based: Similar to an antivirus program, a NIPS can detect an intrusion based on its "signature" or specific characteristics. For example, an intrusion enters through a specific port or from a specific source IP address. A signature-based NIPS/NIDS will not detect attacks that are zero-day or attacks that don't match the signature.
- Heuristic/Behavioral: Like an antivirus program, a NIPS can detect an intrusion based on the way it behaves, more like artificial intelligence. A heuristic-based NIPS can detect zero-day attacks but has a higher rate of false positives.
- Anomaly. An anomaly-based NIPS/NIDS compares new traffic against a baseline. The NIPS/NIDS calibrates itself to understand normal network behavior, and then compares new traffic against that calibration. Traffic that does not match is denied.
- Inline vs Passive. An inline sensor sits between the internet and the internal network. All traffic passes through the sensor, which decides if it should be permitted or denied. An inline sensor can turn off the flow of bad traffic. If the inline sensor is overloaded, it can reduce the speed or capacity of the network. A passive sensor sits on the network but receives a copy of the traffic. A passive sensor cannot turn off the flow of bad traffic.
- In-Band vs Out-of-Band. An in-band sensor is a complete system that monitors traffic and decides whether to allow or prevent it. An out-of-band sensor monitors traffic and sends results to another system that decides whether to block it.
- Rules. Rules are decision making processes that the NIPS/NIDS uses to determine whether the traffic should be permitted or denied. NIPS/NIDS can be preloaded with rules, and an administrator can add additional rules as needed. A NIPS/NIDS with heuristic behavior can automatically create additional rules based on its findings.
- Analytics
  - False Positive. A false positive is when a NIPS or NIDS alerts to an intrusion attempt that is a source of legitimate network activity.
  - False Negative. A false negative is when the NIPS or NIDS allows traffic through that is an intrusion attempt.
  - There must be a balance between false positives and false negatives. Increasing the sensitivity of the NIPS/NIDS will create more false positives. False positives that block legitimate traffic can disrupt the operations of the organization and frustrate users. They require additional administrator attention to correct the false positives. False negatives are dangerous because they allow intrusion attempts. There is no

way to identify a false negative until after it has occurred, and many false negatives go undetected. Lowering the sensitivity of the NIPS/NIDS increases the number of false negatives. A NIPS/NIDS with artificial intelligence can learn from its mistakes.

Router

A **router** connects two or more networks together. A router receives packets of data (from inside and outside the network) and then decides where to forward the packets to.

A router will contain a routing table (a set of static routes), which tell it where to send data based on the subnet of its destination address. In a simple setup, a router may only have one destination to send data to.

The most common type of router security is an ACL or Access Control List. An ACL is a list of source subnets (networks) and their permitted destinations. Like a set of firewall rules, an ACL check each data packed against the ACL and apply the first rule that matches.

A rule can be "always allow" or "always deny". For example
- Always deny traffic from addresses in the range of 252.252.252.0 to 252.252.252.255
- Always allow traffic from 192.168.2.1

A rule can apply to one or more router interfaces and to one or both directions. Each router manufacturer may have a different scheme for configuring a router ACL, but the concept is the same.

Router antispoofing is a process to prevent fake routers from joining the network.

More advanced routers such as Cisco ISRs can also perform some of the following functions
- DHCP server
- DNS Server
- VoIP controller
- Wireless controller

Consider an unfortunately common situation where a rogue or clumsy user connects a router to a network that already has a router. Devices on the network are already configured to communicate with the existing router and will likely ignore the new one, so not much data will flow to it. But if a rogue router is also acting as a DHCP server, then when the DHCP lease expires on any network clients, they may contact the new router for a new IP address. The rogue router will also provide a different default gateway (its own) and begin to intercept traffic.
How to prevent rogue routers? Enforce MAC filtering and other security measures on network switches as discussed further in this section.

Switch

It is recommended for any **switch** that the following security measures are taken during initial configuration

- Create a separate, unused VLAN and shut it down
- Move all unused ports to the unused VLAN
- Shut down all unused ports
- On a physical security level, unused patch panel ports should not be physically patched in to the switch. An exposed data jack can permit a user to connect a device which should not otherwise be connected.

Switches also employ MAC address filtering, which is rarely enabled by administrators in practice

- The switch knows the MAC address of every device on every port. This data goes to a MAC address table.
- Once devices are connected to a network switch, an administrator will have a list of device MAC addresses on the network.
- The administrator can configure the switch to block devices with MAC addresses different from the ones on the list.
- A switch port can be configured to
  - Allow traffic from a single MAC address. In an ideal scenario, each switch port should see incoming traffic from only one MAC address. For example, if a printer is connected to switch port number four, only traffic from the printer should appear on switch port 4.
  - Allow traffic from a limited number of MAC addresses (for example, traffic from up to ten unique MAC addresses is permitted). For example, a user may have only one data jack in their office but must connect multiple devices such as printers and computers. The user would install a small switch in their office. The larger switch would see the MAC address of the small switch and the MAC address of the devices that are connected to the smaller switch. If the switch sees traffic from say eleven MAC addresses on the same port, the switch closes the port.
  - Allow traffic from an unlimited number of MAC addresses. Sometimes users connect and disconnect devices randomly and administrators do not want to be forced to shut down and reopen ports all the time because it can be a drain on their resources and cause disruption to their networks. Therefore, some administrators do not enforce the MAC address rule at all.
- When a switch detects a violation of the MAC address rule, it can
  - Place a warning in the log
  - Shut down the port, in which case no devices will be permitted to connect

Typical switches are "layer two" in the OSI model; that is, they can only forward data frames on the same subnet. Data outside the subnet must be forwarded to a router. A layer three switch acts as a router in that it can forward traffic between different VLANs. Layer three switches have additional security requirements, including Access Control Lists.

Switches also provide the following security features
- **Loop Prevention**. A loop occurs when two or more ports of two switches are connected. It is possible to connect two switches together and make a trunk. Why do we want to do this? What if we have a large network and a single 48-port switch can't handle all the physical connections? We can connect multiple switches together.
    - For example, switch one port 48 and switch two port 48 are connected. When traffic received from a device connected to switch one and intended for a device connected to switch two, switch one forwards the traffic to switch two on port 48. Switch two takes the traffic and forwards it to the appropriate device based on its MAC address table.
    - Switch two registers all the devices connected to switch one (ports one through forty-seven) in its MAC address table as being connected to switch two port 48 (because it sees their traffic only on port 48)
    - Switch one registers all the devices connected to switch two (ports one through forty-seven) in its MAC address table as being connected to switch one port 48 (because it sees their traffic only on port 48)
    - A user might think that the connection between the two switches on port 48 is important and then choose to make it redundant by connecting a second cable. The user could connect the switches together on ports 47 as well. This would create a problem because switch one would learn about all the MAC addresses connected to switch two as being on two different ports, and a loop would result.
    - The loop could cause a data packet to cycle through the switches forever and overload them.
    - Most switches have automatic detection and prevention of loops. This is known as Spanning Tree Protocol.
- **Flood Guard**. A flood occurs when a switch receives a large amount of traffic on a single port. Like many other electronic devices, a switch has a buffer. The buffer stores received data that the switch is waiting to process. A hacker could attempt to bypass a switch's security measures by sending a large amount of traffic and overflow the buffer.
    - Newer switches have security settings in place that can drop additional traffic or shut down the ports.

Proxy

A **proxy** is a device that masks the true source of an internet connection. A proxy is like a VPN. There are several types of proxies

An anonymous (forward) proxy hides the source of the internet connection. For example, if a user visits Google through an anonymous proxy, Google's servers will see the IP address of the proxy as originating the connection, and not that of the user's PC. A popular website (such as Google) may see thousands or millions of requests from the same proxy and may choose to block them to avoid the risk of abuse or SPAM.

A transparent (forward) proxy does not hide the source of the internet connection. For example, if a user visits Google through transparent proxy, Google's servers will see the IP address of the proxy as originating the connection but will also see the IP address of the user's PC. A transparent proxy can be used to cache a website. By caching a website, a transparent proxy reduces traffic on a network.

A reverse proxy sits in front of a set of web servers. Consider that a website may have a single IP address, but multiple (even millions) of web servers. The reverse proxy filters incoming requests and forwards them to the appropriate server. A reverse proxy can
- Provide load balancing
- Encrypt data between the proxy and the user's PC
- Compress web content
- Cache static web content

A proxy can be used to
- Cache web content
- Filter/restrict users from accessing inappropriate web content
- Block malware and viruses
- Allow users to access web content that is blocked in their geographic location
- Eavesdrop on all content transmitted over the internet connection

In a large network, a proxy should be configured to prevent access to malicious websites and enforce the organization's acceptable use policy.

Load Balancer

A **load balancer** distributes traffic among multiple resources. For example, consider that the Google.com website has only one URL (www.google.com), which would ordinarily point to one IP address. That IP address would ordinarily point to one web server. But one single web server would be overloaded by the traffic; in fact, the Google.com website has millions of web servers. The solution is to install a load balancer in front of those servers. The load balancer can distribute the incoming traffic among all the web servers.

DNS load balancing is when a domain name's DNS records point to multiple web servers. For example, Google.com's DNS records could point to both 11.11.11.11 and 12.12.12.12, each of which is assigned to a separate server. This would balance the traffic among two servers (which is not enough for Google). Attempting to balance millions of servers on one DNS record would not work because the customer would not have enough public IP addresses to cover all the servers in use, and the DNS record would be massive.

A load balancer uses a scheduling algorithm to determine how to distribute traffic among the servers connected to it. Consider a scenario where there is one load balancer and three servers, Server A, Server B, and Server C. There are several types of load balancing algorithms

- **First Come First Served** – each request is handled in the order that it arrives; when the servers are busy then additional requests are put on hold. The load balancer sends the first request to Server A, the second request to Server B, and the third request to Server C. The load balancer does not send additional requests to the servers until a server indicates that it has spare capacity (i.e. that it has completed the current request).

- **Round-Robin** – each request is handled in the order that it arrives. The load balancer sends the first request to Server A, the second request to Server B, and the third request to Server C. The fourth request is sent to Server A, the fifth request is sent to Server B, and so on. The round-robin algorithm assumes that all the servers have the same capacity, and that all requests are of the same size. If some requests take longer to process, they could overload the servers. If one server is more powerful then the rest, it could remain idle for extended periods of time (since all servers receive the same number of requests).

- **Weighed Round-Robin** – like round robin, but each server is given a specific weight based on its capacity. For example, if server A is twice as powerful as Server B or Server C, it can be given a weight of two, while Servers B and C are each given a weight of one. Server A would then receive twice as many requests as Server B and Server C.

A sticky session allows a load balancer to remember each client (based on their HTTP session). When a client is recognized, the load balancer sends that client back to the same server that they were previously connected to, regardless of the server load. This allows the server to maintain the client's data locally (and not in a central database). This is also known as affinity.

Load balancers typically work in pairs or groups. This prevents the load balancer from becoming a single point of failure.

In a logical network topology, the load balancer is shown to be connected between the internet and the servers that it is balancing. In the physical reality, the load balancer can be connected anywhere on the network. If a load balancer has 1000 servers connected behind it, it wouldn't have 1000 physical connections to those servers, but instead would route traffic to them over the local network. Regardless of the load balancer's location, it must have a good network connection, typically 1 Gbps or 10 Gbps.

The group of servers connected to the load balancer can be active-passive or active-active. In an active-active configuration, the load balancer distributes the work among all the connected servers. In an active-passive configuration, a group of servers remain active (receive work) and a group remain passive (do not receive work). In the event of a failure of one of the active servers, a passive server is activated and begins to receive work.

An active-active configuration is better because it can quickly respond to surges in traffic and allows the system to fully utilize all its resources.

In a Virtual IP scenario, the load balancer does not exist. Instead, all the servers work together to share the workload. Consider that we have three servers:

Server A has a private IP of 10.0.0.1

Server B has a private IP of 10.0.0.2

Server C has a private IP of 10.0.0.3

The public IP address is 11.11.11.11

Servers A, B, and C communicate with each other over their private IPs 10.0.0.1, 10.0.0.2, and 10.0.0.3. The servers all set 11.11.11.11 as their public IP, and then elect one server to respond to requests. For example, Server A, B, and C choose to have Server B respond to all requests on 11.11.11.11. If Server B is overloaded, it may communicate this fact with Server A and C, which designate Server A to temporarily respond to requests on 11.11.11.11.

The servers continually ping each other to ensure that all the servers are functional. This form of communication is known as a heartbeat. If Server B were to stop responding within a specific period, Server A and Server C would choose to designate Server A to respond to new requests.

The algorithm used to determine which server would respond will vary from scenario to scenario.

Access Point

An **access point** allows a device to connect to a wireless network. Access points should be installed to provide adequate Wi-Fi coverage, considering the location of users, quantity of devices, bandwidth required, and building conditions (size, shape, attenuation due to metal/concrete, etc.)

An access point sends and receives traffic over one or more "WLANs" or Wireless LANs. Each wireless LAN can be mapped to a VLAN.

Each wireless network WLAN is associated with one or more SSIDs (multiple SSIDs can be associated with a single WLAN). The access point broadcasts SSIDs, which client devices can detect and connect to. An SSID can also be hidden. If an SSID is hidden, a client will be required to know its name to connect to it. In theory, hidden SSIDs can prevent hackers from connecting to the network, but SSIDs can be easily cracked.

An **SSID** can be configured as
- An open network, where any device can connect. This is a common setting for guest Wi-Fi.
- As an encrypted network, requiring a user to enter a passphrase. There are several forms of encryption, discussed later.
- As an encrypted network, authenticating through a username/password and RADIUS server/Active Directory server, or authenticating with a certificate.

An access point can be set up to
- Block connections from devices with specific MAC addresses
- Allow connections only from devices with specific MAC addresses. An SSID can be configured to be open, so that devices can connect automatically and without a password, but then configured to allow only specific devices to connect, based on their MAC addresses. In theory, this will work to prevent intruders. A hacker can use a packet sniffer to intercept wireless data and then spoof the MAC address of a rogue device to match an authorized one.

The signal strength of an access point should at least -70 dBm everywhere that Wi-Fi is required. A weaker signal will result in frequently dropped connections.

There are several different wireless bands available for an access point to broadcast on. The two main frequencies are 2.4 GHz and 5 GHz. Each of these bands is subdivided into channels. The 2.4 GHz band has 11 channels, and the 5 GHz band has 54 channels.

An access point will typically broadcast on both frequencies at the same time, but only one channel per frequency at a time. The channel

- May be preconfigured by the administrator and set permanently. The access point operates only on that specific channel.
- May be set so that the access point can choose a channel and change it when necessary.
- Two nearby access points should never broadcast on the same channel at the same time. If they do, signal interference will result, and no clients will be able to connect. Consider a network in an office building, with many access points. Signals from neighboring access points will interfere. Signals from access points on floors above and below will also interfere. Signals from rogue devices and mobile hotspots may also interfere. A particular access point may receive interference from dozens of devices at the same time and must therefore be able to select a specific channel that is free of interference.

Each access point comes with a built-in antenna. Some access points allow for external antennas to be connected. There are many shapes and sizes of antennas, depending on the desired coverage area and signal strength increase.

Special software such as AirMagnet Survey Pro can be used to plan out wireless networks and optimize the placement of each access point. The signal strength of an access point can be affected (reduced by metal shelves, concrete walls, and other construction materials. The quantity of access points may need to be increased in densely occupied areas such as conference rooms and lecture theaters.

Access points can be fat or thin. A fat access point contains software to process the traffic whereas a thin access point sends data back to the controller.

Access points can be controller-based or standalone. When access points are standalone, each access point must be configured separately and operates independently. When there are multiple access points, a wireless controller is optimal. A controller
- Automatically configures access points based on a template; a controller can automatically detect and configure new access points
- Will optimize broadcast channel and power for each access point based on its traffic and signal-to-noise ratio

Access points can connect to a cloud-based controller such as Cisco Meraki.

SIEM

SIEM stands for **Security Information and Event Management**. It can be a dedicated appliance, or it can be a software application. Many SIEM systems are cloud-based and share threat & intelligence data with multiple customers.

Most network devices generate and store security data. For example, a router may detect traffic from an unauthorized location or a server may detect, and log failed login attempts.

An SIEM aggregates this security data from multiple locations including routers, switches, servers, IP Phones, network storage appliances, video recorders. The SIEM may convert the logs and data into a common format. The SIEM allows a security administrator to view all security events in one place (and in one format) instead of having to log in to multiple devices.

The SIEM can also allow a network administrator to correlate events across multiple devices. For example, if a hacker gains unauthorized access to a network through the router and then fails to log in a file server multiple times, both events can be correlated as coming from the same source IP address and occurring at the same time.

The SIEM can automatically send alerts to a network administrator either via SMS or e-mail. The SIEM can be set to trigger alerts when specific events occur.

If network devices are in different time zones, the SIEM can automatically adjust the log times to the time zone of the security administrator. The SIEM can also remove duplicate events from the log.

Some examples of logged data

- Failed log in attempt on a server or router
- Firewall refuses traffic from a specific IP address
- IP address is engaged in port sniffing

DLP

DLP or **Data Leak Prevention** is a technique used to prevent data from leaving an organization. Data leaks can be accidental or deliberate. Data leaves an organization in three ways

- Electronically.
  - A user can attach sensitive data to an e-mail. For example, a user can accidentally e-mail sensitive customer data to the wrong person.
  - A user can upload sensitive data to a file sharing website or blog.
- Physically
  - A user can take physical copies of data (such as documents, blueprints, charts, etc.) from the organization.
  - A user can copy data onto a USB drive and take it out of the organization.
  - A user can photograph sensitive data with a cellular telephone.
- Intellectually.
  - Most of the data leaves the organization through the brains of the employees. Data can include client lists, trade secrets, and other intellectual property.

A Data Leak Prevention appliance is a physical network device that scans outgoing network transmissions and prevents data leaks.

- The appliance is designed to recognize patterns within the data such as credit card numbers (which have 16 digits) or phone numbers (which have 10 digits)
- The appliance may have advanced heuristics to analyse the context of each data transmission, including the contents, the sender, and the recipient, to determine if the data can be sent.
- The appliance may block the transmission, allow the transmission, or trigger a manual review.
- When the data being transmitted is encrypted between the end user's computer and an external network, then the DLP appliance will not be able to read the data. An organization will typically have full, unencrypted access to the e-mail accounts of its users, but will not be able to filter encrypted traffic (such as GMAIL or file sharing websites). These types of websites should be blocked.

The use of USB keys should be prohibited.

- A USB drive allows a user to copy data from a computer and take it out of the organization.
- USB drives can contain viruses, including firmware viruses that cannot be detected by antivirus programs
- At a minimum, an organization should force all users to encrypt their USB drives before being permitted to copy any data onto them

A DLP appliance will only detect patterns in data leaving the network. An organization can take the following additional preventative measures

- Document control system, which logs each time a user views, edits, or prints a document. This will not prevent a user from taking a sensitive document but can aid in detecting a leak after the fact. It will also deter a user from copying many documents if he knows he is being monitored. An organization can monitor and detect users who are opening or printing large quantities of documents or viewing documents that do not relate to their job duties.

- Digital Rights Management, which can permit users access to only the documents that they require to perform their job. DRM can also prevent users from editing or printing documents.

- Prohibit users from bringing cell phones to work. Cell phones can be used to copy sensitive data.

- Searching users before they leave work.

NAC

NAC stands for **Network Access Control**. NAC can be a combination of software, hardware, and policies.

NAC is used to grant access to specific users and specific locations. NAC policies can include
- Who can access the network?
- What resources are they allowed to access (printers, shared drives, servers, VPN)?
- What computers are they allowed to use to access the network (corporate-owned computers only vs personal computer)?
- What times are they allowed to access the network?
- Can they access the network from foreign countries, from home, from specific IP addresses, or only inside the network?

NAC can be **permanent** or **dissolvable**. A **permanent NAC** (also known as a permanent agent or persistent agent) is installed on the client and does not get uninstalled. The client uses the NAC to connect to the corporate network. The NAC may be a combination of VPN software, a security certificate, or other corporate software.

The **dissolvable NAC** is one that is automatically installed when a connection starts and uninstalled when the connection is complete. A dissolvable NAC may be used for contractors/visitors who require temporary access to the network, or for employees who are bringing their own devices to work.

During a connection attempt, the NAC checks the policy server for the policies required by the device. The policies may be company-wide or tailored to the type of device (laptop, desktop, cell phone) or tailored to the type of user. For example, the organization may only permit remote users to connect to the network through a VPN. The organization may only permit devices with strong passwords and disk encryption to connect to the network.

The NAC verifies that the device is compliant with all the policies. If not, the NAC could either trigger an alert but allow the connection, deny the connection, prompt the user to change their settings, or automatically change the user's settings.

Policies can include
- Ability for the organization to remotely erase data on the device
- Device encryption settings (for data stored on the device)
- Device encryption settings for communication
- Up-to-date antivirus software
- Enforcement of specific password policies and two-factor authentication

A NAC can also be **agentless**. An agentless NAC is one that does not include software on the client device. An example of a permanent agent NAC is VMWare Boxer. VMWare Boxer is an application that a user must install to access sensitive corporate resources through their personal phone. The Boxer application encrypts all the data, allows the organization to monitor use of the device, and can erase all device data if necessary. Another example of a NAC is Microsoft Intune.

An example of an agentless NAC is Active Directory group policy. An administrator sets group policies on an Active Directory Domain Server. Each time a device connects to the server, it downloads the required policies and changes its policies to match what is on the server. The device checks the Active Directory Domain Server for policy updates every three hours.

In general, an organization has the legal right to monitor and record all activity that takes place on a company-owned device (such as a cell phone or computer). For best practices, the employees should consent to the monitoring.

A company will have limited rights to monitor or record activity that takes place on a device owned by an employee or contractor, even if that employee consents. An organization could be liable for behavior such as
- Monitoring or recording an employee's personal phone calls, e-mails or web activity
- Erasing an employee's personal information (such as text messages or photographs)
- Monitoring the location of an employee's personal device outside of work hours

Mail Gateway

A **mail gateway** transmits and receives e-mail. A mail gateway may be cloud-based or incorporated into a larger server, such as Microsoft Exchange.

The mail gateway may include a

- SPAM filter to block unsolicited mail. The SPAM filter has multiple possible rules
  - Whitelist – allow all messages from a specific address (e-mail address or IP address)
  - Blacklist – deny all messages from a specific address (e-mail address or IP address)
  - Keyword matching – deny all messages that contain specific keywords
  - Advanced heuristics – uses artificial intelligence to block messages that appear to be SPAM
  - DNS Checking – verify that the server IP address matches what is listed in the DNS record of the domain name
- DLP – Data Leak Prevention, as discussed earlier
- Encryption mechanism. The mail gateway must negotiate an encryption method with the recipient's mail gateway. If the two gateways cannot agree on an encryption method (for example, the recipient does not support encryption), then the message may be sent unencrypted.

Bridge

A **network bridge** is a device that connects two networks to act like one network. A bridge is different from a router, which connects two separate networks.

Consider a network with two devices, having MAC addresses, connected to the bridge on port 1

AAAA.AAAA.AAAA
BBBB.BBBB.BBBB

And another network with two devices, having MAC addresses, connected to the bridge on port 2

CCCC.CCCC.CCCC
DDDD.DDDD.DDDD

The bridge connects the two networks together. A network bridge works like a network switch in that it records MAC addresses of packets arriving on each port. For example, if device AAAA.AAAA.AAAA sends a network packet to device DDDD.DDDD.DDDD, the network bridge learns that device AAAA.AAAA.AAAA is on Port 1.

The bridge does not know the location of the other three devices, so it floods the both ports with the packet intended for DDDD.DDDD.DDDD. When DDDD.DDDD.DDDD responds, the bridge learns that it is located on port 2. Eventually, enough traffic passes, and the bridge learns the location of all of the devices. This is a simplified example as a network may contain hundreds or thousands of devices.

The bridge will eventually learn that AAAA.AAAA.AAAA and BBBB.BBBB.BBBB are on the same segment, and will not forward traffic from AAAA.AAAA.AAAA to BBBB.BBBB.BBBB. In reality, the traffic from AAAA.AAAA.AAAA to BBBB.BBBB.BBBB will not reach the bridge because a properly functioning network switch installed before the bridge will direct the traffic to BBBB.BBBB.BBBB appropriately. A switch on the same network segment as the bridge will have the same MAC address information as the bridge.

Bridges are not common as their functions are typically handled by switches or routers. A bridge can connect more than two network segments at the same time.

An example of a bridge is a point-to-point antenna such as Ubiquiti AirFiber, which allows a bridge to be established between two separate buildings without any wiring.

For example, consider a car dealership having a central show room with network equipment. The dealership has installed IP surveillance cameras on the light poles surrounding the parking lot. The dealership was able to power the cameras through the electrical connection on the poles, but the cost of running data cable to each pole from the central show room was too high. The cameras must be on the same network as the central show room. The solution is to bridge these cameras with the central show room through point-to-point antennas.

SSL/TLS Accelerators/SSL Decryptors

An **SSL accelerator** is a device that provides encryption/decryption support for a network. When two network devices choose to establish a secure connection, they must negotiate specific parameters. Each side must encrypt data that it sends and decrypt data that it receives. This process is computationally expensive (it consumes a substantial amount of processor resources).

Instead of allowing each server to encrypt and decrypt its own data, the process can be offloaded to a dedicated device known as an SSL/TLS Accelerator decryptor/accelerator. The device will have a processor and software that are customized to process SSL/TLS encryption/decryption (as opposed to a general processor that is suitable for general tasks).

The AES (Advanced Encryption Standard) instruction set is a set of instructions that a processor can use to encrypt and decrypt data. Most Intel and AMD processors have the AES instruction set encoded into the hardware. The processor does not need to consult with the software application in order encrypt/decrypt data, improving the speed. Also, the process will be resistant to side channel attacks because the software/operating system layer will not contain any encryption keys/unencrypted data.

Media Gateway

A **media gateway** converts one type of communication medium to another
Some media conversions include

- Convert between a fiber optic signal and a copper ethernet signal. An ISP may need to transport a data signal long distances (where only fiber can carry it), but the network equipment at the customer site only supports copper.
- Convert a POTS (Plain Old Telephone System) line into a digital signal and vice versa for a VoIP system. Voice Gateways can include the Cisco Voice Gateway and Cisco ISR Routers with FXO cards.
- Convert a 3G/4G cellular telephone signal to a digital signal that can connect to the public telephone system. Consider if a user places a cell phone call through a cell tower to a landline phone. The cell tower must be able to convert the signal.

Hardware Security Module

A **Hardware Security Module** manages digital keys for cryptoprocessing. The HSM

- Generates keys
- Stores keys securely
- Encrypts and decrypts data

The most popular HSM is Atalia Box, used by many commercial banks. It allows a customer to verify its identity with the bank and secures the transaction.

An HSM must have

- Logical and physical high-level protection
- Multi-part user authorization schema
- Full audit and log traces
- Secure key backup

2.2 Given a scenario, use appropriate software tools to asses the security posture of an organization

- *Protocol Analyzer*
- *Network Scanners*
  - o *Rogue System Detection*
  - o *Network Mapping*
- *Wireless Scanners/Cracker*
- *Password Cracker*
- *Vulnerability Scanner*
- *Configuration Compliance Scanner*
- *Exploitation Frameworks*
- *Data Sanitization Tools*
- *Steganography Tools*
- *Honeypot*
- *Backup Utilities*
- *Banner Grabbing*
- *Passive vs Active*
- *Command Line Tools*
  - o *ping*
  - o *netstat*
  - o *tracert*
  - o *nslookup/dig*
  - o *arp*
  - o *ipconfig/ip/ifconfig*
  - o *tcpdump*
  - o *nmap*
  - o *netcat*

Protocol Analyzer

A **protocol analyser** captures data over a transmission channel. There are many types of transmission channels and protocols, including

- Telecom
- Internet Protocol
- Satellite

The protocol analyser can be used to intercept and monitor some or all the data transmissions over the protocol.

The analyser can also be used to analyse the quality of the connection. For example, an internet router may communicate over a copper or fiber optic cable and use OSPF, BGP, and RIP protocols. These protocols require the connection to perform at a specific standard that may include a minimum speed, a maximum latency, and a lack of dropped packets. The analyser can stress test the connection to ensure that it performs in accordance with the standard.

Questions to ask

- Is this protocol secure or can any intruder gain access to it?
- Is this protocol performing to the necessary standard required by the business?

Network Scanners

A **network scanner** detects hosts on a network. When given a range of IP addresses, the network scanner pings each IP address in the range. The scanner also checks for open ports The scanner will return a list of IP addresses, hostnames, device descriptions, and open ports corresponding to each device. The scanner will help identify devices that are unsecured.

The scanner may be software based or hardware based. A scanner can run on demand or can be scheduled to run automatically. The scanner may report its results via e-mail.

The scanner can be used to detect rogue systems – systems that are not authorized to be on the network. Of course, proper switch, router, and WLAN configurations can mitigate the presence or impact of rogue systems on a network.

The scanner can also be used to map out a network whose members were previously unknown. If the network has a large hierarchy (to include core, intermediate, and edge switches), the scanner will not be able to determine the exact topology. The scanner will assume a linear topology for the network, but an administrator can further build the topology by considering the MAC address tables of the switches on the network.

A secure device may not respond to the network scanner. For example, a server might be configured to accept requests only from a specific set of IP addresses. The server might respond to requests from 192.168.2.5, but if the network scanner is running on a computer that has an IP address of 192.168.2.6, then the server will not respond. That doesn't mean that the server is secure, just that it won't respond except to specific IP addresses (192.168.2.5 might be an address of a computer that should not be able to access the server).

A popular scanner is the Advanced Network Scanner, available for free on the internet. What can the scanner tell us?
- Hostnames of active devices on the network
- IP address/MAC address of each device
- Network card manufacturer of each device
- Open ports on each host

The scanner sends a packet to every possible IP address/port combination on that network segment. Some packets are returned, and some will time out. The possible results are
- Open port (the port is willing to establish a connection)
- Closed port (the scanner does not receive a response)
- Filtered port (connection is blocked by a firewall)

Wireless Scanners/Cracker

A **wireless scanner** detects available wireless networks.

The scanner will be able to identify
- The SSID of the wireless network (if it is not hidden)
- The type of encryption used by the wireless network
- The MAC address of the access point broadcasting each SSID
- The signal strength of each access point

A popular wireless scanner is Wireshark.

A wireless scanner can also capture the packets transmitted by the networks (including packets not addressed to the host). Remember, a wireless access point is an antenna – it does not know the exact location of each connected device, and the device does not know the exact location of the access point. The AP broadcasts data addressed to the host's MAC address in all directions, and the host broadcasts data addressed to the AP's MAC address in all directions.

In general, a wireless NIC will only accept traffic that is addressed to its own MAC address. A few manufacturers include a "promiscuous mode" option on their NICs, which allow it to collect packets that are addressed to other NICs. A wireless scanner combined with a NIC that has promiscuous mode enabled or combined with a packet sniffing NIC (such as Riverbed AirPcap) can collect all data being transmitted over a wireless network.

This data is still encrypted between the host and the access point and is useless without the encryption key. There are three main forms of wireless encryption

- **WEP** encryption uses a password to authenticate the host with the access point. A packet sniffer can intercept packets and easily crack the password. WEP has been known to be insecure since 2005 but is still in use today.
- WPA and **WPA2** uses a password to create a handshake (which creates a unique one-time password) between the host and the access point. A packet sniffer can intercept packets during the handshake process and identify the password.
- **WPA Enterprise** uses a RADIUS server to authenticate the identity of the host attempting to connect. The host will typically present a digitally signed certificate to the RADIUS server (i.e. the host computer must have a certificate installed to connect to the network). Another option is for the host to sign in to the wireless network by entering a username and password. Certificate-based WPA Enterprise is difficult to break, provided that the certificates are digitally signed using a strong algorithm and that there are no other flaws in the access point or RADIUS server. Username/password based WPA Enterprise can be

broken if the username/password are intercepted. An attacker could set up a rogue access point broadcasting the same SSID and then intercept usernames/passwords.

Password Cracker

A **password cracker** allows a user to crack a password. Password crackers can be online or offline:

- An online password cracker is one that is connected to a live system. For example, attempting to crack a password on a Windows computer connected to an Active Directory domain controller, or attempting to crack a password on an Apple iPhone. In an online attack, the host is verifying each password attempt, and may lock the account or self destruct after several incorrect attempts.

- An offline password cracker is not connected to a live system. For example, attempting to crack a password on a ZIP file or a password-protected Excel document. The ZIP file or Excel document does not know how many attempts a user has made. A user might take an online system and turn it into an offline system
    - For example, a Windows computer connected to an AD domain controller will cache the most recent correct passwords on the computer. A hacker could disconnect the computer from the AD controller by removing the network cable, and then attempt to guess the password.
    - For example, a computer will self destruct after ten incorrect password attempts. The computer records the number of incorrect attempts on a file. If the hacker had access to the file system or physical hard disk drive, he could make a copy of the computer's data, try the password attempts on the copy, allow it to self destruct, make another copy, and then try again, repeating the process until the correct password is obtained.

There are several strategies for cracking a password

- Brute force; the cracker tries every combination of password. A computer or cellular phone may lock the account/self destruct if too many incorrect passwords have been attempted. The brute force cracker may have rules for the type of characters included (numbers, letters, special characters, etc.)
- Educated guess; the cracker tries common passwords such as the name of the user's dog, the name of the user's children, etc..
- Algorithm exploitation. A password cracker may attempt to exploit the underlying algorithm that has secured the password. If the password is stored as a hash, and the mathematics underlying the hash is weak, then mathematical methods may be used. Rainbow tables are a popular method for cracking password hashes.

If the system itself is weak, then cracking the password may not be the best method for gaining access.

If the users themselves are weak, then stealing the password from a user through social engineering may be a better method.

Vulnerability Scanner

A **vulnerability scanner** is a general term for a device that detects security flaws and weaknesses. It may be software based or hardware based.

The scanner will have specific items that it looks for, which could include
- Open ports
- Weak passwords
- Computers without malware scanners
- Computers without required patches or updates
- Switches without port security

A scanner may
- Report the detected vulnerabilities to an administrator
- Automatically repair or rectify the detected vulnerabilities
- Quarantine or disable the affected device

Configuration Compliance Scanner

A **configuration compliance** scanner verifies that a device is configured in accordance with organizational policies. Some devices allow an automated system to verify their configuration and some do not.

For example,

- A computer connected a Microsoft Windows Active Directory domain controller can verify that its policies match what is on the server (for example, BitLocker encryption enabled, Internet Explorer proxy settings are set, antivirus program is installed)
- A cellular phone with mobile device management software can verify that it has correct configuration such as a lock screen password, encryption, and no malicious applications installed

Windows Server can automatically verify that all Windows computers connected to it have the correct policies (encryption, internet security, etc.)

Exploitation Frameworks

An **exploitation framework** is a hacking tool that can be used to simulate an attack on a network. A network security tester can run the exploitation framework to simulate an attack and identify areas of weakness. A hacker can use the exploitation framework to attack the network.

Metasploit is a popular exploitation framework written in Ruby. Metasploit has over 1500 common vulnerabilities, with additional vulnerabilities being added. The framework is used to infiltrate networks, collect data, and launch additional attacks once inside.

Data Sanitization Tools

A **data sanitization tool** is a software or hardware device that erases data from a storage device. Data can be stored on

- Hard Disk Drives & Solid-State Drives
- Cellular phones
- Surveillance cameras
- Network switches, routers, and access points

A data sanitization tool might be software-based, or hardware based. For example, erasing data on a hard disk drive is commonly accomplished with a degausser. Erasing data on a hard drive installed in a computer can be completed with a bootable USB containing a data sanitization application.

It is important to choose a data sanitization tool that is best for the device being erased. Sometimes it is not possible to erase a device without physically destroying the device.

An organization may have a specific policy for destroying data. A government organization may have a specific policy for destroying data that is the law.

The Department of Defense uses **DoD 5220.22-M Wipe Method** to erase data. This process writes random data overtop of the drive three times, each time verifying the data that was written.

Steganography Tools

Encryption converts plaintext data so that it can appear in the open without being read. A **Steganography Tool** does not encrypt data but hides it instead. If an unauthorized user were able to locate the hidden data, he or she would be able to read it. For added security, the hidden data can also be encrypted.

Steganography is used when encryption or encryption alone cannot protect the data. For example, a user is in a country where transmitting encrypted data is illegal or would raise suspicions but needs to send a secure message.

In steganography
- **Carrier**. The carrier is the medium carrying the hidden message. It could be a phone call, an e-mail, or a file transmission. The carrier is modified to carry the hidden message. It is important that
  - The carrier is much larger than the message. If the message increases the size of the carrier substantially, then spies will detect the modified carrier.
  - The carrier must be unique. If the carrier is publicly available, then the modified carrier can be compared against the original.
- Data can be split among multiple carriers
- **Carrier engine**. A carrier engine injects hidden data into legitimate data with an algorithm. The types of algorithms include adaptive substitution, frequency space manipulation, injection, generation, and metadata substitution.

Honeypot

A **Honeypot** is a network device that appears to be vulnerable but is in fact designed to detect hackers. A network security administrator creates a honeypot to identify hackers and/or to distract them from legitimate network resources. A honeypot allows an organization to understand the motives behind the attacks (which can be used to better protect network and other resources), and the type and sophistication of the hackers.

There are several types of honeypots

- **Pure honeypot** – a production system with a monitoring device on the network interface. The pure honeypot can be detected.

- **High interaction honeypot** – runs on a physical or virtual machine and imitates many production systems. The high interaction honeypot consumes a substantial amount of resources. When run on a virtual machine, the honeypot can be quickly regenerated.

- **Low interaction honeypot** – simulates only necessary services, allowing more honeypots to operate with fewer resources

- **SPAM honeypot** – spammers will locate servers that use open relays (an open relay is an e-mail server that allows an unauthenticated user to send an e-mail) and use them to send e-mails. The spammer will attempt to send e-mail test messages through the SPAM honeypot; if successful, the spammer will continue to send e-mail through the honeypot. The honeypot can detect the SPAM messages and also detect the spammer.

Backup Utilities

A **backup utility** backs up data. The utility could be set to operate automatically or manually. The utility may back data from a server, computer, network video recorder or other device. The back-ups can be stored on a storage appliance, tape, removable drive, or in the cloud.

It is important to back up data regularly. A large organization may have an individual or group dedicated to maintaining back ups.

- Back up all data regularly (incremental and full back ups)
- Verify that the data has been backed up
- Retain a copy of the backed-up data on site and retain a copy off site (in case of a natural disaster)

When planning a back-up strategy, think about whether it allows the organization to resume normal operations, and how quickly. The speed of the recovery should be weighed against the cost of the back-up strategy. Disaster recovery is discussed in more depth further on.

Banner Grabbing

Banner Grabbing is an attempt to obtain information about a system. If a system is not secured (or even if it is), it may respond with some data about itself when a user attempts to log in.

For example, an HTTP server will respond with the type of server that it is and some details about itself.

A network administrator can query a server to obtain an inventory of the devices in use. A hacker could also query the server to obtain details about the server.

Command Line Tools

ping   Ping tests the availability of a network host

The ping protocol sends a small packet to the host, and the host responds

Ping measures the round trip time that the packet travelled

A user could ping a hostname or an IP address; in the event of pinging a hostname, the user's device will contact a DNS server to obtain the IP address and then ping the IP address

A ping could fail if

- The host is offline
- The host is online but has a firewall that is blocking the pings (a good secure host will not respond to pings)
- The user's computer is offline (no pathway to the host)
- The DNS server could not translate the hostname to an IP address or translated it to an incorrect IP address

The command is

ping *hostname*

```
Pinging 8.8.8.8 with 32 bytes of data:
Reply from 8.8.8.8: bytes=32 time=32ms TTL=56
Reply from 8.8.8.8: bytes=32 time=33ms TTL=56
Reply from 8.8.8.8: bytes=32 time=30ms TTL=56
Reply from 8.8.8.8: bytes=32 time=35ms TTL=56

Ping statistics for 8.8.8.8:
    Packets: Sent = 4, Received = 4, Lost = 0 (0% loss),
Approximate round trip times in milli-seconds:
    Minimum = 30ms, Maximum = 35ms, Average = 32ms
```

netstat   Netstat lists all the active network connections on a computer

This includes

- Whether the connection is TCP or UDP
- The local address and port of the connection
- The remote address and port (protocol) of the connection
- The state of the connection

The connections can be filtered by status or connection type.

The command is

netstat

Connection states

- Listening – a program is listening. A software program can listen on a socket (a socket is a combination of a port and protocol). For example, a web server may listen on TCP port 80 for incoming HTTP requests.
- Close_Wait – the remote host has closed the connection, but the local host is still waiting for packets to arrive
- Time_Wait – the local host has closed the connection, but the local host I still waiting for packets to arrive
- Established – an active connection

To show only sockets, a user can type

netstat a

```
C:\Users\xxy401003>netstat

Active Connections

  Proto  Local Address          Foreign Address        State
  TCP    10.0.0.168:56744       ec2-52-6-197-42:https  ESTABLIS
  TCP    10.0.0.168:56745       ec2-52-2-221-190:https  ESTABLI
  TCP    10.0.0.168:56746       ec2-18-215-111-224:https  ESTAB
  TCP    10.0.0.168:57051       72.21.91.29:http       CLOSE_WA
  TCP    10.0.0.168:58607       relay-0e394848:http    ESTABLIS
```

tracert   tracert shows the route from the local host to the remote host. A user can run a tracert on an IP address or on a hostname; in the event of running a tracert on a hostname, the user's device will contact a DNS server to obtain the IP address and then tracert the IP address.

Since data must typically travel through multiple computer networks before it reaches its final destination, the tracert command will send three packets to each router in the route, and then display the round-trip travel time.

Each destination in the trip is known as a hop. The route that a packet takes may vary from network to network and from time to time. Just like there are multiple pathways to fly an airplane from one city to another, data packets may have multiple routers that they can pass through. The pathway that is selected depends on current network congestion, and the route that the user's ISP has negotiated with downstream carriers.

Tracert can be used to identify if routers along the pathway are correctly configured. If the ping test fails, but the remote host is online, then the next step would be to run a tracert and see how the packet is travelling (and why it is not reaching its destination)

nslookup/dig   nslookup provides the name of the name server associated with a specific domain name, or the domain name associated with a specific IP address.

The command is
nslookup *ip address or hostname*

For example, when running nslookup on dns.google, the server will return the following results

```
C:\Users\xxy401003>nslookup dns.google
Server:   nsc4.ar.ed.shawcable.net
Address:   2001:4e8:0:4004::14

Non-authoritative answer:
Name:    dns.google
Addresses:   2001:4860:4860::8844
         2001:4860:4860::8888
         8.8.4.4
         8.8.8.8
```

nslookup allows a user to determine if the name server for a specific hostname is correctly configured.

arp   ARP or Address Resolution Protocol

Each network device keeps a table (known as the ARP table) of other network devices on its network; the table contains the device's physical (MAC address), IP address, and whether the address is static or dynamic. Each time a device receives data from another network device, it creates a new entry in the table (or updates an existing entry if the MAC address matches).

When a device chooses to send data packet over the network, it uses the MAC address of the device (provided that both devices are on the same network segment).

The ARP command is

215

arp -a

The ARP command lists all of the entries in the ARP table. A user can troubleshoot a network connection on a local network segment by checking the ARP table. If a remote host is not reachable and does not appear in the ARP table, then the local host does not see it.

```
Interface: 10.0.0.168 --- 0x8
  Internet Address      Physical Address      Type
  10.0.0.1              bc-9b-68-aa-90-50     dynamic
  10.0.0.27             44-00-49-af-7a-e7     dynamic
  10.0.0.62             02-0f-b5-7f-23-54     dynamic
  10.0.0.210            94-53-30-b6-74-e3     dynamic
  10.0.0.255            ff-ff-ff-ff-ff-ff     static
  224.0.0.22            01-00-5e-00-00-16     static
```

ipconfig/ifconfig

ipconfig shows the network interface configuration of the device. A device may have multiple network interfaces, including an ethernet interface, a wireless interface, and VPN interfaces

The ipconfig command will show the
- DNS Suffix
- IPv4 addresses
- IPv6 addresses
- Subnet mask
- Default gateway
- DNS Server IP address
- DHCP Server IP address

Additional functions of ipconfig
- flushdns – erases current DNS cache
- release – released currently set DHCP addresses
- renew – renews the currently set DHCP addresses

The command is
ipconfig /a

The ipconfig command allows a user to see if the computer's network interface is configured correctly. Some problems

- There is no IP address – an IP address is not configured, the device is not reaching the DHCP server, or the network interface is disconnected or not functioning
- The assigned IP address is a link-local address – the device did not reach the DHCP address
- The IP address is in the wrong subnet – the wrong static IP address may have been set or the device is connected in the wrong VLAN

tcpdump   tcpdump lists the packets being transmitted and received over a network interface. It does not function in Windows.

The packets can be saved to a file.

nmap   nmap is an open-source application that provides network scanning.

nmap has many functions
- Scan a single IP address or host for open ports
- Scan a range of IP addresses and/or port ranges for open ports
- Scan TCP or UDP protocols
- Detect malware
- Detect the operating system version of a remote host

netcat   netcat reads from and writes to TCP/UDP connections

netcat can
- Intercept inbound and outbound TCP/UDP connections
- Check forward and reverse DNS settings
- Scan for open ports on a remote host or range of IP addresses
- Dump intercepted data to a text file

2.3 Given a scenario, troubleshoot common security issues

- *Unencrypted Credentials/Clear Text*
- *Logs and Events Anomalies*
- *Permission Issues*
- *Access Violations*
- *Certificate Issues*
- *Data Exfiltration*
- *Misconfigured Devices*
  - *Firewall*
  - *Content Filter*
  - *Access Points*
- *Weak Security Configurations*
- *Personnel Issues*
  - *Policy Violation*
  - *Insider Threat*
  - *Social Engineering*
  - *Social Media*
  - *Personal Email*
- *Unauthorized Software*
- *Baseline Deviation*
- *Licence Compliance Violation (Availability/Integrity)*
- *Asset Management*
- *Authentication Issues*

Unencrypted Credentials/Clear Text

Unencrypted credentials describe when a user login script sends login data to a remote host without encryption. Unencrypted credentials happen when

- The remote host is not configured with an SSL/TLS encryption
- The remote host and the local host cannot agree on an encryption protocol, and revert to no encryption (instead of closing the connection)
- The user credentials are hardcoded into a URL or script that sends data in plain text

Credentials must never be sent in plain text because hackers will intercept them and use them to log in to the affected systems. If a system is sending unencrypted credentials, there are probably hundreds of other things wrong with it.

Logs and Events Anomalies

Most network and computer devices keep **logs**. A computer may have hundreds of different logs, which could show

- Logins and failed log in attempts
- Attempts to access a server or server port
- Application errors

Consider having a web server running the Windows Server Operating System. The server may have logs that show

- Each time an administrator logs in or attempts to log in to the server
- Each time a web user attempts to access the server (their remote IP address, the page they attempted to access, the date and time of the access attempt, and the data that was transmitted)
- Errors in retrieving the web site data (such as 404 – page not found, 401 – user unauthorized to access the particular web page/data, etc.)

The logs can be analysed to determine if a security event has occurred and if remedial action should be taken. Software applications can be used to automatically detect security events and alert administrators.

Permission Issues

A **permission issue** occurs when

- A user has permission to access resources that he or she does not require – a user should be able to access only the resources that he or she needs to perform his job. For example, a user in the marketing department should not be able to see sensitive human resources records.
- A user does not have permission to access resources required to do his job – the user will not be able to perform his job, which will result in lost productivity.

An organization must have an efficient process to

- Allow new and existing employees to request access to resources
- Review requests to access resources and determine if the requests should be granted or denied
- Grant access to resources; the requests should be reviewed and granted quickly so that the requesting employees can remain productive
- Review existing access permissions and revoke access to resources that users no longer require

Access Violations

An **access violation** is when a user attempts (successfully or unsuccessfully) to access a resource that he/she should not be able to access.

An access violation may be accidental or deliberate. A deliberate access violation may be the result of a person's curiosity or may be malicious (an attempt to steal or destroy data).

All access violations should be investigated
- A successful violation is caused by a system or resource that is not configured correctly. The system must be configured to prevent unauthorized access.
- An unsuccessful violation may be caused by a user who is attempting to steal or destroy data, or who legitimately requires access to the resource, but has not been granted access.

Certificate Issues

Local and remote devices will use **certificates** to authenticate themselves and to encrypt data prior to exchanging it. For example, when a user attempts to log in to a bank website, the bank's server presents a certificate to the user. This certificate demonstrates that the website/server legitimately belongs to the bank.

Certificates are issued by certifying authorities. A certifying authority is an organization that is trusted to issue certificates. When issuing a certificate, the CA signs the certificate with its own certificate (known as a root certificate). Most network devices and computers have the root CA installed (i.e. they trust the root certificate).

Certificates used on public websites must be signed by a CA to be trusted. Certificates used inside an organization can be self-signed – they are trusted internally only.

Certificate Issues
- A certificate that is not trusted. The certificate is not trusted because it is not signed by a root certificate issued by a CA, or the root certificate is not installed on the computer.
- A certificate that is expired. A certificate typically expires after one year, and then must be renewed.
- A certificate mismatch. A certificate may be issued to a specific organization, domain name, and/or IP address. A certificate secures only that specific domain name or IP address. If the certificate is installed on an incorrect domain or IP address, it will not be trusted.

Data Exfiltration

Data exfiltration is the theft of data. Data could leave through
- Paper documents
- USB drives
- The minds of the employees
- The internet

What do people steal
- Usernames and passwords
- Cryptographic keys
- Trade secrets
- Personal information such as names, social security numbers, and credit card numbers
- Customer lists

Data leaks can be prevented by
- Using proper security measures on firewalls, routers, and computers
- Prohibiting the use of USB drives and cell phones at work
- Installing Data Leak Prevention appliances
- Searching employees when they leave the work site

Misconfigured Devices

A misconfigured network device can present a massive security risk

- Firewall
    - Firewall firmware not updated
    - Default usernames/passwords not changed
    - Unnecessary firewall ports left open
    - Remote connections not blocked
- Content Filter
    - Content filter not enabled or not set to block malware/malicious content
- Access Point
    - Access point configured without a secure WPA2 password
    - Access point firmware not updated

Weak Security Configurations

A **weak security configuration** occurs when a device is not configured securely. Examples could include

- Not updating the firmware on the device
- Not updating/changing default username/password
- Not enabling two-factor authentication when available
- Enabling remote access or enabling remote access from a broad range of IP addresses; enabling remote access through a weak security protocol
- Leaving open ports and protocols that are not in use
- Not setting up proper access control lists
- Not enabling Windows User Account Control
- Not installing antimalware software

Personnel Issues

A **personnel issue** is usually handled by HR or enterprise security, not by the IT Department. The IT Department may detect the issue, but will report it to HR. This could include an

- **Acceptable Use / Information Security Policy Violation**. The user has violated a specific policy such as accessing an inappropriate website, stealing information, or not taking precautions to safeguard sensitive organizational data.
- **Insider Threat**. The user has engaged in activities to steal information or create backdoors in the organization's network.
- **Social Engineering**. The user is a victim of social engineering (as discussed previously). Users should be well educated to prevent them from becoming victims of social engineering.
- **Social Media**. The user has a social media account and has posted sensitive corporate information or has posted critical information about his employer. Employees should be reminded that they do not speak on behalf of the company – that role is handled by Public Relations. At the same time, an employee represents the company, and their poor public conduct can portray the company negatively. The employee's public (and online) behavior should reflect the values of his employer.
- **Personal E-mail**. The user has used personal e-mail to communicate work related matters. This is unacceptable because it does not allow the organization to monitor/retain e-mails, which could be in violation of various laws (HIPPA, Sarbanes-Oxley). It may also be in violation of the confidentiality agreements between the organization and its clients. The personal e-mail provider may not take proper measures to secure its servers or may store data in other countries.

Unauthorized Software

Unauthorized software is any software installed on a computer or server that was not approved by the organization. Preventing the use of unauthorized software can be accomplished through the following steps

- Standard software should be centrally deployed through a configuration manager such as SCCM. An administrator can automatically install required software across all computers
- Users should be prohibited from installing software themselves (via technological measures and organizational policies)
- Users requesting custom software should obtain approval from an administrator, who can verify that
  - The organization has a proper license for the software
  - The software does not present a security risk for the organization
  - The software will not consume an excessive amount of resources
  - The user has a valid justification and need for using the software
- When a user leaves the organization or no longer requires the software, the license should be released so that it can be reused

Risks of unauthorized software

- If the organization does not obtain a proper license, use of the software could lead to civil fines or criminal charges
- The organization must be able to keep track of all the licenses it purchases and pays for, so that it does not overpay for software
- Software can introduce malware or introduce security holes
- Software can consume excessive computer or server resources

Baseline Deviation

The **baseline** is the specific standard software set and configuration that an organization issues to a user. The baseline can vary by

- Location (remote location, urban location, warehouse, production center, etc.)
- User type (remote user, administrator, clerk, executive, etc.)
- User role (HR, marketing, sales, engineering, etc.)
- Computer type (laptop, standard desktop, powerful desktop, thin client, etc.)

The baseline includes

- Operating system version and build
- Standard software set (Antivirus, Microsoft Office, Adobe Reader, etc.)
- Operating system patches
- Configuration (desktop icons, computer name, firewall settings, encryption, etc.)

An administrator can create a standard image that includes all the baseline components and then deploy it to new and existing computers.

A deviation in the baseline must be authorized. Prior to deviating from the baseline, the organization must determine that

- There is a legitimate business justification
- The deviation will not present an unmitigated security risk to the organization.
- The benefit of the deviation outweighs the cost

Licence Compliance Violation (Availability/Integrity)

Each software program that the organization installs must be licensed. A **license** may be

- Free
- Free for non-commercial use
- Charged once per computer or per simultaneous user (per seat)
- Charged per user on a monthly or yearly basis (per seat per month or per seat per year)
- Charged for the entire organization on a monthly or yearly basis

Licenses can also be found on network equipment such as routers, switches, and VoIP phones.

Some software programs automatically enforce the license terms through a license server or online system, while others do not. For example, a software publisher may not be able to automatically enforce a license that prohibits non-commercial use.

An organization must be able to keep track of all the licenses in use and ensure that it does not violate the terms of any license agreement. Automated programs can keep track of licenses. The IT department may need to charge the cost of each license to the department or business unit that requires it.

The organization must be able to keep track of all the licenses that it purchases. An organization should not purchase more licenses than it requires and should be able to reuse licenses from computers that are disposed of, and from users who no longer use the software or leave the organization.

Asset Management

Asset Management is the process of keeping track of the organization's assets, especially electronics. Assets that should be tracked include

- Desktops
- Laptops
- Servers
- Printers and Scanners
- Routers, Switches, Firewalls, and Access Points
- AV equipment

The organization may also choose to keep track of smaller items such as computer monitors, mice, or keyboards. The cost of such tracking may exceed the cost of the item.

An organization must track their computer equipment to ensure that

- Each item is issued to a specific individual or department according to the business justification. For example, a user should not be issued two computers; a mobile worker should not be issued a desktop computer; a secretary should not be issued a powerful CAD/development workstation.
- Items are not lost or stolen. The replacement cost of a lost or stolen item should be billed to the department or user that is responsible for the item.
- Items are retrieved when the user leaves the organization.
- Each computer is monitored to ensure that it has the correct software and configuration baseline, operating system updates, and malware protection.
- Items that are subject to recalls or security holes can be quickly identified and patched/repaired
- Items that break while under warranty can be repaired without cost to the organization.
- The cost of each item, especially consumables, can be billed to an appropriate business unit. This allows the organization to track the expenditures of each business unit and determine if it is profitable. It also prevents waste because it forces each user to justify the cost of purchasing equipment, rather than offloading the cost to the IT Department's budget.

At a minimum, the organization should track

- Item make and model
- Item serial number
- Hostname, MAC address, and IP address (for devices that are on a network)
- Warranty status
- Date of purchase
- User and business unit that the item is issued to

- Item location

Assets can be tracked through software such as
- Microsoft Excel spreadsheet
- Snipe-IT
- Service Now
- xAsset
- Spiceworks
- A custom-built application

Authentication Issues

An **authentication issue** is when a user is unable to connect to a service.

There are two scenarios for issuing user credentials
- Typically, a user will be issued a single credential (username/password or smartcard/PIN). This credential is issued through a TACAS or Active Directory server. Each application that the organization uses (computer, payroll, HR, etc.) allows the user to access it through a "single sign on"; when the user logs in to the application, the application verifies the user's access through the TACAS server. There is a back-end connection between the TACAS and the application.
- Sometimes, the user will be issued a separate set of credentials for some or all the separate applications. Some applications are not compatible with single sign on.

There are several causes for authentication issues:
- The user's username or password is incorrect
- The user is not permitted to access the specific resource
- The user's account is locked
- The user is accessing the resource from an unauthorized location (such as from a remote location)
- The user is accessing the resource from an unauthorized device (such as a personal cell phone)
- The resource is not available
- The resource is not able to connect to the TACAS server and verify the identity of the user

2.4 Given a scenario, analyze and interpret output from security technologies

- *HIDS/HIPS*
- *Antivirus*
- *File Integrity Check*
- *Host-Based Firewall*
- *Application Whitelisting*
- *Removable Media Control*
- *Advanced Malware Tools*
- *Patch Management Tools*
- *UTM*
- *DLP*
- *Data Execution Prevention*
- *Web Application Firewall*

HIDS/HIPS

A **HIDS** is a **Host-Based Intrusion Detection System** and a **HIPS** is a **Host-Based Intrusion Prevention System**. The HIDS is installed on each computer and mobile device (subject to regular updates). The HIDS monitors the device for intrusion attempts

- Has the file system been changed?
- Are new or unauthorized applications installed on the file system?
- Have the contents of the RAM been changed?
- Are unauthorized or new programs running in the RAM?
- Have programs attempted to change portions of the file systems that they should not be able to?

A HIDS may keep track of critical system components by generating a checksum for each item, or recording each item's attributes (file size, last modified date, location, etc.). A HIDS must also be able to prevent a malware/attacker from modifying components of the HIDS. If the HIDS is modified, then it cannot continue to protect the system.

A HIDS only detects intrusions and reports intrusion attempts to an administrator. A HIPS prevents intrusions as well. In a large organization, an administrator may not be able to fully investigate every notification from every HIDS in use; thousands of notifications may be generated each day. The notifications should be categorized based on their severity and quantity, and the most common and serious threats should be investigated and patched.

Antivirus

An **antivirus program** detects and removes viruses. Currently, very few antivirus programs target only viruses. More commonly, organizations deploy anti-malware programs that can protect against viruses, trojans, worms, SPAM, intrusion attempts, and other malicious attacks.

Antimalware programs must be deployed on every computer in the organization and must be updated regularly. The installation and updates must be enforced by policy.

A detected virus or other security threat must be investigated. The administrator must find out
- How the threat was introduced into the organization
- The quantity of devices that are affected
- Whether the threat can spread to other devices
- Whether any data has been compromised
- How to remove the threat and whether affected devices must be quarantined
- How to prevent the threat from reappearing

File Integrity Check

A **File Integrity Check** verifies that a file has not changed. Malware can be hidden inside a legitimate file such as an operating system DLL or application. To detect whether a file has changed, the existing file's size, date, and location can be compared with the original file's size, date, and location. However, malware can modify a file without changing its size, date, or location. Therefore, a hash of the file must be taken. A hash is a fingerprint that will change even if a small portion of the file changes (and even if its size remains the same).

No system is foolproof. An antimalware program may not be able detect every piece of malware, especially new, stealthy malware that have just been introduced. Malicious actors spend millions of dollars and thousands of hours attempting to create malware that cannot be detected. Therefore, the antimalware application must be used in combination with other methods.

Critical files should be checked regularly. If a file has changed, the device should be quarantined, and the file should be replaced with a clean version.

Host-Based Firewall

A **Host-Based Firewall** is an application (usually software) that monitors network activity and blocks dangerous connections

An organization will typically have a hardware firewall that protects the entire network, but the hardware firewall is only one layer of security. Why is a second firewall required?

- Protects the device from threats occurring on the internal network
- Provide additional threat protection that the hardware firewall could not
- Provide threat protection for devices that are taken outside the company network (for example a laptop taken home by an employee, or a server that is installed in the cloud)

An organization must ensure that each host-based firewall is properly configured. The organization may deploy and update the configuration through a central server.

A host-based firewall will not protect devices that are not capable of running software applications, such as
- Network switches & routers
- NVRs
- Storage appliances
- HVAC equipment

They must be protected by a physical firewall.

Application Whitelisting

An **application whitelist** is a list of approved applications that can be installed on a computer. An organization may have different whitelists for

- Different types of users (administrators, engineers, executives, etc.)
- Different business units (marketing, sales, manufacturing, etc.)
- Different types of computers (laptops, desktops, servers, thin clients)

Prior to adding an application to a whitelist, the organization should ensure

- The application will not introduce any security risks to the organization; the application should be properly patched and configured
- The organization has obtained appropriate licenses for the application
- The application is compatible with the equipment that it will operate on

Whitelisted applications can be deployed automatically (and silently) or on demand through a server such as SCCM.

The whitelist should be reviewed and updated on a regular basis to ensure that

- The latest stable release of each application is available so that users can take advantage of new features (where the release is compatible with the goals and security policy of the organization)
- The organization continues to maintain applicable licenses for each application
- Whether existing applications can be replaced by new applications that are more secure, more cost-effective, have additional features, or are more user-friendly
- Applications with newly discovered security threats are patched or removed
- Unnecessary applications are removed (applications removed from the whitelist should be automatically uninstalled from the computers)
- New, in demand, applications are added when they meet the necessary criteria

Devices should be scanned regularly. Applications that appear on the devices but are not on the whitelist should be removed. How can an application appear on a computer if it is not on the whitelist?

- Device was acquired from another organization and added to the network without being reimaged. Existing software remained on the device.
- Application was installed when it was on the whitelist, and then later removed from the whitelist
- Application or user was able to circumvent user access control settings and install the application without requiring admin privileges (for example, Google Chrome can be installed in a user's temp folder without requiring admin privileges)

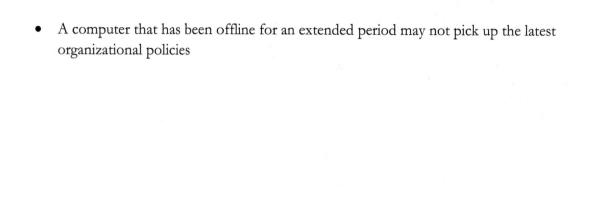

- A computer that has been offline for an extended period may not pick up the latest organizational policies

Removable Media Control

Removable Media Control is any portable device that can store data. It includes
- USB drives and keys
- Flash memory such as SD Cards
- CD-ROMs, DVDs
- iPods, Tablets, cell phones

A user can connect removable media to a computer, copy data, and then take the removable media outside the organization. Sometimes, removable media has a legitimate use.

An organization can
- **Allow all removable media.** This will put the organization at risk
  - Removable media can contain viruses in the firmware, which antivirus programs are unable to detect
  - Users can use removable media to steal data.
  - Removable media used for legitimate purposes can become lost or stolen. Data on the media can be compromised.
- **Allow only encrypted removable media and/or only for specific purposes**
  - An organization can enforce a policy (technically and legally) to ensure that only specific types of removable media are used (for example, USB drives that support hardware-based encryption or BitLocker)
  - An organization can monitor the use of every piece of removable media and by whom
  - The organization can monitor each time a file is copied to a piece of removable media, by whom, and when
  - The organization can restrict copying of data to removable media to specific users, and only for specific types of data
- **Prohibit all removable media**
  - Prohibiting all removable media is a practice in some organizations, especially where data storage is subject to government regulations (for example banks, insurance companies, and hospitals)
  - Files can be shared over the internet to users inside and outside the organization (through services such as OneDrive or Windows File Share). An organization can enforce more granular control over files shared through an application. An organization can monitor each time a file is accessed and by whom.

Advanced Malware Tools

An **advanced malware tool** is one that can detect advanced forms of malware. It uses heuristics, cloud-based threat analysis, and other features to detect malware. Most commercial/enterprise malware systems use the cloud. Threats emerge quickly, and traditional antimalware applications will not be able to detect them before the damage is done.

Patch Management Tools

A **patch management tool** keeps track of patches for each computer, network appliance, and software application in use at an organization.

Items that require patching include
- Software applications
- Operating systems
- Computer hardware drivers
- Network equipment firmware
- Surveillance camera and other IoT device firmware
- VoIP phones

An organization may have thousands or even hundreds of thousands of applications and devices to maintain. It is impossible to manually patch each one (and verify the status of each patch).

A patch management tool keeps track of the patch status of each item. For example, an organization has 10,000 computers. 5,000 of them use Microsoft Office 2016. Microsoft released a patch for the Microsoft Office 2016 application. The administrator will automatically deploy the patch to all 5,000 computers. It is best to install the patch on a few test computers to ensure it works as planned prior to deploying it across the entire organization.

An administrator can query the patch management tool to identify the 5,000 computers that require the patch and use it to deploy the patch. The application will verify that all 5,000 devices have receives the patch successfully (or if some have failed to patch, then the application will determine which ones failed and for what reason). If the patch installation continues to fail, the administrator may choose to ignore the issue, manually install the patch on each of the failed computers, or quarantine the failed computers (if the lack of a patch represents a serious security risk).

UTM

UTM stands for **Unified Threat Management**. It is the term given to most modern enterprise firewalls, which can include antivirus, antimalware, SPAM filtering, and intrusion detection tools. A threat from a single malicious actor can enter the organization through multiple routes. For example, a hacker could enter an organization's network through an unsecured firewall, log in to a server that has weak credentials, and install a piece of malware that allows him to copy the corporation's sensitive data.

UTM devices can detect patterns in network traffic and user activity. They can send this data to the cloud where it can be further analysed to determine whether it is a threat.

A UTM must be connected to the internet to be effective. Like any other threat management application, a UTM must be properly configured.

DLP

As mentioned previously a **Data Leak Prevention** appliance is a physical network device that scans outgoing network transmissions and prevents data leaks.

- The appliance is designed to recognize patterns within the data such as credit card numbers (which have 16 digits) or phone numbers (which have 10 digits)
- The appliance may have advanced heuristics to analyse the context of each data transmission, including the contents, the sender, and the recipient, to determine if the data can be sent.
- The appliance may block the transmission, allow the transmission, or trigger a manual review.
- When the data being transmitted is encrypted between the end user's computer and an external network, then the DLP appliance will not be able to read the data. An organization will typically have full, unencrypted access to the e-mail accounts of its users, but will not be able to filter encrypted traffic (such as GMAIL or file sharing websites). These types of websites should be blocked.

Data Execution Prevention

Data Execution Prevention prevents a program from executing malicious code. The computer will designate some portions of the memory (RAM) as protected. Only Windows can store data and execute code in these protected locations. Computer programs are not allowed to talk directly with the computer hardware or to other programs. They must talk to Windows, which decides whether to pass on the message.

If a program attempts to execute code in an area that is prohibited, Windows will shut down the program.

DEP was introduced in Windows XP Service Pack 2. DEP is integrated into all major computer hardware. It can be enforced at the hardware (processor) level, preventing malware from attempting to disable it.

Some older programs are not compatible with DEP because they are not able to choose where in the memory they would like to store their data (remember that each part of the memory has an address). These programs may not operate correctly unless DEP is disabled. Older legacy programs should be carefully evaluated to ensure that they do not pose a security threat and should be replaced when feasible.

DEP can be
- Enabled for all programs (default)
- Disabled for all programs
- Disabled for specific white-listed programs

Web Application Firewall

A **Web Application Firewall** protects a web server from threats including

- Cross-Site Scripting
- SQL Injection
- Cross-Site Forgery

A Web Application Firewall only protects against Layer 7 attacks (the application layer). It does not protect against attacks to the server itself. The firewall can be hardware or software based.

2.5 Given a scenario, deploy mobile devices securely

- *Connection Methods*
    - *Cellular*
    - *Wi-Fi*
    - *SATCOM*
    - *Bluetooth*
    - *NFC*
    - *ANT*
    - *Infrared*
    - *USB*
- *Mobile Device Management Concepts*
    - *Application Management*
    - *Content Management*
    - *Remote Wipe*
    - *Geofencing*
    - *Geolocation*
    - *Screen Locks*
    - *Push Notification Services*
    - *Passwords and Pins*
    - *Biometrics*
    - *Context-Aware Authentication*
    - *Containerization*
    - *Storage Segmentation*
    - *Full Device Encryption*
- *Enforcement and Monitoring For*
    - *Third-Party App Stores*
    - *Rooting/Jailbreaking*
    - *Sideloading*
    - *Custom Firmware*
    - *Carrier Unlocking*
    - *Firmware OTA Updates*
    - *Camera use*
    - *SMS/MMS*
    - *External Media*
    - *USB OTG*
    - *Recording Microphone*
    - *GPS Tagging*
    - *Wi-Fi Direct/Ad Hoc*
    - *Tethering*
    - *Payment Methods*

- *Deployment Models*
  - *BYOD*
  - *COPE*
  - *CYOD*
  - *Corporate-Owned*
  - *VDI*

Connection Methods

There are many ways to connect a cell phone to an outside network, but the two most common methods are Cellular and Wi-Fi. Typically, voice and SMS do not function over Wi-Fi, but a phone can run on multiple connections at the same time.

Some applications do not function over cellular by default to reduce costs associated with cellular data transfer.

Cellular A cellular phone connects to a cellular network through its cellular modem. The phone will contain a SIM card that allows it to authenticate with that network.

The subscriber will typically pay for a cellular plan with a specific carrier (Bell, Telus, AT&T, Verizon, etc.). A cellular phone may be locked to a specific cellular network (Bell, Telus, AT&T, Verizon, etc.) or unlocked (in which case it can connect to any network)

Some cellular phones have room for two SIM cards, in which case a phone can connect to two networks at the same time (or two connections to the same network).

When a phone is outside the range of its default network (for example, when it is in another country), it is roaming, and can connect to any number of available networks. The user may incur additional charges for roaming.

GSM and CDMA are the two main types of cellular radio networks. Most cellular networks are currently GSM, except for Sprint and Verizon. Some phones can operate on both GSM and CDMA networks. A carrier will operate their radios on several different frequencies (for example, Sprint operates over the CDMA 800 MHz and 1900 MHz frequencies). For a phone to connect to a carrier's network, it must have a modem that operates on at least one of that carrier's frequencies.

Most newer phones are also compatible with the 4G LTE network (which only supports data, but at a higher speed). GSM and CDMA only operate at a 3G speed. Thus, a phone should operate either GSM or CDMA and on 4G LTE.

When selecting a phone
- Ensure that the phone's modem is compatible with the chosen carrier
- The carrier has adequate network coverage

250

- The cost of the cellular data and voice plan is known in advance

Wi-Fi   A phone can be connected to cellular and Wi-Fi at the same time. A phone will attempt to transmit data through the Wi-Fi connection instead of the cellular connection.

It is important to connect a phone only to secured, trusted wireless networks. Unsecured networks can compromise user data.

SATCOM   A satellite phone will typically not connect through Wi-Fi or Cellular. A cellular phone will only be able to connect when it is within the range of a cell tower, but a satellite phone will be able to connect when it is within the line of sight of a satellite. Therefore, while cellular phones do not function in rural areas that have no cell towers, satellite phones can function almost anywhere.

The cost of placing a call through a satellite phone is highly expensive.

The two main satellite providers are Globalstar and Iridium.

Some governments prohibit the use of satellite phones because they are unable to monitor or intercept the calls.

Bluetooth   A cellular phone will connect to other devices via Bluetooth. Bluetooth allows a cellular phone to connect to vehicles, headsets, and other peripherals. The Bluetooth connection shares contacts, missed calls, GPS data, and other data.

It is important to carefully verify the identity of each Bluetooth device before connecting to it. For example, it is a bad idea to connect a Bluetooth phone to a rental vehicle (data may be copied to the vehicle and then exposed to other renters).

NFC   NFC is Near Field Communication. NFC allows a phone to connect to another device over a short distance. NFC is commonly used for contactless payments, electronic identity, and key cards. For example, Hilton hotels allows guests to use their phones as hotel keys.

Data can be stolen from a phone through NFC, but a malicious user must be able to get close enough to the phone. It is recommended to turn off the NFC function unless it is in use. For example, turn off the NFC until the you are ready to make a transaction.

ANT   ANT is a proprietary technology that allows a phone to connect to devices like fitness sensors. Many devices can connect to a single phone over ANT at the same time.

The ANT technology is still new and likely will be exploited. Caution should be exercised.

Infrared   Infrared communications allow a phone to communicate with another phone or with another infrared device such as a television.

Infrared is an outdated technology and very few phones are being manufactured with it.

USB   Almost every phone available is equipped with a USB port. A USB port allows a phone to communicate with another device such as a computer, a phone, or a peripheral.

A USB connection between the phone and the computer can give the computer access to the phone's root folder. A USB connection may be required to back up the phone or to upgrade its operating system.

It is important to connect a phone only to a trusted device that is running an antimalware program.

Mobile Device Management Concepts

MDM or **Mobile Device Management** allows an enterprise to keep track of their mobile devices. The MDM software acts as an administrator of the phone.

MDM is compatible with Android and iOS devices. Some iOS devices can allow a user to remove the MDM software (but the phone must be erased).

The most popular MDM applications are
- Apple Mobile Device Management (Device Enrollment Program)
- Mobile Iron

What can an MDM do?
- Allow an administrator to automatically enroll and track mobile devices. The organization can determine how many mobile devices are deployed, and to whom.
- Automatically configure mobile devices
- Automatically download and install apps and download and install updates
- Prohibit users from changing device settings or installing unauthorized apps
- Encrypt data stored on the device (entire device or only specific corporate data)
- Automatically lock the device and set specific lock screen settings
- Enforce password complexity settings
- Enforce biometric locking of the device
- Remotely wipe the entire device or remotely wipe corporate data
- Track the location of the device
- Automatically lock or disable the device when it is taken outside a specific location (geofencing). This might be out of the country or simply off the corporate network.
- Restrict the type of networks (cellular, Wi-Fi, and Bluetooth) that the device can connect to
- Send the device notifications
- Context-Aware Authentication. The device will understand the context in which the user is attempting to log in. Many organizations have deployed two-factor authentication but forcing a user to authenticate at every location can be tedious. Instead, the device can recognize if the employee is on a corporate network and not have him authenticate.
- Containerization. Containerization allows an application to run in a virtual environment instead of directly on the device. A base operating system interacts with both the device and the application creating a container.
- Storage Segmentation. Store corporate data in a separate area from the user data.
- Disable the camera, microphone, or other components of the mobile device.

How much Mobile Device Management does an organization need?

- The device should be registered with a mobile device management tool that cannot be removed.
- The organization should be able to deploy antimalware applications on the device
- The device should be encrypted
- The user should be required to choose a complex password; the device should automatically wipe when incorrect passwords have been entered
- The organization should be able to remotely wipe the device
- The organization should be able to update device firmware and applications. The user should not be able to install new applications.
- In some organizations, the administration should be able to record phone calls and text messages
- The organization should be able to track the location of the device, but only when necessary. Tracking the location of employees who are off work can lead to liability.

Enforcement and Monitoring

The organization must be able to enforce and monitor policies related to the mobile device. How strict the policy must be depends on the role of the employee and the risk to the organization. For example, disabling the camera may be a bad idea if the employee uses the phone to take photographs for work, but might be a good idea if the employee is working at a research facility with sensitive data.

Areas that can be enforced

- **Third party app stores**. An employee should not be able to install applications unless they come from a legitimate app store (such as iTunes or Google Play). An employee should not install applications unless they have a legitimate business need. A corporate device should not be used to play games.

  Many applications have undetected security vulnerabilities that could expose sensitive data. Prohibiting unnecessary applications will mitigate this risk.

- **Rooting/Jailbreaking**. Rooting or Jailbreaking is the process of gaining root access to the device and bypassing security restrictions. These methods take advantage of bugs in the existing iOS and Android operating systems. Rooting takes place on Android devices while Jailbreaking takes place on Apple devices. It is impossible to completely prevent a technically savvy user from rooting or jailbreaking a device because flaws exist in every operating system. An organization can reduce the risk of rooting/jailbreaking:
  - Enforce an HR policy to prohibit employees from rooting or jailbreaking their devices
  - Ensure that the devices are upgraded to the latest available operating systems
  - Choose devices whose hardware verifies and enforces digital signatures before loading software (a rooted device will load software that is not digitally signed by the manufacturer). Samsung devices are noted for their hardware security features such as Knox and a Trusted Execution Environment. Each time the phone boots, it checks that the operating system software is digitally signed, and refuses to load unsigned software.
  - Use a mobile device manager that can verify that the device has not been rooted/jailbroken.

- **Sideloading**. Sideloading is a method of installing an app without going through the app store. On an iOS device, sideloading is impossible unless the device is jailbroken. On an Android device, a user can download an application file (known as an APK) and run it on the phone. By default, an Android phone will not allow a user to run an APK; the user must enable the use of apps from unofficial sources. A user may choose to install an APK because
  - The app is no longer available in the app store
  - The app has been updated, but the user would like to run an older version

- **Custom Firmware**. A user may choose to install custom firmware on a device to unlock additional capabilities or bypass manufacturer restrictions. The use of custom firmware should be prohibited but may be technically impossible to prevent.

- **Carrier Unlocking**. Some mobile devices are locked to a specific carrier. For example, devices purchased from Verizon will only work on Verizon's network. A user would have to pay a fee to unlock the device and use it on alternative networks. The organization will not necessarily need to prohibit a user from carrier unlocking the device, but the cellular carrier will not provide the unlock code directly to the user.

- **Firmware OTA Updates**. The phone may receive firmware updates "over the air" either from the device manufacturer or from the carrier. Newer versions of firmware improve performance, patch security holes, and add additional features. Firmware updates should be permitted.

- **Camera Use**. Many employees require the camera in the performance of their duties. The camera should not be prohibited unless it presents a security risk.

- **SMS/MMS**. SMS/MMS is useful and may be required by employees in the performance of their jobs. The use of SMS/MMS can be used to bypass data leak prevention devices. Sending sensitive information over SMS/MMS can be a violation of applicable privacy laws. In addition, SMS/MMS communications are not recorded and may cause the organization to violate eDiscovery and data retention laws. SMS/MMS should only be disabled when it presents a risk.

- **External Media**. Some mobile devices can store data on removable media, such as SD Cards. The media is not encrypted, and if lost, can present a serious information leak. Many smartphones contain adequate internal storage (up to 1TB), resultantly, the use of removable media is not necessary. The organization should prohibit external media unless necessary.

- **USB OTG**. USB OTG is a feature that allows a smartphone to connect to other USB devices such as mice and keyboards. USB OTG does not pose a significant security risk as of now.

- **Recording Microphone**. The microphone is used to record audio and to transmit audio in telephone calls. The microphone should only be disabled if the phone is used in sensitive locations where recording audio could pose a security risk.

- **GPS Tagging**. GPS tagging allows a phone to tag the GPS coordinates of any photograph within the EXIF data. GPS tagging may be useful because a user can identify the location that a photograph was taken, but could also pose a privacy risk,

- **Wi-Fi Direct/Ad Hoc**. Wi-Fi Direct allows a phone to connect to a wireless device such as an access point without having to enter a password. Wi-Fi Direct is not a secure connection method and should be prohibited.

- **Tethering**. Tethering allows a user to connect a phone to a computer or other device and share its internet connection. Tethering can consume a substantial amount of data and increase costs. Tethering should be permitted for mobile workers who need internet access while out in the field.

- **Payment Methods**. A phone can be used as a payment method through NFC communication. An organization will not require payment methods.

Deployment Models

There are many ways to introduce mobile devices into an organization

- **BYOD**
    - **Bring Your Own Device**
    - Each employee is permitted to bring their own personal device (subject to restrictions), and connect it to the corporate network
    - An employee can use their own personal device and not have to carry two devices.
    - The organization must be able to provide technical support for a wide range of manufacturers and models.
    - The organization must be able to ensure that all employee-owned devices can be secured
    - There may be legal restrictions on what the organization can do with an employee-owned device (such as GPS tracking, data erasing, encryption). The organization may be required to reimburse employees for the use of their phones.

- **COBO**
    - **Company Owned, Business Only**
    - Also known as Corporate-Owned
    - The company supplies mobile devices. Employees may be permitted to choose from a limited set of models.
    - The company can control every device, track its location, and implement security policies without limitation
    - The organization will not have to support a wide range of devices
    - Employees will have to carry two devices (one personal, one business), and may be forced to learn to use a device that they are not familiar with

- **COPE**
    - **Company Owned, Personally Enabled**
    - The company supplies mobile devices. Employees may be permitted to choose from a limited set of models.
    - An employee will only have to carry a single device
    - The company can control every device, with some limitations considering that personal data will be stored. The company must be careful to keep personal and corporate data separate.
    - The organization will not have to support a wide range of devices
    - Employees may be forced to learn to use a device that they are not familiar with
    - The personal use of the phone may be considered a taxable benefit, and the employee may be taxed on it.
    - An employee may not be comfortable using a corporate owned phone for personal use

- **CYOD**
    - **Choose Your Own Device**

- o A user can select any device that they want, but it will be owned by the organization
- o CYOD may be part of COBO or COPE
- o The organization must be able to support a large range of devices but will be able to control every device

- **VDI**
  - o **Virtual Desktop Interface**
  - o Any mobile device can be used to connect to a virtual desktop using an app or a web browser
  - o The corporate data and applications are stored on a corporate server, but only accessed through the phone; no data is ever stored on the phone
  - o Personal and corporate data do not mix

2.6 Given a scenario, implement secure protocols

- *Protocols*
  - *DNSSEC*
  - *SSH*
  - *S/MIME*
  - *SRTP*
  - *LDAPS*
  - *FTPS*
  - *SFTP*
  - *SNMPv3*
  - *SSL/TLS*
  - *HTTPS*
  - *Secure POP/IMAP*
- *Use Cases*
  - *Voice and Video*
  - *Time Synchronization*
  - *Email and Web*
  - *File Transfer*
  - *Directory Services*
  - *Remote Access*
  - *Domain Name Resolution*
  - *Routing and Switching*
  - *Network Address Allocation*
  - *Subscription Services*

Protocols

There are many secure communication protocols that can be implemented in an organization.

DNSSEC   **Domain Name System Security Extensions**

Recall that DNS is a method for a computer to resolve a domain name (human readable) into an IP address (machine readable)

What happens when the DNS sends inaccurate data, such as when it is hijacked by a hacker?

With DNSSEC, all DNS data is digitally signed. Therefore, a DNS resolver can verify that the DNS data is the same as the data owned by a DNS server.

Each domain name owner digitally signs their own domain names. The digital signature keys are published along with the DNS information. If the domain name owner has not digitally signed their domain name, or if the class of domain names does not support DNSSEC, then DNSSEC will not be available.

DNSSEC is important for security of the internet, but many organizations have not adopted it yet. DNSSEC should be used in critical applications that use DNS.

SSH   **Secure Socket Shell** (or Secure Shell) allows a user to connect to a remote computer. SSH authenticates the identity of the remote computer to the user and the user to the remote computer.

SSH creates a tunnel between the user and the remote computer. The user will require an SSH client such as PuTTY, and the remote computer will require an SSH daemon.

Each remote computer must be set up to accept SSH logins (typically over port 22). Network firewalls must be configured to allow traffic over port 22. The user's IP address should be whitelisted on the firewall (do not allow SSH connections from any IP address)

S/MIME   **Secure / Multipurpose Internet Mail Extension**

S/MIME allows a user to send an encrypted and digitally signed e-mail. The digital signature verifies the identity of the sender, while the encryption protects its contents.

Each user who sends or receives S/MIME messages must configure a certificate that allows them to decrypt messages sent to them, and a certificate that authenticates their identity to recipients.

S/MIME uses public key cryptography

- A user creates a private key (which can only be used to decrypt messages); the private key is kept secret
- A user uses the private key to generate a public key (which can only be used to encrypt messages); the public key is shared
- A sender finds the recipient's public key and uses it to encrypt messages sent; the recipient uses its private key to decrypt the message

S/MIME does not work well with webmail clients. Encrypted e-mails can contain viruses.

SRTP   **Secure Real-Time Transport Protocol**

Provides encryption, message authentication, and integrity for real time data such as VoIP phone calls. It is a protocol that allows encrypted communication over a network where packet loss is expected to take place.

LDAPS   **Secure Lightweight Directory Application Protocol**

LDAP is an open source protocol for sharing directory information such as employee names, telephone numbers, and e-mail addresses. For example, a scanner with a scan-to-email function may connect to a server and obtain directory data.

LDAPS uses a secure protocol to transmit/receive data. It requires that the directory server have an SSL certificate installed.

FTPS   **Secure File Transfer Protocol**

FTP is a protocol for transferring files between two devices

FTPS adds a security layer to the file transfer. It requires that the server have an SSL certificate installed. The entire session can be encrypted or only specific portions of it.

SFTP   **SSH File Transfer**

SFTP is a file transfer protocol within the SSH protocol. Provided that the SSH session is secured and properly configured, then the SFTP session will be as well.

SNMPv3   **Simple Network Management Protocol (version 3)**

In SNMP one or more computers manage, monitor, and administer other computers or network devices. Each managed device will have an agent software installed on it. The agent allows it to connect back to the management server.

Version 3 is the latest version of SNMP and the only version with cryptographic security. Older versions of SNMP allowed a manager to authenticate with a network device via a password sent over plaintext.

Older versions of SNMP have additional security holes and should be patched. They can expose an organization to DOS attacks as well.

SSL/TLS   **Secure Sockets Layer / Transport Layer Security**

SSL is no longer considered secure and has been replaced with TLS.

TLS allows two devices to
- exchange encryption keys
- encrypt their data, ensuring security
- authenticate with each other; each party can verify the identity of the other party
- ensure that the transmission is reliable (that the message has not been modified during transmission)

TLS requires that each party obtain a third-party certificate from a trusted certificate issuer, such as Symantec. The certificate verifies the identity of the sender.

Once the two parties are ready to communicate, they must agree on a method to exchange encryption keys. The parties must exchange encryption keys so that each party has a key to encrypt data, and a key to decrypt data. There are over a dozen algorithms that can be used for key exchange including RSA and Diffie-Hellman.

The strength of the key is directly related to its length and the current recommended length is 2048 bits.

Most modern browsers support TLS.

HTTPS   **HTTPS is Hyper Text Transfer Protocol Secure**

It is the same as HTTP in that it allows website traffic to be transmitted between a server and a user. HTTP uses Port 80, while HTTPS uses port 443.

HTTPS requires that a certificate be installed on the server. The HTTPS certificate must be issued by a trusted third party.

Secure POP/IMAP   **Secure Post Office Protocol / Internet Message Access Protocol**

These protocols allow users to send and receive e-mail messages. The secure versions of the protocol use SSL/TLS to send and receive messages. Like other protocols, the e-mail server must have a certificate installed. The e-mail client and the server can negotiate a key exchange.

Use Cases

What are scenarios that require the use of secure protocols?

Voice and Video	SRTP
Time Synchronization	SRTP
Email and Web	DNSSEC
	Secure POP/IMAP
	HTTPS
	SSL/TLS
	S/MIME
File Transfer	SFTP
	FTPS
Directory Services	SSL/TLS
	LDAPS
Remote Access	SSH
Domain Name Resolution	DNSSEC
Routing and Switching	SNMPv3
Network Address Allocation	SRTP
Subscription Services	LDAPS

Part D: SY0-501 3.0 Architecture and Design

3.1 Explain use cases and purposes for frameworks, best practices and secure configuration guides

- *Industry-Standard Frameworks and Reference Architecture*
  - *Regulatory*
  - *Non-Regulatory*
  - *National vs International*
  - *Industry-Specific Frameworks*
- *Benchmarks/Secure Configuration Guides*
  - *Platform/Vendor-Specific Guides*
    - *Web Server*
    - *Operating System*
    - *Application Server*
    - *Network Infrastructure Devices*
  - *General Purpose Guides*
- *Defense-In-Depth/Layered Security*
  - *Vendor Diversity*
  - *Control Diversity*
    - *Administrative*
    - *Technical*
  - *User Training*

Industry-Standard Frameworks and Reference Architecture

A **Framework** is a set of rules or best practices that an organization can adopt to secure their infrastructure, reduce risk, and improve processes.

A framework can be regulatory or non-regulatory. A regulatory framework is one that is imposed by a local, state, or federal government. An organization subject to a regulatory framework must follow it. A non-regulatory framework is one created by an industry organization or trade group. An organization is not required to follow a non-regulatory framework, but it is recommended. The organization may have to choose between multiple non-regulatory, industry-specific frameworks.

Frameworks can be national or international. An organization may do business differently in different countries and therefore may require the use of different frameworks.

By adopting a framework, an organization may secure additional contracts or gain recognition. For example, an oil company may only hire vendors that have recognized health and safety policies. An organization that does not adopt an industry-recognized framework may be held liable in the event of an incident. For example, a vendor who does not have a health and safety policy may be held criminally negligent in the event of an easily preventable accident.

An organization may need to hire an industry expert or lawyer to ensure that they have implemented the correct frameworks.

Examples of regulatory frameworks
- State and federal occupational health and safety regulations (personal protective equipment, working at heights, lock out)
- Food and Drug Administration Food Safety and Drug Safety regulations
- Health Insurance Portability and Accountability Act (regulates health information)
- Sarbanes-Oxley (regulates publicly traded corporations)

Examples of non-regulatory frameworks
- Payment Card Industry Data Security Standards (regulates payment card data security and storage)

Examples of industry-specific frameworks
- Nuclear safety regulations
- Financial Crimes Enforcement Network

Benchmarks/Secure Configuration Guides

A **Benchmark** is a minimum standard that an organization can use to ensure that their devices are properly configured. A benchmark may also be known as "best practices"

The benchmark may be issued by a specific vendor such as Cisco, Juniper, or Fortinet. For example, Cisco publishes a Cisco IOS Security Configuration Guide, which is over 3000 pages long. This guide covers the best security practices for configuring Cisco routers, switches, and access points. A vendor will usually know best about how its devices should be configured.

A benchmark may also be issued for a type of platform such as a web server, operating system, application server, or network device. This benchmark is not vendor-specific, and is written in general terms, and is therefore not exhaustive.

A General-Purpose Guide outlines general security policies for an organization, but is not specific to a device or technology.

Defense-In-Depth/Layered Security

Vendor Diversity is a practice of using multiple vendors for network devices. For example, using a Fortinet firewall with a Cisco router and a Juniper switch. If a security hole affects multiple classes of devices manufactured by the same vendor, then the entire chain of devices will not be affected.

Another form of vendor diversity is to use multiple devices made by multiple vendors. For example, an organization can install two firewalls (one Fortinet and one Juniper) between their internet connection and the internal network. This may be more expensive to implement and maintain, but the possibility that both firewalls suffer from the same security vulnerability is low.

Control Diversity is a practice of having multiple layers of security. Administrative diversity involves having multiple security policies and standard operating procedures. Administrative controls are rules and regulations that deter or prohibit specific activities. Technical diversity involves using software or hardware to prevent security violations.

User Training involves educating individuals to prevent security threats. Teaching people to recognize security threats that cannot be detected by technological measures (such as social engineering) is important. User training adds another layer of security.

The possibility that a threat penetrates a single layer of security might be high, but the possibility that it penetrates multiple layers of security is much lower.

3.2 Given a scenario, implement secure network architecture concepts

- *Zones/Topologies*
    - *DMZ*
    - *Extranet*
    - *Intranet*
    - *Wireless*
    - *Guest*
    - *Honeypots*
    - *NAT*
    - *Ad Hoc*
- *Segregation/Segmentation/Isolation*
    - *Physical*
    - *Logical (VLAN)*
    - *Virtualization*
    - *Air Gaps*
- *Tunneling/VPN*
    - *Site-to-Site*
    - *Remote Access*
- *Security Device/Technology Placement*
    - *Sensors*
    - *Collectors*
    - *Correlation Engines*
    - *Filters*
    - *Proxies*
    - *Firewalls*
    - *VPN Concentrators*
    - *SSL Accelerators*
    - *Load Balancers*
    - *DDoS Mitigator*
    - *Aggregation Switches*
    - *Taps and Port Mirror*
- *SDN*

Zones/Topologies

DMZ
The DMZ is the **Demilitarized Zone**. The DMZ is a zone where devices that need to access the internal and external network can be placed.

Hosts that require internet access and that are vulnerable to attack (such as e-mail servers, web servers, and VoIP servers) should be placed in the DMZ.

The best setup is to install a firewall between the internet and the DMZ, and another firewall between the DMZ and the internal network.

Always assume that a device in the DMZ has been compromised.

Intranet
An intranet is an internal website or group of websites. An organization may place corporate news, HR information, or other data on the intranet. The intranet is usually accessible from inside the organization.

An intranet web server may block traffic that originates from outside the organization. An organization may allow intranet access from outside the organization using a VPN or username/password.

Extranet
An extranet typically contains a subset of the data available on the intranet and is usually made available to vendors or customers. The extranet provides authorized users with limited data.

An organization may call their extranet a "vendor portal", or a "customer portal".

Wireless
A wireless zone exists when users can connect to an organization's wireless network. The wireless zone may provide a user with access to the entire organization's network resources or only to limited resources.

A user may be required to authenticate to the wireless network through a certificate or username/password.

A wireless LAN (WLAN) should map to a specific VLAN on the network. A WLAN for authenticated users could map to the same VLAN as that of authenticated ethernet users.

Guest   A guest zone can be an ethernet zone or a wireless zone. A guest zone has limited privileges and should be a separate VLAN that cannot access network resources.

Honeypots   A honeypot is a trap that allows an organization to detect hackers, as explained previously.

The honeypot may be located inside the DMZ and not the internal network.

NAT   NAT is **Network Address Translation**

An organization will have many internal hosts that must access the internet, but only a limited set of public IP addresses. NAT allows a router or firewall to map one public IP to multiple internal hosts and allow all of them to access the internet at the same time.

NAT also allows an internal host to hide its true IP address from the external world.

Ad Hoc   An Ad Hoc wireless network is one that exists between two devices, and only temporarily. When an Ad Hoc network is established, two devices agree on a set of encryption keys (this is known as a handshake)

Ad Hoc capabilities should be disabled wherever possible, because they do not offer good security. During the handshake process, the encryption keys can be intercepted by a third party, which could then decrypt all further communications undetected.

Ad Hoc is commonly found on residential-grade devices such as IoT devices and printers (which do not have the capability to accept long WPA2 passwords)

273

Segregation/Segmentation/Isolation

It is important to isolate different types of data. For example, a retail store may have the following types of data on its network

- Point of Sale system information, including product inventory, transactions, and customer records, which may be shared with an in-store server and also with an external server or data center such as Microsoft Dynamics
- Back office data including e-mail, sales forecasting, payroll, and scheduling, which may be shared with different cloud apps such as Microsoft Office 365, and ADP
- Credit card transaction information
- Music (retail stores use media players that automatically download music from the internet)
- Traffic counting camera system (such as Shopper Trak)
- VoIP phone system
- Surveillance camera footage that may go to an NVR or to a server (accessible by all employees or only by loss prevention)
- Wi-Fi for store-owned devices such as mobile point of sale devices
- Guest Wi-Fi

Guest Wi-Fi should not mix with any other type of traffic. Credit card transaction information should go directly to the bank and not mix with any other type of traffic (but a point of sale system must be able to communicate with a credit card terminal for creating a transaction). Third party vendors such as the music company, the VoIP company, and the traffic counting company should be able to access their own devices, but no other devices.

If each type of traffic was to be physically separated, the store would have to build a separate physical network for each class of devices. That would require a separate internet connection, router, firewall, switch, and access points, which would be expensive to maintain and operate.

A separate physical network is the second most extreme type of network segmentation
- It is the most expensive because it requires separate hardware and wiring; operating costs are greatly increased
- Physical network separation should be used when the risk of any data leak is too high, or when the damage resulting from a data leak is too high. For example, classified information and unclassified information should never be on the same physical network.
- It may not always be possible to install a new separate physical network (there may not be enough space or adequate wiring). For example, if a retail store has
  - A cash counter with one cash register
  - One ethernet cable, which connects the cash register to the network equipment at the back of the store

- The store wishes to add a new credit card machine at the cash counter, which will require a separate physical network
- Even if the store could install a set of new network equipment at the back of the store, it may not be able to run a second ethernet cable to the cash counter; thus, a separate physical network may not be possible

A **logical network** (VLAN) is the next step, when a physical network cannot be implemented

- A **VLAN** is a **Virtual Local Area Network**
- Each network switch port can be assigned to one or more VLANs (each with a different default gateway)
- Each network device can be assigned to a different VLAN
- A device on one VLAN cannot communicate with a device on another VLAN (even if they are on the same switch and even switch port), unless it goes through a gateway. The gateway can permit or deny the traffic.
- A VLAN allows multiple types of devices to coexist on the same set of network equipment
- In the example of the retail store, each type of device (point of sale, back office, surveillance cameras) can be on a different VLAN. The store can set rules for if and how devices can communicate with each other.
- A VLAN requires the use of a managed switch. Unmanaged switches cannot be configured to accept traffic tagged with VLANs.

A virtual network is one that exists in a virtual environment. Consider an organization with a large physical server. That server is connected to a physical switch. That server runs a hypervisor, which runs ten virtual servers. Those virtual servers must be connected to each other (and in some cases to the outside world).

Each virtual server can contain one or more virtual network interfaces. The hypervisor can contain a virtual switch, with any amount of ports. This switch can be configured just like a physical switch, and through software, can "connect" to the virtual switch interfaces. Thus, there is a network virtualization, also known as software defined networking. The virtual switch ports can also be mapped to the physical server's network interfaces to allow the virtual switch to communicate with the external network.

An air gap is the most extreme type of network segmentation. A single device can be air gapped or a large network can be air gapped. An air gapped system is one that is not physically connected to any other network.

Air gapping is necessary when the harm from compromise greatly outweighs the cost of the air gapping. For example, a nuclear power plant's control system should be air gapped. An air gapped computer should have its network interfaces physically removed where possible. Remember, it is impossible to predict when or how a network device is compromised. Security holes exist in everything and it is always possible that a device known to be secure contains a major flaw.

Tunneling/VPN

A **Site-to-Site VPN** allows two separate networks to act like one network. It is established between two routers, which create a tunnel. A router should only pass traffic through the tunnel if it is intended for the other site. Since a tunnel has limited capacity, passing all traffic through the tunnel can degrade its performance.

Remote access allows a user working from home to connect to the corporate network through a VPN. Once connected, a user's network interface receives an IP address on the corporate network and can access network resources (subject to limitations placed by the administrator). All a user's network traffic is passed through the VPN. For example, if a user accesses a shared drive, that traffic passes through a VPN.

If a user access YouTube, that traffic also passes through the VPN. A VPN may have limited capacity and have high latency. There is usually no need for a user to access YouTube through the VPN. Thus, a VPN can be configured to route internal traffic through the VPN and external traffic through the user's primary internet connection. This is called **split tunneling**.

Security Device/Technology Placement

The placement of security devices is important.

- Sensors should be placed wherever they are required to collect data. For example, a motion sensor should be in the room where motion is being monitored.
- Collectors should be placed along a location where they can collect data. A collector can be placed anywhere in the network.
- Correlation Engines can be placed anywhere on the network
- Filters blocks specific content. The filter can be placed anywhere between the source and destination. A filter may be software-based and placed on the device whose data is being filtered.
- Proxies should be placed on the edge of the network, between the host accessing the content and the internet connection.
- Firewalls must be placed between the internet connection and the network, but as close to the edge of the network as possible. A firewall protects all the network's internal components.
- VPN Concentrators can be placed at the edge of the network. A VPN Concentrator must connect to external users.
- SSL Accelerators can be placed at the edge of the network; possibly before the firewall so that the firewall is able to monitor unencrypted traffic.
- Load Balancers can be placed anywhere on the network, because they receive connections from the outside and forward it to devices within the network. A Load Balancer must have a high-speed connection.
- DDoS Mitigators must be placed at the edge of the network, possibly before the firewall. A DDoS Mitigator will prevent malicious traffic from entering and overloading the network.
- Aggregation Switches must be placed after the router and connect to smaller switches directly.
- A Tap is a physical device that copies all traffic on a cable. The tap must be physically installed on the cable to be monitored. A Port Mirror can be a software application that allows a switch to duplicate the traffic of one port onto another port.

SDN

An **SDN** or **Software Defined Network** is a concept that allows a network to become virtualized. Configuration of network devices and routing/traffic decisions happen on a software layer instead of a hardware layer.

Software Defined Networking is supposed to operate regardless of the device manufacturer. SDN allows an organization to purchase and configure devices regardless of the vendor. The SDN software may translate the virtual (software-based) configuration into hardware configuration for each device.

In reality

- All networks require physical components
- All physical devices such as servers, must physically connect to network devices
- Dedicated network hardware is required (a computer server cannot operate well as a switch)
- The software defined network only operates as well as the underlying hardware. An administrator could create a 10Gbps switch port in the software, but if the physical network switch supports only 10/100 Mbps, then that will be the maximum speed.
- The configurations created on the software layer must be passed to the hardware layer to be executed

3.3 Given a scenario, implement secure systems design

- *Hardware/Firmware Security*
  - *FDE/SED*
  - *TPM*
  - *HSM*
  - *UEFI/BIOS*
  - *Secure Boot and Attestation*
  - *Supply Chain*
  - *Hardware Root of Trust*
  - *EMI/EMP*
- *Operating Systems*
  - *Types*
    - *Network*
    - *Server*
    - *Workstation*
    - *Appliance*
    - *Kiosk*
    - *Mobile OS*
  - *Patch Management*
  - *Disabling Unnecessary Ports and Services*
  - *Least Functionality*
  - *Secure Configurations*
  - *Trusted Operating System*
  - *Application Whitelisting/Blacklisting*
  - *Disable Default Account/Passwords*
- *Peripherals*
  - *Wireless Keyboards*
  - *Wireless Mice*
  - *Displays*
  - *Wi-Fi-Enabled MicroSD Cards*
  - *Printers/MFDs*
  - *External Storage Devices*
  - *Digital Cameras*

Hardware/Firmware Security

It is important to select computer hardware that is secure. Some common security features include

- **FDE (Full-Disk Encryption) / SED (Self Encrypting Drives)**. Full Disk Encryption is a process where the hard disk drive automatically encrypts and decrypts its data. SEDs usually have dedicated encryption/decryption chips. A self encrypting drive removes the encryption/decryption workload from the computer's processor (otherwise, drive encryption could slow a computer down by up to 30%).
  - The drive randomly generates an encryption key, which it uses to encrypt and decrypt the data. The user chooses a password. The drive secures the encryption key with the password and stores the encrypted key on the drive.
  - When the computer boots up, the user must enter his password. The drive uses the password to decrypt the key. It loads the key into memory and uses it to decrypt the data.
  - If the user forgets the password, it would be impossible to retrieve the key.
  - Many organizations use BitLocker (a software-based encryption method). BitLocker encryption keys can be stored in Active Directory and retrieved.
  - FDE can be attacked. Some SEDs have firmware with security vulnerabilities that can be attacked. If the drive is running, then the encryption key will be stored in memory and can be stolen. The drive remains decrypted while it is powered on. A running drive can be moved to another computer (without removing power), and then data on it can be accessed.

- **TPM**. A **Trusted Platform Module**. The TPM is a chip, and the purpose of the TPM is to ensure that a piece of computer hardware boots up using trusted hardware and software. A TPM prevents a malicious person from booting a computer with a modified operating system.
  - For example, BitLocker encrypts the entire disk with a random key. It stores the key inside the TPM (protected by the user's password). When the user enters a password, the TPM releases the key. The TPM verifies that the Windows operating system has not been modified. If a user removes the hard drive from the computer and attempts to boot it in another computer, it will not boot because the TPM is missing (and therefore so is the key).
  - The Department of Defense requires that all new computer hardware (including desktops, laptops, phones, and tablets) contain TPMs

- **HSM (Hardware Security Module)**
  - A Hardware Security Module manages digital keys for cryptoprocessing. The HSM
    - Generates keys
    - Stores keys securely

- Encrypts and decrypts data
  - An HSM must have
    - Logical and physical high-level protection
    - Multi-part user authorization schema
    - Full audit and log traces
    - Secure key backup

- **UEFI/BIOS** or **Unified Extensible Firmware Interface** / Basic Input Output System. UEFI has replaced the legacy BIOS. UEFI/BIOS allow the operating system to interact with the physical system devices.

- **Secure Boot** and **Attestation**. Secure Boot is a feature of UEFI/BIOS that ensures that a foreign operating system does not load. Each operating system is signed with a key ensuring its authenticity. When an operating system is first installed, its public key is stored in the Secure Boot section of the UEFI/BIOS. The Secure Boot section is then locked. Afterwards, each time that the computer boots, the UEFI/BIOS uses the public key to ensure that it matches that of the operating system being loaded.

- **Supply Chain**. A supply chain is a set of vendors that deliver a product. It starts at the manufacturer (or possibly the manufacturer's vendors), and continues through the distributors, transportation companies, and possibly the retail stores. For example, if a computer might be manufactured by HP. The components of the computer start at the vendors (Western Digital hard drives, Nvidia graphics cards, Intel processors). These vendors manufacture computer components and ship them to the HP factory. The HP factory manufactures the computers and hires a trucking company to ship them to a distributor. The distributor ships the product to the organization or to the retail store where it is purchased.

  Devices can be compromised at any stage of the supply chain, in any factory, sitting in any warehouse, or during any form of transportation. A rogue version of the device firmware or operating system can be loaded, or a chip capable of spying on the device can be installed.

  Threats to the supply chain can be reduced by
  - Using digitally signed firmware and software
  - GPS tracking of sensitive components
  - Applying physical security seals on equipment packaging and chassis when they leave the factory
  - Using tamper resistant screws and fasteners

- **Hardware Root of Trust**. The hardware root of trust builds on the secure boot and other security components. It prevents a device from loading a rogue operating system.

Consider that each operating system, software application, or boot loader is digitally signed with a private key (that can be verified by a public key). When a software application attempts to load, the operating system will first check that it is digitally signed. How can a computer prevent a rogue operating system from loading?

The operating system's public key is physically burned into the computer's hardware. This key cannot be changed. When the operating system (or boot loader) loads, the hardware uses the public key to verify that it is loading a legitimate operating system. If the signature does not match, then the computer hardware does not allow the operating system to load.

The Hardware Root of Trust is a feature found on Apple iPhones. It is not possible to load an operating system on an Apple iPhone unless it has been digitally signed by Apple. If the operating system is replaced or becomes corrupted, the phone will not boot and will require the user to reload the original operating system.

- **EMI/EMP** or **Electromagnetic Interference/Electromagnetic Pulse**. An electromagnetic pulse is a surge of electricity that can destroy a device. Electromagnetic Interference can cause undesired operation in an electronic device (such as static on a phone call). It is important to protect against EMI/EMP through shielding, but high energy EMPs cannot be protected against.

Operating Systems

There are multiple types of operating systems

- **Network Operating System**. A network operating system runs on a router or switch. Examples include Cisco IOS and FortiOS. A network operating system may be proprietary to the hardware that it runs on.

- **Server Operating System**. A server operating system runs on a server (or turns regular computer hardware into a server). Server operating systems can run on a wide range of hardware. A server operating system may include software applications such as web hosting, e-mail, and file storage. Examples include Windows Server and UNIX.

- **Workstation**. A workstation operating system runs on a personal computer such as a laptop or desktop. Examples include Microsoft Windows and Apple OS X. Workstation operating systems are subject to frequent updates.

- **Appliance**. An appliance operating system runs on an appliance such as a firewall, network storage appliance, or network video recorder. It is typically written by the manufacturer of the device and is proprietary. It will contain only the features necessary to run that device. Examples include FortiOS, which runs only on Fortinet firewalls and switches.

- **Kiosk**. A kiosk operating system is a hardened operating system that runs on a public device that is subject to abuse. It could include Microsoft Windows (with special software to lock out most of the features) or Microsoft Windows PE (Portable Edition).

- **Mobile OS**. A mobile OS runs on a mobile device. It may include features that allow it to interact with mobile device components such as vibration generators and accelerometers. A mobile operating system may run on a wide range of devices (such as Android) or only on a single device (such as Apple iOS).

Prior to deploying an operating system, an organization must plan
- How will this operating system interact with the hardware in use at this organization?
- Does it include the correct drivers for all of the hardware used by the organization?
- Is it compatible with the types of software used by the organization?
- Is it user friendly (do users have adequate training)?
- Are multiple versions of the operating system required (for different user roles, locations or hardware types)?
- Does the organization have a license to deploy the operating system?
- Can the organization deploy the operating system automatically?
- Does the operating system provide mechanisms to secure the user data?

The organization should test different versions of the operating system on a small scale prior to deploying it across the entire organization.

Consider the following
- Most operating system manufacturers release patches which provide additional compatibility with peripherals, improve device security, and additional features. A patch may cause undesired operation.
  - An administrator must be able to deploy patches across all devices automatically, but must test the patches on a few sample devices first
  - Some organizations may allow users to automatically receive updates (such as through Windows update)
- Unnecessary ports and services are found on every operating system. Each unnecessary port or service could contain multiple security vulnerabilities, and the more unnecessary items running in the background, the wider the attack surface. An organization should remove any unnecessary item.
- Least functionality. Least functionality asks the question: what is the minimum set of components required for a user to perform his/her job? Any extraneous components (such as games) are removed or disabled.
- Secure configuration. A secure configuration is one that does not allow any unnecessary changes to the operating system.
- Trusted operating system. A trusted operating system is one that is recognized by the computer hardware as being legitimate. All other operating systems are prohibited from loading.
- Application whitelisting/blacklisting. Application whitelisting is the process of allowing only specific applications to load/be installed. Blacklisting is the process of denying specific applications from loading/installing.
- Disable default account/password. Many operating systems come with a default admin account/password. If a user or malicious individual finds this account, he could log in to the computer and compromise it. The default account should be disabled, and/or the username/password should be changed.

Peripherals

An organization should carefully evaluate the use of any peripheral that it deploys. It should ask

- Does this peripheral have a legitimate business need?
- Is the peripheral cost-effective?
- Does the peripheral pose a security risk?
- Is the peripheral compatible with existing computer hardware or software?
- What is the cost of supporting the peripheral?
- Can the firmware on the peripheral be updated automatically?

Some peripherals

- **Wireless Keyboard / Mouse**. A wireless keyboard / mouse can communicate with a computer through a wireless dongle or via Bluetooth (less common). The connection between the keyboard / mouse and the computer can be compromised. Keystrokes can be logged. The connection can also be used to hijack the computer and to introduce malware. It is important to select wireless keyboards / mice that offer encryption.

- **Display**. A computer monitor is not typically thought of as something that can be compromised, especially an analog display. A display's video cable can be compromised with a sophisticated device that could intercept and split the video signal. This would require physical access to the display. All displays should be equipped with privacy filters, especially those in public places. Some displays have wireless capabilities (the ability to transmit or receive a wireless video signal). This type of display can be hijacked. Some displays can connect to the internet (such as digital signage or drive thru screens).

- **MicroSD Card** (with Wi-Fi). Full sized SD cards can be equipped with Wi-Fi, but it is rare to find a MicroSD Card with Wi-Fi (practically impossible to put a Wi-Fi chip and antenna into a card that size). The purpose of a MicroSD card with Wi-Fi is so that a hacker can steal all the photographs. The second purpose of the Wi-Fi is to allow a non-Wi-Fi camera to connect to the Wi-Fi and transfer the photographs. Technically, the Wi-Fi card connects to the Wi-Fi and then a user could transfer photographs through their smartphone or computer. A Wi-Fi card will first create an ad hoc network that a user would connect to. The user can then configure proper WPA2 settings. It is important to select a card that is secure enough to prevent others from connecting to it via its ad hoc network, and that uses at least WPA2 security.

- **Printers/MFDs**. A printer can be compromised in over one thousand ways. It is impossible to list every way that a printer can be compromised.
  - A user could send a document to a printer and forget to pick it up, or arrive at the printer after another individual has viewed it

- A printer may allow users to view documents printed or scanned by other users, either through its GUI or through a web interface
- A printer may allow users to reprint documents printed by other users
- A printer may allow a user to e-mail a scanned document to a user outside of the organization, bypassing DLP
- A printer may allow a user to e-mail a scanned document to a user via an unsecured method
- A printer may have access to network file shares to store scanned documents; a user could take the printer's login credentials and use them to compromise the server. The printer may store its login credentials (active directory) in plain text, which could be viewed through its web interface. Once, an administrator set up a printer and entered his own admin credentials in the LDAP settings. Each time a user scanned a document, the printer used the administrator's login credentials (instead of an account dedicated for the printer) to access the file server. A user who accessed the printer's web interface could have learned the administrator's username and password.
- A printer may have firmware that has been compromised or that contains security vulnerabilities, allowing hackers to connect to it
- A printer may connect to an external service (for example Xerox printers automatically report their toner levels to an external server and reorder supplies when they are low). This external connection could be used to download malware.
- A printer could allow a user to connect a USB drive which would introduce malware
- A printer's default username and password may not have been changed.
- In November 2018, a hacker known as TheHackerGiraffe compromised over 50,000 printers. He sent a document advertising a YouTube channel to each printer over an open network port.

- **External Storage Devices** such as USB drives should be prohibited unless necessary. As explained previously, USB drives can lead to the compromise of sensitive data and can introduce viruses into the organization.

- **Digital Cameras**, also known as "web cams" are used to transmit video. A hacker can compromise a web cam and use it to spy on a user's most intimate moments (such as them picking their nose) and then blackmail them. Most modern laptops have physical shutters on the camera; the camera is physically blocked from the outside world. A camera may be physically integrated into a laptop. It is important to select a laptop with a physical shutter and close the shutter when not in use. An external camera should be unplugged.

3.4 Explain the importance of secure staging deployment concepts

- *Sandboxing*
- *Environment*
  - *Development*
  - *Test*
  - *Staging*
  - *Production*
- *Secure Baseline*
- *Integrity Measurement*

Sandboxing

A **Sandbox** is a highly controlled environment for testing new applications. Each time that an organization chooses to modify an existing (in house) application, develop a new application, or deploy a new (off the shelf) application, it should subject it to extensive testing.

Testing can identify
- Security vulnerabilities
- Data corruption
- Undesired operation
- Applications that consume excessive system resources
- Applications that allow users to gain administrative access into the system

The sandbox is an environment that does not allow the application to obtain additional privileges or modify sensitive system components. It can be a virtual server, or a physical server that is air gapped. Many application development systems contain sandboxes; they include
- Linux
- Google APIs
- HTML5
- Java Virtual Machines
- .NET Code Access Security

Environment

The Development, Test, Staging, Production hierarchy is common in software architecture. All hierarchies start at development and end at production but may include other stages.

- **Development**. The development environment is where the program is written. The development environment may be different from the target machine. For example, a developer may use a Windows machine to develop an application for a smartphone running an Android operating system.

  The development environment may be limited to a single machine or could include many machines and servers. In software development, it is common for changes to be logged gradually (so that a developer can revert to a previous revision). Each time a major change occurs, the developer stops and records that change. A git repository is good for recording changes.

- **Test**. The test environment is where the program is tested. Ideally, the program should be tested on the same types of machines that it will be deployed on. This is not always possible (for example developing an application for a smartphone that has not been released). For a developer writing a program for a mass market, there may be millions of combinations of hardware and operating systems, and it is not possible to test on all of them.

  No test is perfect. Results from testing will catch the most common errors which will be fixed. It may be necessary to release the program to the marketplace and allow users to report their feedback.

  The testing may be automated and/or may use human subjects. What are some items that should be tested?
  - User interface (is the application user friendly?)
  - Does the application perform as intended?
  - Does the application consume excessive system resources?
  - Does the application crash or halt unexpectedly?
  - Will entering invalid data (for example, negative numbers for a measurement, text in a numeric field, etc.) damage the program?

- **Staging**. The staging environment is an environment that is exactly like the production. It is used to install, test, and configure the program. In some environments, the staging environment is where the program is set up. For example, a retail store may set up (stage) cash registers at a warehouse and then ship them to a store for final installation.

- **Production**. The production environment is where the software is used. The production environment is the most important environment. Errors will continue to be detected in the production environment, but the harm caused by the errors may be less than the cost of delaying deployment of the software. It is not possible to detect all the errors.

Secure Baseline

The **Secure Baseline** defines how a software application will perform including

- Firewall rules/ports that must allow application traffic
- Patches for the operating system and other applications
- Operating system settings

The Secure Baseline can be created through an analysis tool such as the Microsoft Baseline Security Analyzer. The baseline can be adjusted from time to time (as new security vulnerabilities are discovered, or adjustments are required)

Integrity Measurement

Integrity Measurement guarantees that the software on a machine has not been tampered with. It is important to ensure that malware has not infiltrated a machine.

Recall that Integrity management uses a TPM and hashes of the software or data to determine if changes have taken place.

Each operating system type has its own form of Integrity Measurement.

For example, Linux contains Integrity Measurement Architecture (IMA), a system that supports additional integrity measurement. It is up to each software developer to write code that works with IMA.

IMA has two subsystems: measure, and appraise
- The measurement subsystem collects hashes from important files.
- The appraise subsystem verifies that those hashes are correct.
- In the event of a hash mismatch, the file is not permitted to run.

3.5 Explain the security implications of embedded systems

- *SCADA/ICS*
- *Smart Devices/IoT*
  - *Wearable Technology*
  - *Home Automation*
- *HVAC*
- *SoC*
- *RTOS*
- *Printers/MFDs*
- *Camera Systems*
- *Special Purpose*
  - *Medical Devices*
  - *Vehicles*
  - *Aircraft/UAV*

An embedded system is a computer that is inside a larger device. Embedded systems are installed inside consumer electronics and inside critical systems such as medical equipment and control units for nuclear power plants. Many of these systems are vulnerable for the following reasons

- They represent a high value target for hackers (a hacker could exploit a vulnerability in a nuclear power plant and hold it ransom, or a hacker could discover a security hole in a popular consumer electronic and hijack thousands or millions of devices)
- An embedded system may be in a remote area and its firmware cannot be readily updated. Some device manufacturers do not include a mechanism for updating firmware, either as planned obsolescence, to reduce costs, or to prevent end users from modifying their equipment.

SCADA/ICS

SCADA stands for **Supervisory Control and Data Acquisition** while **ICS** stands for **Industrial Control System**. These systems are found at power plants, factories, utilities, and other critical forms of infrastructure.

An ICS is designed to operate reliably 24 hours per day, 7 days per week for many years, without interruption. Multiple ICSs can be combined to operate redundantly. An ICS may consist of many PLCs – Programmable Logic Controllers. A PLC is a special type of industrial computer that collects input from sensors, uses an algorithm to make decisions, and send an output to different control units.

For example, a PLC could be connected to a water pump that is filling a tank with water, and a sensor that is monitoring the tank's water level. The PLC continuously monitors the tank's water level. When the tank is empty, the PLC directs the pump to pump water, and when the tank is full, the PLC directs the tank to turn off.

Multiple ICSs can be connected to a SCADA system. The SCADA system collects data regarding a process. For example, the SCADA system can collect data from an oil refinery to determine the quantity of crude oil being turned into gasoline and can collect data from thousands of steps along that process. This data is typically sent to a control room where operators can analyse the data and detect discrepancies.

The different components of the SCADA system can be housed close together or may be far apart. SCADA system components may communicate over a standard IP network via copper or fiber links.

Ideally, a SCADA system should be air gapped and isolated from any commercial network. This is not always possible because a SCADA system may control facilities that are physically separated by hundreds of kilometers. For example
- SCADA system that controls the traffic lights in a major metropolitan city
- SCADA system that controls the power grid in the North Western United States
- SCADA system that monitors multiple oil refineries in a state

The SCADA system's communications should be
- Securely encrypted
- Air gapped and isolated from any commercial network, where possible
- On a dedicated WAN connection where air gapping is not possible due to distances

Yet there are many SCADA systems in use today that are accessible remotely (due to the negligence of the installer or manufacturer), some without a password. It is possible to locate these systems simply by running a port scan.

SCADA should be physically isolated from the commercial network. For example, a nuclear plant should not allow any part of the SCADA network to interact with the plant's commercial network. SCADA systems should not communicate wirelessly unless necessary, and where extreme precautions have been taken to ensure that all data is encrypted.

Many components inside the SCADA system may communicate without encryption. An air-gapped SCADA network can be easily disrupted if a malicious user has physical access to any SCADA network equipment or wiring. A malicious individual could splice the wiring between two SCADA system components and

- Disrupt the communication. For example, a conveyor belt is being used to load a truck with fertilizer. A hacker could cut the wire between the PLC and the conveyor belt motor, in which case no trucks could be filled. This behavior would disrupt operations.
- Spy on the communication. For example, a hacker could spy on the content of the communication to determine the quantity of oil being refined; the hacker could use this data to predict oil prices on the open market and place trades.
- Substitute inaccurate data inside the communication. For example, SCADA systems are used to control traffic lights in many major cities. These systems connect over unencrypted wireless systems or analog telephone lines. A hacker could disrupt the traffic patterns and bring intersections to a halt.

According to **NIST Guidelines for SCADA Systems** (**NIST Special Publication 800-82**), good SCADA security should

- Restrict logical access to an ICS network (using firewalls, multiple network layers, a DMZ, and unidirectional gateways)
- Restrict physical access to an ICS network
- Protect ICS from exploitation (install and test patches when available, disable unused ports and services, restrict user privileges to only those that need it, monitor and audit use of the system, check for file integrity)
- Restrict modification of data
- Detect security incidents (detect security events before they become incidents, detect failed ICS components and overloaded resources)
- Maintain functionality during adverse conditions (ensure that there is no single point of failure, that critical components have redundant counterparts, that the failure of a specific component does not create additional traffic or cascading effects, that if the system is to operate in a degraded state it does so gracefully)

- Restore the system after an incident (organization should have an incident response plan which includes key roles for all individuals involved, a well documented system, back up of all configuration, readily available replacement parts, and support from manufacturers and vendors)

An example of a virus that affects SCADA systems is Stuxnet. The Stuxnet virus
- Infected computers and hid its presence through a root kit
- Infected the firmware on USB drives inserted on those computers (the firmware on a USB drive does not contain any user storage and is typically inaccessible by any form of operating system or antivirus program)
- Searched for and infected any computer running the Siemens Step7 software application (which controls PLCs)
- Once locating a PLC, modified the code on the PLC so that it would cause damage, but returned normal values to the computer (so that the operator was unaware as to the harm that was being caused)

Smart Devices/IoT

Smart Devices include the Apple Watch and the Nest thermostat. The harm resulting from a single smart device's exploitation is small, but since the most popular devices have millions of units deployed, a hacker could exploit many of them.

Recently, the smart devices have been exploited to launch botnets.

HVAC

HVAC stands for **Heating, Ventilation, and Air Conditioning**. HVAC systems can be connected to computerized controls, which can be connected to the internet for several reasons

- Allows multiple buildings to be monitored at the same time
- Allow configuration changes to be made remotely

In 2013, Target stores was hacked when an HVAC contractor's credentials were compromised. Specifically,

- Target posted detailed information about its network architecture on its own vendor portal and allowed Microsoft to publish detailed case studies with the same information
- Target uses a vendor management application known as SAP Ariba
  - SAP Ariba is connected to other Target computer systems
  - In particular, it is connected to Active Directory and Single Sign On
  - A user with access
- The hacker sent a phishing e-mail to Fazio Mechanical, one of Target's HVAC contractors
- The hacker installed Zeus malware (a keylogger) on Fazio's computers and waited until it detected Fazio's login credentials (which provided access to Target's systems)
- Fazio did not use an antivirus program or may have used the free version of Malwarebytes. In any event, the antimalware application did not detect the Zeus malware.
- The hackers used Fazio's login credentials to gain access to SAP Ariba, and then used their SAP Ariba access to gain access deeper into Target's network
- The hackers deployed malware known as Trojan.POSRAM which infected Target's point of sale systems
  - The malware scraped the RAM of each point of sale system, looking for credit card data
  - The malware sent the data to a compromised server on Target's internal network (since a point of sale system is unable to directly access the internet)
- The hackers then copied the stolen credit card data from the internal server to an external server
- After the data breach, Target agreed to
  - Improve monitoring and logging of system activity
  - Improve firewall rules and policies
  - Limit or disable vendor access to their network
  - Reduce privileges on over 445,000 Target personnel and contractor accounts
  - Expand the use of two-factor authentication
- This attack was fully preventable
  - Fazio did not have good anti-malware software
  - Target's POS did not have good anti-malware software

- Target provided its contractors with logins that did not include two-factor authentication
- Target provided its contractors with access to more systems that they did not require

SoC

An **SoC** is a **system on a chip**. A system on a chip is a complete set of components – processor, memory, storage – integrated into one unit.

SoCs can be found in many types of devices such as medical devices. The use of a SoC can be risky, but sometimes an organization has no choice.

- The software on a SoC cannot be modified.
- It is difficult or impossible to determine how the SoC works because the circuitry and software is proprietary. The SoC will not accept monitoring or an antivirus program.
- It might be impossible to determine if a SoC that has been exploited by a hacker
- If the SoC operates a critical device such as a medical monitor, an MRI, or an ultrasound machine, deactivating the device may be impossible. It may take months to find a suitable replacement.

RTOS

An **RTOS**, or **Real-Time Operating System** is one that processes data in real time. Devices that run RTOS's include PLCs and other devices that could not afford to fail.

An RTOS must not have any memory leaks. It must be able to run forever without a reboot. The RTOS can also fail if something interferes with its ability to deliver a response in real time. Therefore, an RTOS must operate at the highest levels of security.

Printers/MFDs

There are thousands of ways to hack a printer, as explained earlier.

Camera Systems

A Camera System is important for physical security. **Cameras** in sensitive places can be hijacked. It is important that

- Each camera is physically secure so that it cannot be removed or manipulated
- The connection between the camera and its monitoring station is encrypted
- The camera software is secured. Cameras connected to the internet can be exploited by botnets.

Special Purpose

Harm to a special purpose device such as a medical device, a vehicle, or an aircraft can cause loss of life. It is important to keep these devices physically isolated from the network.

This is not always possible because

- Medical devices need to be monitored. For example, a nurse can monitor the vital signs of multiple patients and be alerted in the event of a code. The vital signs can be automatically inserted into the patient's electronic health record
- Medical device manufacturers must go through a lengthy approval process when they need to update the software
- Vehicles now have connections to GPS, traffic, and software updates.
- Aircraft are subject to monitoring by the airline and by the engine manufacturer

As of 2008, all vehicles must contain a device known as a CAN bus. The CAN bus allows the different vehicle computer systems to talk to each other. Hackers have demonstrated that they can hijack vehicles remotely and cause them to accelerate.

Hackers have also demonstrated that the in-flight entertainment systems on airplanes are connected to the aircraft cockpit systems, and only separated by a firewall instead of a physical network. that means it might be possible for a passenger to hijack an airplane through the inflight entertainment system.

3.6 Summarize secure development and deployment concepts

- *Development Life-Cycle Models*
  - o *Waterfall vs Agile*
- *Secure DevOps*
  - o *Security Automation*
  - o *Continuous Integration*
  - o *Baselining*
  - o *Immutable Systems*
  - o *Infrastructure as a Code*
- *Version Control and Change Management*
- *Provisioning and Deprovisioning*
- *Secure Coding Techniques*
  - o *Proper Error Handling*
  - o *Proper Input Validation*
  - o *Normalization*
  - o *Stored Procedures*
  - o *Code Signing*
  - o *Encryption*
  - o *Obfuscation/Camouflage*
  - o *Code Reuse/Dead Code*
  - o *Server-Side vs Client-Side Execution and Validation*
  - o *Memory Management*
  - o *Use of Third-Party Libraries and SDKs*
  - o *Data Exposure*
- *Code Quality and Testing*
  - o *Static Code Analyzers*
  - o *Dynamic Analysis (e.g. Fuzzing)*
  - o *Stress Testing*
  - o *Sandboxing*
  - o *Model Verification*
- *Compiled vs. Runtime Code*

Development Life-Cycle Models

There are two main development life cycles.

In the **Waterfall** life cycle, changes are implemented every period. The developer releases a software version, comes up with a list of new features, spends months or years updating the software, and then releases a new version. Each release contains many new features. By the time the software is released, the software is no longer relevant.

In the **Agile** life cycle, changes are implemented every two weeks. Each iteration works as follows
- At the beginning of the development iteration, the developer comes up with a list of new features that have been demanded by the users
- The new features are ranked by priority
- The development team attempts to complete as many of the new features as possible
- The software is released
- The next iteration begins. Some features that were not completed in the previous iteration return to the new list. Some are no longer relevant. The ranking of each feature may change.

It is easier to implement new security features in an Agile lifecycle because changes can be made quickly. In the Waterfall lifecycle, adding security features requires the developer to return to the planning phase of the project.

Secure DevOps

Secure DevOps is an idea where a company combines their systems operations and application development teams. In DevOps all stakeholders (management, marketing, product development, etc.) work together. Each time a change is ready, it is released.

Development of a secure system must include the following features

- Security Automation. DevOps allows security processes to be automated, reducing costs and freeing up labor.
- Continuous Integration. DevOps allows developers to update the codebase frequently and allows them to test even minor changes. By testing every minor change, the developers can isolate every possible error.
- Baselining. A baseline is a default configuration. After each update, DevOps can determine if the changes have improved the system or if they have reduced its functionality.
- Immutable Systems. An immutable system is one that cannot be changed after it has been deployed. An immutable system cannot be patched; it can only be replaced with a new system.
- Infrastructure as a Code. IaaC is a form of IaaS (Infrastructure as a Service). IaaC allows a developer to build systems with code instead of through manual configurations. This ensures that the code is efficient and reproducible.

Version Control and Change Management

Each time a new version of an application is released, it should contain a version number. The current stable version is the latest version of the program that can be used in a production environment. A developer should ensure that all users are updated to the latest stable version.

There may be additional, later versions that are still in production or are being tested. These are known as beta versions.

Each version should document the changes that have been made. If that version is rolled out and causes problems, then it can be rolled back to the previous version. Since DevOps allows for software updates to occur frequently, rolling back to a previous version will only cause minor changes.

A git repository is a tool that can store multiple versions of a software application.

Provisioning and Deprovisioning

Provisioning is the process of assigning a user permission to access an object. Deprovisioning is the process of removing that permission.

A process in a software application can be provisioned when it requires a higher level of permission (for example, when it needs to access a system file). It should be quickly deprovisioned when it no longer requires that level of permission.

Secure Coding Techniques

The Software Development Lifecycle Methodology provides many best practices for secure coding. At the time of writing, the top 25 coding errors are

- Improper Restriction of Operations within the Bounds of a Memory Buffer
- Improper Neutralization of Input During Web Page Generation ('Cross-site Scripting')
- Improper Input Validation
- Information Exposure
- Out-of-bounds Read
- Improper Neutralization of Special Elements used in an SQL Command ('SQL Injection')
- Use After Free
- Integer Overflow or Wraparound
- Cross-Site Request Forgery (CSRF)
- Improper Limitation of a Pathname to a Restricted Directory ('Path Traversal')
- Improper Neutralization of Special Elements used in an OS Command ('OS Command Injection')
- Out-of-bounds Write
- Improper Authentication
- NULL Pointer Dereference
- Incorrect Permission Assignment for Critical Resource
- Unrestricted Upload of File with Dangerous Type
- Improper Restriction of XML External Entity Reference
- Improper Control of Generation of Code ('Code Injection')
- Use of Hard-coded Credentials
- Uncontrolled Resource Consumption
- Missing Release of Resource after Effective Lifetime
- Untrusted Search Path
- Deserialization of Untrusted Data
- Improper Privilege Management
- Improper Certificate Validation

Good coding practices include

- **Proper Error Handling**. The developer must predict all possible errors, including errors caused by user-generated content and have a method of handling each one. When an application is unable to handle an error, it crashes and may leak sensitive data. The error should get stored in a log file. It should never be outputted to the user, where he can use it to manipulate the system. An error could contain SQL queries, filenames, variable names, etc..

- **Proper Input Validation**. The developer must be able to sanitize all inputs. For example, number field should be a number and text field should be text. The system should sanitize the input on the client side and again on the server side. It is always possible for a malicious end user to bypass the sanitization on the client side.

- **Normalization**. Normalization is the process of converting an input into a standard format so that it can be compared and processed. Different users and systems use different text encoding format such as Unicode, UTF, etc.. A developer must choose an encoding format that is suitable for his program and then convert all inputs into that format.

- **Stored Procedures**. Each common procedure should be stored as a script that can be called. The developer can call the script when he needs to. In SQL, stored procedures are also known as prepared statements. The prepared statement prevents a user from injecting SQL code into an input that could harm the underlying database.

- **Code Signing**. The developer should digitally sign the code with a certificate. By default, Windows will not run unsigned code. Signed code ensures that the application has not been modified.

- **Encryption**. The application should be able to encrypt all data shared between two sources. A developer should implement an open source cryptographic library and try to build his own.

- **Obfuscation**. Obfuscation is a method of hiding code and variables to reduce exploitation.

- **Code Reuse/Dead Code**. The developer should be careful not to reuse code that is not verified. The developer should delete code that is not in use (dead code). This code may be executed by an end user or behave unpredictably. It also increases the volume of the application. A complier may automatically remove dead code.

- **Server-Side vs Client-Side Execution and Validation**. Validating inputs on the client side allows for reduced load on the server, but it can cause data leaks. Data should always be validated at the server. For convenience and to reduce server load, it should also be validated on the client.

Code execution can take place on the client or on the server, depending on the type of code. Code such as JavaScript can only run client-side, while code such as PHP can only run server-side. The developer should be careful to ensure that critical code runs only on the server.

- **Memory Management.** It is important to reduce the amount of memory used. A program will occupy memory to store its variables. Some languages have an automatic garbage feature collect to release memory not in use, but some languages do not (such as C). When programming, a developer should be careful to release unused memory locations.

- **Third Party Libraries.** Third Party Libraries are convenient. They allow a developer to introduce new functions without having to write additional code. The developer must take care to ensure that the library is from a trusted source. It would not be practical (or even possible) to thoroughly test an entire library and ensure it is secure.

- **Data Exposure.** Data must be protected when in transit and when at rest through cryptography. Exposed data can be modified or leaked.

Code Quality and Testing

Code Testing can use the following techniques

- **Static Code Analysis**. Static analysis reviews the actual source code without running the program.
    - o Code can be reviewed by a human or through an automated tool such as a static code analyser
    - o Tools can look for syntax, logic, use of unapproved libraries, etc.
- **Dynamic Analysis**. Dynamic analysis reviews the program as it is running.
    - o The program is fed a set of pre-defined test inputs and the outputs (or resulting errors) are verified
    - o Thousands or hundreds of thousands of inputs can be entered using automated tools. This is known as fuzzing. Everything can be fuzzed including network protocols, files, and web protocols. Fuzzing allows for a wide range of errors to be detected.
- **Stress Testing**. A Stress Test is where the system is overloaded to examine its response under pressure. A developer will want to examine how the program responds when it is overloaded and background issues such as buffer overflows occur. The developer will also see how much the program slows down.
- **Sandboxing**. A sandbox is an environment that isolates untrusted code from an external environment. When testing a new application, a developer must be careful not to introduce it into an environment that is in use. The application could open security vulnerabilities or damage existing systems.
- **Model Verification**. The 'model' is design that the software is supposed to look like. Model verification is a method for verifying that the actual software looks like the model.

Compiled vs. Runtime Code

Complied code is code that is written in a language and converted to machine code. This code is difficult to reverse engineer. The languages can include C++, C, and Visual Basic. Complied code can run on any machine regardless of the original language.

Runtime code is code that stays in a code file and is executed by an emulator. The runtime code is executed by the emulator at runtime. Runtime code is not secured. The end user could potentially modify the code and run it again, if it is not server side. The run time code can only be executed by a machine or device that has the emulator installed on it.

Run time code includes HTML, Java, and JavaScript (run on the client side), and ASP and PHP (run on the server side).

3.7 Summarize cloud and virtualization concepts

- *Hypervisor*
    - *Type I*
    - *Type II*
    - *Application Cells/Containers*
- *VM Sprawl Avoidance*
- *VM Escape Protection*
- *Cloud Storage*
- *Cloud Deployment Models*
    - *SaaS*
    - *PaaS*
    - *IaaS*
    - *Private*
    - *Public*
    - *Hybrid*
    - *Community*
- *On-Premise vs Hosted vs Cloud*
- *VDI/VDE*
- *Cloud Access Security Broker*
- *Security as a Service*

Hypervisor

A **hypervisor** is a software application that acts like a virtual machine. A hypervisor allows a user to run multiple virtual servers on a single physical server. The hypervisor allocates hardware resources to each virtual server. There are two types of hypervisors

- **Type I** – runs directly on the system hardware. This is known as a bare metal hypervisor. Examples include Microsoft Hyper-V and VMware vSphere.
- **Type II** – runs on top of a host operating system. Examples include Oracle VirtualBox.
- **Application Cells/Containers** – an application cell allows multiple virtual server containers to share a single operating system. Each cell only maintains separately the files that it needs to perform its function. By containerizing the operating system, overhead is reduced, and applications can be ported to different servers. In other words, a container is like a virtual machine with a preinstalled operating system.

VM Sprawl Avoidance

Virtual Machine Sprawl is a concept where too many virtual machines are created, and nobody is keeping track of them. The organization should keep track of each virtual machine, and its purpose. It should verify – on a regular basis – that each virtual machine is still in use and terminate those that aren't.

VMware provides tools to manage virtual servers.

VM Escape Protection

The virtual machine must be able to protect from applications escaping either to the host operating system or to another virtual machine. A hypervisor must be able to detect and prevent VM escapes.

Cloud Storage

Cloud Storage is increasingly used by organizations. In cloud storage, an organization pays for data storage that it uses each month, and the amount of data transfer that takes place.

Popular cloud storage applications include
- Amazon S3
- Microsoft Azure

A cloud storage provider may use the same physical hardware to house data belonging to multiple customers. If the system is not secure, a malicious customer may gain access to the data of another customer. An organization must encrypt all of its data prior to transferring it to the cloud.

Cloud Deployment Models

There are several Cloud Deployment Models in use today

IaaS

Infrastructure as a Service

A company will rent their physical infrastructure and pay per month or per hour. Customer will not deal with up front costs or hardware maintenance.
Customer will see system components and will be responsible for configuring them.

Examples include Amazon Web Services

SaaS

Software as a Service

Software is licensed on a per hour or per month basis.
The software is centrally hosted. The customer will not have to install software, manage licenses, or manage servers.

Examples include Microsoft Office 365 and Salesforce

PaaS

Platform as a Service

Hybrid of IaaS and SaaS

Platform is licensed per hour or per month. Customer will not deal with hardware directly but is free to run any applications they want.

Advantage is ability to run applications without having to build the underlying infrastructure.

Example is AWS Hadoop

Public Cloud

A public cloud is available to the public. The hardware resources inside a public cloud are shared amongst all customers, which improves efficiency and reduces cost.

Private Cloud

Multiple customers may be provided access to the same physical server without realizing it (cloud software should prevent data leaks)
A private cloud is built by one organization for its internal use.

A large organization can use a private cloud to share resources amongst different departments.

Hybrid Cloud

A mix of a private cloud and a public cloud.

A company may decide that some applications are too sensitive to host with a public cloud, or that some applications will not run properly when they are off site but would like to take advantage of the public cloud.

Applications that can run on the public cloud are placed there, and remaining applications are placed on a private cloud.

The private cloud and public cloud are connected via a WAN or VPN.

Community Cloud

Like a private cloud except that infrastructure is shared by several organizations.

Several organizations that trust each other pool their computing resources. For example, several different municipal government agencies (fire department, police department, infrastructure, etc.) pool their servers together.

On-Premise vs Hosted vs Cloud

An **On-Premise Cloud** is where the devices are in the organization's physical buildings.

A Hosted system is where the organization rents the devices from a third-party. Another option is for the organization to purchase or lease the physical hardware but install them in a data center owned by a third-party ta center (known as co-location facility). The organization takes advantage of enhanced monitoring, internet connections, and power.

VDI/VDE

Virtual Desktop Infrastructure and **Virtual Desktop Environment**. This allows an organization to host end users' desktop and application in the cloud. A user will access his desktop via a remote desktop tool or a thin client.

VDI provides enhanced security because all the data is stored on an encrypted server in a physically secure data center, and none of it resides on the end user's computer. If the end user computer is lost or stolen, the data is not compromised.

An example of a VDI is Amazon Workspaces.

Cloud Access Security Broker

A **Security Broker** is a firewall that determines if a user is given access to the cloud. It also ensures that the organization's policy is enforced on the cloud devices.

Security as a Service

Security as a Service is a new concept where a security provider provides security and peace of mind to an organization. Security as a Service could include protection from viruses and ransomware, consulting, penetration testing, employee background checks, enforcement of group policies, physical security, and internal investigations.

Many companies that have traditionally provided physical security (such as G4S) are branching into cyber security. Most businesses will benefit from the expertise of an experienced security firm. Even if a company has an excellent security program, it may be beneficial to have a "second set of eyes" look at their security policy.

The Security provider may guarantee their service, in that they may indemnify or compensate the client in the event of a security breach.

3.8 Explain how resiliency and automation strategies reduce risks

- *Automation/Scripting*
  - *Automated Courses of Action*
  - *Continuous Monitoring*
  - *Configuration Validation*
- *Templates*
- *Master Image*
- *Non-Persistence*
  - *Snapshots*
  - *Revert to Known State*
  - *Rollback to Known Configuration*
  - *Live Boot Media*
- *Elasticity*
- *Scalability*
- *Distributive Allocation*
- *Redundancy*
- *Fault Tolerance*
- *High Availability*
- RAID

Automation/Scripting

Automation can reduce risks because the organization will have an automatic, pre-defined response for each common scenario.

- Saves the administrator time in not having to manually act on each situation
- Reduces the risk of typos in common configurations, which are now implemented through automated scripts
- Each time a script is run, its use can be logged and audited. A query can determine how many systems were affected by a script.

Some Automation Frameworks

- *NIST Security Content Automation Framework*
- *Common Vulnerabilities and Exposures*

The organization implements

- Automated courses of action. NIST Special Publication 800-53 provides a set of standards for automating courses of action, suitable for US Federal Government computer systems.
- Continuous Monitoring. A system must be continually monitored in real time, instead of being inspected when an event takes place. An administrator must be able to monitor each system and determine if it is functioning properly.

  Status data from each device must be aggregated into a database and unusual or out-of-bound scenarios can be highlighted, so that an administrator does not have to sort through thousands or hundreds of thousands of entries.
- Configuration Validation. Configuration Validation is a method for determining whether a system is operating exactly the way that it is supposed to. A system must do exactly what it was designed to do and must not do anything that it was not designed to do. Systems change, software is updated automatically, applications crash, and users make modifications. After each change, the administrator must again verify that the system continues to operate exactly as it is supposed to.

Templates

A **template** is a document that outlines a specific goal. For example, if an organization has hundreds of network switches, it could create a common switch configuration template.

Each time the organization implements the template, it could modify minor details such as the switch host name and the number of ports on the switch.

The template is good because it
- Saves time; the organization does not have to create a new configuration each time
- Improves security; if the organization manually created a new configuration, they would miss some security features due to human error
- The template can be updated when new vulnerabilities are updated and pushed out to all the connected devices

Master Image

The **master image** is a premade image of an operating system and/or software configuration. It is typically a full disk image of a standard issued computer, server, or network device used by the organization. Each time an organization deploys a computer, it loads a copy of the master image onto the computer.

The master image can be updated from time to time. There can be multiple master images (for different types of devices and scenarios). The master image must be carefully protected. The master image can be deployed over a network boot protocol (PXE) or via a bootable USB drive.

The master image saves an administrator from having to manually install software applications and configurations on each computer that he deploys. It also ensures that critical security protocols are always followed, since they do not have to be implemented manually.

In the event of a software corruption or viral infection, the master image can be used to reload the operating system on a computer.

Non-Persistence

Non-Persistence is a concept where changes to a system are not permanent. If somebody makes a change to a system that causes harm, it can be returned to its previous working state.

- **Snapshots**. A snapshot is an image (a replica) of a system at a point in time. If a system fails due to a change in its configuration, it can be reverted to the time when the snapshot was created. Snapshots are more common with Virtual Machines.
  - Data created between when the snapshot is created and when it is used will be lost. User data such as documents can be stored in a separate volume and protected with backups and the Volume Shadow Copy so that they are not affected by snapshots.
- **Revert to Known State**. Reverting to a point in time when the configuration was good.
  - An example of this feature is Windows Restore, which regularly creates internal "snapshots" each time an important update is installed. These are known as "restore points". A user can restore his computer back to a time when the restore point was created. Windows Restore preserves user data such as documents and photographs
  - Applications can automatically create system restore points when they are installed.
  - An administrator can disable Windows Restore in an enterprise setting.
- **Rollback to Known Configuration**. This is a Windows feature, also known as the "last known good configuration".
  - When run, Windows restores the registry to a previous version. Applications and user files are preserved.
  - This tool is not always effective because while most configurations are stored in the registry, many are stored in INI files.
  - This feature was removed in Windows 8
- **Live Boot Media**. A live boot medium could be a network boot source (PXE boot) or a bootable USB drive. These systems may be able to back up user data, reimage the computer, and the reload the backed-up data.
  - Using Live Boot Media is a last resort when other methods have not worked.

Elasticity

Elasticity is a concept in cloud computing where a system can expand to meet the needs of its users. The system should be able to expand in real time to avoid disruptions or bottlenecks. An organization does not want to pay for more resources than it can consume, but also it needs to be able to access all the resources that it needs.

Cloud computing services allow users to create scripts that monitor demand in real time, and provision/deprovision additional resources when required. Scripts can also provision/deprovision additional resources at specific times of day or days of the week (when demand is predicted to be high or low).

Elasticity is the idea of being able to "scale out" – for example, adding more servers identical to the ones that are in use.

Scalability

Scalability is the concept that the system needs to grow with the needs of the users.

It is different from elasticity in that the system can "scale up" – the system can move to larger, more powerful servers when required.

Distributive Allocation

The system should be able to automatically distribute incoming requests against multiple resources. For example, if an organization hosts a website over 1000 servers, it should be able to balance incoming traffic evenly against all 1000 servers.

This can be accomplished through a software or hardware-based load balancer. In a stateful system (such as a database) requests must be sent to the same database server each time.

Redundancy

Redundancy is where the system has eliminated single points of failure. The goal of any system is to keep operating, and the presence of a single point of failure represents an unacceptable risk.

Redundancy should be considered when the system is designed. In the cloud (as a service), redundancy is built into the physical infrastructure. Redundancy is implemented in the

- Internet connections
- Power supply
- HVAC
- Load balancing
- Network infrastructure
- Physical server components – hot-swappable RAID drives, hot-swappable processors, other hot-swappable components

When the organization has an on-premise cloud, they will be responsible for implementing all these redundancy measures. As mentioned before, an organization should maintain a supply of spare parts for critical hardware components.

Fault Tolerance

Fault Tolerance is the ability of the system to continue operating even when encountering an error. An example of a fault tolerant system is a RAID array. If a single drive in a RAID array fails, the system continues to operate without data loss.

Fault tolerance is expensive, and the organization must weigh the cost of fault tolerance against the cost of not having it (data loss, disruption to its operations, damage to its reputation).

High Availability

High Availability is the state that Fault Tolerance gives us. Fault Tolerance is simply a design goal that results in a system with High Availability.

High Availability means that the system continues to operate even when there is a disruption.

One system that provides High Availability in a server environment is VMware VSphere – Fault Tolerance. VSphere is a hypervisor that allows a user to create multiple virtual servers on a physical machine. High Availability by VMware distributes the virtual server workload on multiple physical machines, which can be in different geographic locations. In the event of a failure of a server component, or even a physical server, the system continues to operate as normal. VMware also provides a system called High Availability.

RAID

RAID stands for Redundant Array of Independent Disks. It is a computer server set up where multiple hard disk drives store the same data.

There are multiple versions of RAID, and each has benefits and drawbacks.

RAID 0	Data is split across two or more disks
	Each disk contains half of the data
	If one disk fails, all the data is lost. Therefore, RAID 0 is twice as risky as storing the data on a single disk.
	RAID 0 is faster than a single disk because we can access data from two disks at the same time

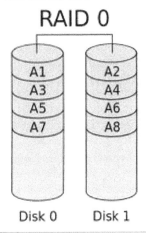

RAID 1	Data is replicated across two disks
	Each disk contains all the data
	If one disk fails, no data is lost
	When reading data, RAID 1 is faster than a single disk because we can access data from two disks at the same time.
	When writing data, RAID 1 is the same speed as a single disk.

RAID 1

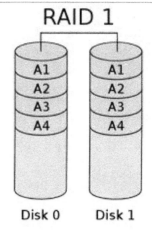

Disk 0   Disk 1

RAID 5

RAID 5 is faster and has redundancy

Parity is distributed across multiple drives

It requires at least three disks

- We split the data across three (or more disks)

- In this example, we split the data "A" across Disk 0, 1, and 2.

- We calculate the parity bit Ap (the sum of the data bits A1, A2, and A3

- If a disk fails, we can rebuild the disk by recalculating the data from the parity bit (or by recalculating the parity bit)

- Notice that parity is distributed across multiple drives

- If we were to store all the parity bits on a single drive, that drive would become overloaded. That is why we distribute the parity.

RAID 5

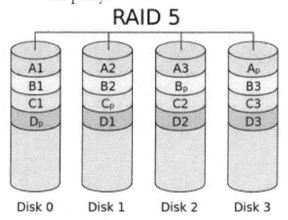

Disk 0   Disk 1   Disk 2   Disk 3

RAID 10	RAID 10 is a nested RAID level It combines RAID 0 and RAID 1 We split the data across two drives, and then we make a copy of each of those drives This gives us faster speeds (because we can read data from four drives at the same time) and redundancy (because we have two copies of the data) RAID 10 is the best choice for storing data where we have lots of reads and writes. We can write twice as fast because we only write half the data to each set of drives. We can read four times as fast because we can read from four drives at the same time.

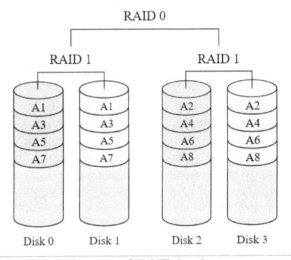

RAID 1+0

RAID 01	RAID 01 is a nested RAID level It combines RAID 0 and RAID 1 We copy the data across two ore more drives, and then we split each drive onto two drives This gives us faster speed (because we can read data from four drives at the same time) and redundancy (because we have two copies of the data)

RAID 0+1

RAID 1

RAID 0   RAID 0

A1	A2		A1	A2
A3	A4		A3	A4
A5	A6		A5	A6
A7	A8		A7	A8

Disk 0   Disk 1   Disk 2   Disk 3

Other types of RAID

Other types of RAID include

RAID 2

RAID 3

RAID 4

RAID 6

RAID 50

RAID 60

RAID 100

But these are less common

3.9 Explain the importance of physical security controls

- *Lighting*
- *Signs*
- *Fencing/Gate/Cage*
- *Security Guards*
- *Alarms*
- *Safe*
- *Secure Cabinets/Enclosures*
- *Protected Distribution/Protected Cabling*
- *Airgap*
- *Mantrap*
- *Faraday Cage*
- *Lock Types*
- *Biometrics*
- *Barricades/Bollards*
- *Tokens/Cards*
- *Environmental Controls*
  - *HVAC*
  - *Hot and Cold Aisles*
  - *Fire Suppression*
- *Cable Locks*
- *Screen Filters*
- *Cameras*
- *Motion Detection*
- *Logs*
- *Infrared Detection*
- *Key Management*

Proper physical security is important in any facility. Different levels of physical security have different costs. The cost of physical security should be proportional to value of the assets being protected or to the harm that would result from a compromise of those assets.

Lighting

Proper **lighting** is important for

- Physical safety of people walking. Hazards can be illuminated. It is important to provide bright lights on all entrances and walkways
- Making things visible. Intruders and criminals are more tempted to access buildings at night.
- Emergencies. Emergency lighting is necessary and may be required under various building codes. Emergency lighting is battery-operated and activates in the event of a power outage.

Bad people can hide in dark corners and then sneak into the building or mug people walking by.

Signs

Proper **signage** is important
- Identify entrances and exits
- Direct visitor traffic and deliveries (humans and vehicles)
- Show people where to enter and exit to reduce confusion
- Tell people where they can go and where they can't go!
- Warn people about hazardous conditions
- Warn intruders against trespassing (may be necessary to avoid legal liability)

Fencing/Gate/Cage

A **Fence** or **Gate** or **Cage** keeps people out or keeps people in. For example, a tool storage area inside a building/warehouse might be fenced in.

Consider

- Who you are trying to stop. A chain-link fence can be cut with wire cutters easily. Even a barbed wire fence can be cut. Fences are good for slowing down random people who are trying to climb over but are not so good for vehicles or sneaky people. In those cases, a concrete wall may be required.
  - o An electric fence is more effective at keep people out but may introduce unwanted legal liability. An electric fence must have clear signage that identifies it as such. It should also be separated from the public by a normal fence so that people cannot inadvertently contact it.
- Whether the fence is opaque or transparent (chain link). The fence may need to be opaque so that people can't see inside.
- The height of the fence. A tall fence may stop people from climbing or seeing over it, but it is irrelevant if people can cut through the fence or fly drones into the facility.
- Fences can be used in combination. The fence provides a buffer zone. It slows people down. By the time a person has penetrated the fence, security will have been able to intercept them. The fence can be monitored with cameras, security patrols, and sensors.

Inside a building, chain link fencing can be used to set up cages for controlled physical access. It is cheaper to build a cage than a physical room.

Security Guards

A **security guard** is a human who provides security. The security guards may be stationed in key areas, may walk around, or may drive patrol vehicles.

Proper training is important. A security guard who is not vigilant will not be effective. Security guards who use excessive force, are disrespectful, or are perceived to be incompetent, will cost the company money, introduce legal liability, and damage its reputation.

Security guards may be outsourced from a company like G4S or Guarda. There is no good reason to outsource, except for cost. When renting security guards, it is important to ensure that the security company sends the same people each time, so that they become familiar with the premises. Many companies outsource security so that they do not have to risk legal liability in the event that a security guard acts inappropriately.

A larger organization may be able to better train an internal security force, even with as few as 50 security guards.

The security guard's most important tool is his brain. Security guards also have other tools like guns, handcuffs, batons, and pepper spray, depending on the state/province that they are in. The organization must decide if it should risk the liability and cost of training to supply security guards with weapons.

Artificial intelligence is no substitute for a human brain. It is important to ensure that the security guard is aware of his surroundings. A security guard who is complacent may be worse than no security guard at all. Security guards are human and can be manipulated through social engineering techniques.

In general, a security guard is not a law enforcement officer. A security guard is entitled to
- Enforce the law when seeing an actual commission of a crime on the organization's property
- Use reasonable force to protect himself or another human being from physical harm or death
- Use reasonable force to protect the physical property of his organization
- Detain an individual who the security guard knows has committed a felony (an indictable offense in Canada), and promptly turn him to a law enforcement agent
- Use reasonable force to prevent a trespasser from entering a secured facility

Security guards may also have dogs that can detect for food, drugs, or explosives. Like a weapon, the use of a dog can also subject the organization to serious legal liability.

A security guard also keeps track of visitors

- Signs visitors in and out
- Verifies that the visitors are legitimate
- Ensures that visitors have been briefed on the organization's security and safety policies and that they are wearing appropriate personal protective equipment (PPE), if required
- Escorts visitors to the appropriate locations

Alarms

An **alarm** is necessary to protect critical assets. The two main types of alarms
- Intruder alarm – detects intrusions
- Environmental alarm – detects a fire, flood, high temperatures, etc.

The alarm will have multiple components
- **Sensor**. The sensor detects an event
  - Motion Sensor detects motion, which could indicate the presence of an unauthorized person
  - Glass Break Sensor detects if glass has been broken based on the specific sound frequency that broken glass makes
  - Door/Window Contact detects if a door/window is closed or if has been opened. The sensor consists of a magnet that sits on the door/window and a contact that sits on the door/window frame. This creates a closed circuit. When opened, the door/window breaks the circuit, and an alarm activates
  - Smoke Detector detects for the presence of smoke but can also sound a false alarm. It can be triggered by dusty conditions.
  - Flood Detector detects moisture content. This may be installed in a server room.
  - Thermostat detects temperatures that are too high or too low. High temperatures can lead to equipment damage. Cold temperatures can cause water pipes to burst.
- **Controls**. The controls allow the alarm to be programmed. The controls collect data from the sensors and decide if an abnormal event has occurred, in which case the alarm is triggered. The controls send an alert to another device.
- **Alerts**. The alarm must make an alert, or else it will have no purpose. It must notify somebody that an abnormal condition is present. Some forms of alerts
  - Siren/Flashing Lights can scare intruders but are by themselves just a nuisance. Some intruders will ignore the alarms, especially when there are many false alarms. A police department will probably not respond to an audible alarm unless they are specifically notified that a crime is in progress.
  - Alert on a control panel. The alarm can notify a monitoring station so that the responsible people can verify that the alarm is real and take additional action such as calling the police, calling for emergency services, or dispatching a security guard to investigate.
  - Automated phone call/email/SMS alert to the responsible people

When an alarm is triggered, a security guard might first review the surveillance cameras in the relevant areas to determine if there is a problem. The security guard would then physically investigate the areas and act as appropriate. If nothing out of the ordinary is present, the security guard may turn off the alarm and record his findings.

An alarm system can be divided into multiple zones. Each zone is subject to its own rules. For example, a zone can be always armed, or it can be armed at night. A server room might always be armed unless somebody needs to access it. An office might only be armed at night when nobody is present.

When an alarm is in an armed state, any sensor activity will trigger an alarm.

The control system for an alarm must be in a physically secure room. The control system must itself be alarmed (connected to a tamper-detecting sensor), so that any attempt to disable it is detected.

Safe

A **safe** protects valuables against fire and intruders. The safe can be opened with

- A numeric combination
- A key
- A key and a numeric combination

Safes come in many sizes. The larger safes are called vaults. The safe can also be connected to an alarm, which can be triggered if the safe is opened. Many jewelry stores have two separate alarm sensors connected to their safes (and possibly two separate alarm systems provided by different vendors). This eliminates a single point of failure in the alarm system.

The safe is subject to

- Fire. It is important to choose a safe that is rated to withstand at least one hour of fire.
- Physical removal. Thieves will first attempt to steal the entire safe and crack it later. It is important to bolt the safe down to the ground so that it cannot be stolen.
- Damage. Thieves will try to break through the safe. On many safes, it is difficult to pry open the door with a crowbar, but it is easy to cut through the side wall. Many safe manufacturers put a lot of effort into reinforcing the door, but very little effort in reinforcing the walls.
- Cracking. Many safes are flawed in their design, either through poor design or gaps in the door. The safe can be cracked by inserting a magnet or small pry bar tool inside. It is important to choose a safe that cannot be cracked.

A safe can be hidden. It is a good idea to hide a safe to provide an additional layer of security.

Secure Cabinets/Enclosures

A **secure cabinet**/enclosure can hold items or documents. It is not as secure as a safe but can protect against unauthorized access. Secure cabinets are designed to protect large volumes of documents.

Protected Distribution/Protected Cabling

Protected distribution ensures that the cables are physically secure. An intruder could physically penetrate a data cable and hijack a connection such as a camera or a printer. This is an unlikely scenario, but still possible.

Cables should be protected against damage. They should be installed inside conduit and cable trays.

It is important to physically secure devices such as cameras and wireless access points (which can be hidden inside the ceiling space).

It is also important to not patch in cables that are not in use.

Airgap

An **air gap** is a physical separation of a network. An air gap is necessary to protect against vulnerable networks where the risk of intrusion or damage is so high that the cost is justified. Networks that require air gaps include

- Networks that contain classified information
- Nuclear facilities
- Public utilities such as water, power, and gas
- SCADA and other industrial control networks

Mantrap

A **man trap** is a door that only allows a single human to enter or exit at a time. The man trap door is typically used in combination with a card access/biometric authentication.

The user presents his credentials to a card reader and/or security guard. The first door opens, and the user enters a small hallway or room. The first door closes, and when the first door is closed, the second door opens. The man trap may be outfitted with a camera that detects if multiple individuals are present.

Faraday Cage

A **Faraday Cage** is a container that prevents the transmission of electromagnetic radiation (such as cellular or Wi-Fi signals). A Faraday Cage can be used to

- Isolate a device. For example, a cell phone seized during an investigation could be remotely wiped by the defendant. It must be secured in a Faraday cage so that it cannot transmit or receive data.
- Prevent data leaks. To prevent users from transmitting data without authorization, a Faraday Cage can be built around a room. This type of cage doesn't work because users can secretly record data and leave with the recording device.
- Protect a device from EMI. Most devices have some EMI shielding.

A good substitute for a Faraday Cage is aluminum foil. Wrapping a cell phone with aluminum foil is just as effective as a commercial Faraday Cage.

Lock Types

There are many types of locks. Locks can be three things

- **Mechanical Key lock**. The mechanical key lock is used when there are only a limited number of keys required (such as a person's office) and where it is not practical (or too expensive) to install electrical/network cabling and components for an electronic lock. The mechanical lock is excellent for this.

  The disadvantage is that the mechanical lock requires physically creating keys for each user. If an individual loses a key or it is stolen, then the lock must be physically rekeyed. All users must then receive new keys corresponding to the lock.

  A set of locks can be keyed with individual user keys and with a master key that opens all the locks.

- **Combination lock**. The combination lock is for low security but where there are multiple users. The combination can be changed in the lock. A combination lock may be electronic or mechanical. Combination locks are frequently installed in lunchrooms and staffrooms.

- **Electronic lock**. The electronic lock is most important because it allows multiple people to access the system, and has the following features
  - Restrict access based on time of day
  - Restrict access based on location
  - Allow a user to access multiple doors and locations with a single key card
  - Use the key card in combination with the multi-factor authentication
  - If the key card is lost or stolen it can be disabled without having to rekey the locks

- Lock that can be opened with both an electronic lock and a mechanical key. The mechanical key must be kept secure, and it is used to access the building in case a power outage disabled the electronic portion of the lock.

In a mechanical key lock, there are two ways in

- It can be broken. The thief who is willing to break the lock is one who does not care if the entry is later detected (somebody who is stealing something like money). The thief will break whatever is weakest – a nearby window, the door, or the lock. Therefore, it is important to make sure that the building is physically secure, not just the lock. The lock must be physically secure in that it cannot be broken or drilled.

  Many mechanical locks exist for bicycles and laptops. These locks can be easily cut or broken. They prevent only the most casual of thefts, and it is better to ensure that these items are never left unattended.

- It can be picked. The thief who wants to pick the lock is more sophisticated and does not want to be detected (somebody who is stealing data or planting a listening device/spyware). Some locks can be bypassed due to poor design. Otherwise, they can be broken or picked depending on how they are designed.

An electronic lock cannot be picked, but some can be bypassed
- Hacking into the electronic system that manages the lock, and commanding it to open the door
- Creating a replica of a valid key card and using it to gain access
- Using a magnet to unlatch the door (some electronic door locks contain magnets that are easily bypassed)

Biometrics

Biometrics are used in combination with other devices to provide an additional layer of authentication. These include
- Facial recognition
- Finger print reader
- Voice recognition
- Palm reader
- Retinal scan

The biometrics takes a photograph of a human body part and then converts it into a mathematical model. For example, a fingerprint reader understands the bumps and ridges on a fingerprint and compares their relative sizes. There are many different algorithms and each one is different.

Not every scan is perfect. Most biometrics have a false positive because of the algorithm. The false positive rate is approximately 1 in 50,000.

A biometric reader does not (and cannot) create a pixel-by-pixel comparison of a person. Imagine taking a photograph of your face 100 times. Each photo will be slightly different. The lighting, the reflection, the angle of your head, and the position of your hair will be slightly different each time.

Barricades/Bollards

A **barricade** or **bollard** is a physical device that keeps vehicles from crashing through a building. The barricade can be made of metal, concrete, or plastic (filled with sand or water). A barricade can be designed as part of a landscape architecture so that it is aesthetically pleasing.

The barricade is used to provide an additional layer of security next to a fence. A fence can keep people from climbing over won't stop a vehicle, and a barricade can stop a vehicle but won't stop a person.

Tokens/Cards

A **token** is a device that a user uses to access a secure area. The token identifies the user and is a physical device.

Many companies issue identification cards (ID cards) to their employees, contractors, and visitors. The ID card may also function as an access card, which permits access to a physical facility, and possibly as a smart card, which permits access to a computing device.

Environmental Controls

In a data center, there are three main types of environmental controls

- **HVAC**. The goal of the HVAC is to cool down the facility. The warm air is taken from the data room and pumped outside where it is cooled. There are many ways to transfer the heat. Most commonly, cold water (or another chemical such as a refrigerant) is pumped through the data center. It absorbs the heat. The now-hot water leaves the data center where it passes through a device known as a heat exchanger. The heat exchanger cools down the liquid, allowing it to pass through the data center again.

  An organization may locate their data center in an area that has a body of water or in cool climate. Cooling and electrical costs are a major factor in deciding where to construct a new data center.

- **Hot and Cold Aisles**. Proper design includes hot and cold aisles. Most rack-mounted equipment is designed to pull air through horizontally. The front of the device pulls cool air in. The air travels through the device, warms up, and is ejected through the rear.

  In a standard rack, the devices should be installed so that the air intake is on one side and the air output is on the other side. Racks are installed facing back-to-back and front-to-front. Then the result is that front-to-front aisles are cool, and back-to-back aisles are warm. The data center can then pump cool air in the front-to-front and eject warm air from the back-to-back.

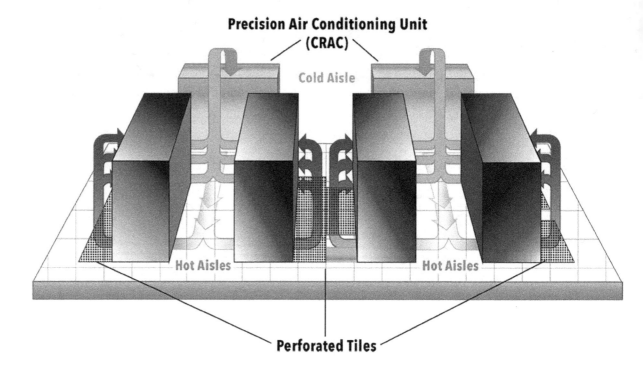

Precision Air Conditioning Unit (CRAC)

Cold Aisle

Hot Aisles   Hot Aisles

Perforated Tiles

- **Fire Suppression**. Fire Suppression keeps the facility from burning down. There are four types of fire suppression:
    - **Sprinklers**. A sprinkler system sprays oily water. This will stop the fire, but it will also damage the electronics. Many commercial buildings are required to have sprinkler systems by law, but these should not be installed in data centers.
    - **Low Oxygen System**. Air is 21% oxygen. When the oxygen levels drop to approximately 16%, a fire won't start (fire needs oxygen to burn). People can still breathe normally. The low oxygen fire suppression system lowers the oxygen levels to approximately 15%. This system is also known as Hypoxic Air, and while it works, it is not popular.
    - **Clean Fire Extinguishing Systems**.
        - The 3M Novec system sprays a gaseous fire suppressant that quickly puts out the fire. Novec evaporates fifty times faster than water and can put out a fire in seconds. 3M Novec does not damage electronics because it is non-conductive. Thus, servers continue to operate even in an emergency.
        - Carbon Dioxide. Carbon Dioxide suppresses oxygen, which puts out the fire.
    - **Handheld Fire Extinguishers**. Before using a fire extinguisher
        - Know that a fire can spread quickly. A handheld fire extinguisher may not be powerful enough to put out a large fire.

- It may be better to call the fire department, especially if you do not have proper training to use a fire extinguisher.
- Make sure to use the correct type of fire extinguisher
  - **A – Common Combustibles** – wood, cloth, or plastic. The fire extinguisher will contain water or a foam chemical.
  - **B – Combustible Liquids** – petroleum products. The fire extinguisher will contain Carbon Dioxide.
  - **C – Electrical Fire** – electrical wiring and power tools. The fire extinguisher will contain Carbon Dioxide.
  - **D – Flammable Materials** – metals such as magnesium. The fire extinguisher will contain copper or sodium chloride.
  - ABC fire extinguisher can put out A, B, and C-type fires

- **Flood Protection**. There are three considerations
  - The data center should be built on a raised floor. In the event of a flood, water will drain below the equipment
  - Do not run water pipelines through the data center if possible. This factor depends on the size of the data center, and the location in the building.
  - Install moisture alarms. These detect moisture/water and can alert a supervisor to take further action.

Equipment should be
- Installed by a trained professional
- Maintained regularly
- Tested to ensure that it is operational and working correctly
- Monitored so that alerts can be identified and responded to

Cable Locks

A **cable lock** is a lock that secures a computer or other hardware to a desk or other physical furniture. Most computers, monitors, and docking stations have ports that accommodate a cable lock. The cable lock is inserted into the port, wrapped around a physical piece of furniture (such as table leg) and then locked.

A cable lock can be easily cut with a bolt cutter, and only provides protection against casual theft. Some cable locks are alarmed and will trigger an alert when cut.

There are also locks that can alarm when the computer is moved. An example is a mount for an iPad, which has sensors that alert when the mount is lifted.

Screen Filters

A **screen filter** is a device that fits on top of a laptop or computer monitor. The device prevents others from viewing the content of the screen. It is also known as a privacy filter. The filters come in several standard sizes but may need to be cut to size. The filter prevents people from viewing the screen if they are too far to the left or the right of the user, but not if they are directly behind him.

The HP EliteBook has a built-in electronic privacy filter that is integrated into the laptop monitor. It gives the monitor a strange appearance, even when deactivated. The privacy filter is available on the EliteBook x360 and EliteDisplay E243p.

The privacy filter should not be thought of as a guarantee of protection, especially in a public place. There is always the potential for the user to be within the viewing angle of another person and/or a surveillance camera/hidden camera.

Cameras

A surveillance camera is used to monitor a physical area. Cameras should be placed

- At all entrances
- At locations where money is counted or exchanged
- At locations where valuables are stored
- At areas where thefts or acts of violence can occur
- At other areas where video monitoring is required

Cameras can be used with software that can

- Perform facial recognition and automatically detect/identify individuals and known trespassers
- Provide data analytics to understand traffic patterns
- Monitor entrances and exits

Cameras are available in a wide variety of models and features

- Analog or digital. Digital cameras are better because can connect to an NVR over a network, can be powered by PoE, and offer higher resolutions
- Resolution measured in megapixels (at least 3MP)
- Digital and analog zoom
- PTZ – ability to pan and tilt, which can be manual or automatic
- Optional heater for outdoor cameras
- Indoor and outdoor ratings (designed to withstand cold weather)
- Water/dust ingression rating of at least IP66
- Vandalism proof
- Integrated speaker/microphone
- Internal storage (some cameras contain flash memory and can directly record video, negating the use of an NVR)
- Night vision

The camera video feed is recorded onto a network video recorder (a dedicated device or a computer with video recording software). The NVR can connect directly to each camera, or the cameras can connect to a network switch.

The organization must decide how many days (weeks/months) worth of video they require. This affects the amount of storage space required (and then also the size of the NVR required). The amount of space required depends upon the

- Quantity of cameras
- Video resolution

- Frame rate
- Whether the camera records 24/7 or only when the camera detects motion

Some cameras have built in storage capacity so that they can record more data even when the NVR is offline. Some cameras can be cloud managed, where they upload their video to the internet. This can consume substantial network resources. A network may not be capable of uploading all of the video generated by the cameras.

Motion Detection

As previously discussed, motion detectors can detect motion. The sensitivity of the motion detector must be adjusted so that it can be easy to avoid a false alarm (small animals, leaves blowing in the wind, etc.).

The motion detector is typically connected to the alarm system. The motion detector is used in combination with secure doors, windows and fences. It can also be used in combination with a surveillance camera.

Logs

Logs are used in conjunction with physical security controls. The logs allow access/access attempts to be audited.

The logs should identify
- The identity of the person who accessed the resource
- The date and time that it was accessed
- The resource that was accessed
- How the identity of the person was verified and how the entitlement was verified

Each time a visitor enters or leaves a building, their entry/exit should be logged. Each time a person enters a server room, their presence should be logged.

Infrared Detection

Infrared detection identifies individuals and other objects through the heat patterns that their bodies generate. IR can be integrated into a surveillance camera or can part of a standalone sensor. IR detectors are more useful at night.

Key Management

Key management is a system that tracks the quantity of keys issued. There are automated systems (key lockers) that can automatically manage keys for contractors and vendors. There are also software applications that keep track of keys issued.

Keys should be marked as "do not duplicate". Most locksmiths will not duplicate keys marked as such, but this warning can be bypassed with a 3D printer/scanner.

Part E: SY0-501 4.0 Identity and Access Management

4.1 Compare and contrast identity and access management concepts

- *Identification, Authentication, Authorization and Accounting (AAA)*
- *Multifactor Authentication*
  - o *Something You Are*
  - o *Something You Have*
  - o *Something You Know*
  - o *Somewhere You Are*
  - o *Something You Do*
- *Federation*
- *Single Sign-On*
- *Transitive Trust*

Identification, Authentication, Authorization and Accounting (AAA)

How does a secure system provide access to an individual? Through **IAAA** – also known as **AAA** (**Authentication, Authorization, and Accounting**)

- **Identification** is the process of identifying a person. The person has presented credentials to the system (such as a smart card, an access card, an identification card, or a username). It is possible that the credentials have been compromised, so the system has not verified the person's identity at this stage.
- **Authentication** is when the person has been positively identified. Circumstances where authentication takes place
  - User presented a smart card and entered their PIN correctly
  - Presented an identification card to a security guard who positively compares the photograph on the card with the face of the individual
  - Entered the correct username and password into a computer
  - Scanned an access card at a card reader (the access card is a weak form of authentication because a lost/stolen access card can be used by an unauthorized individual)
- **Authorization** is the process of providing the user with access to the resources that he requested. Just because a user requested access and entered the correct username/password does not mean that the user is entitled to access.
  - For example, a user comes to work on a weekend but is not permitted. The security guard recognizes the employee as a legitimate employee and verifies his identification but does not permit access.
  - A user logs in to an HR system with the correct username and password but is not authorized to access the system.
- **Accounting** is the process of keeping track of who accessed what. Accounting is important for audits, and to ensure that all access attempts are legitimate. For example, patients have the right to know who accesses their personal health data. A nurse at a hospital may have the ability (authorization) to access the electronic health records of any patient at the hospital but should only do so if she has a legitimate need (and not because she is curious). The system should be able to track every time a patient record was accessed.
- We should log the following
  - What credentials were used (username, password, etc.)?
  - What system did they log in to (computer, door, entrance, etc.)?
  - What resources did they access (shared folder, printer, etc.)?
  - When did the access take place?

Multifactor Authentication

The principles of **multifactor authentication** (formally two-factor authentication) are important. The three main factors are Something You Are, Something You Have, and Something You Know. Basic authentication methods combine Something You Have (a username/access card) with either Something You Know (a password) or Something You Are (biometric).

- **Something You Are** – something you are refers to a biometric identity such as facial recognition, fingerprints, voice recognition, or a retinal scan. Select the best type of biometric for your environment. A construction site or hospital may have employees with gloves or
- **Something You Have** – something you have refers to a smartcard, identification card, or username; it could also refer to a randomly generated password (such as an RSA SecurID or authenticator app)
- **Something You Know** – something you know refers to a password or PIN
- **Somewhere You Are** – somewhere you are refers to your physical location. In the case of connecting to the internet, somewhere you are is your IP address. If a hacker compromises a username/password and logs in through a computer or network location that is not recognized, then the login may be denied. Websites have sophisticated ways of detecting users – IP address, web browser version, computer version, date/time of the login, other user behaviors. If the username/login is correct, but the other factors aren't it could be that the account was compromised, or it could be that the user is travelling/bought a new computer. The site can ask the user for additional verification (such as through an automated phone call)
- **Something You Do** – something you do is an observation of the user's action's or behaviors. In Windows a user can choose a picture password; in an Android phone the user can interact with a pattern.

Federation

Federation is a process where two computer systems establish a trust relationship. Federation allows a user to access resources located in multiple domains.

For example, a user working at Google can use Skype for Business to communicate with users working at Yahoo. The Skype system at Google and the Skype system at Yahoo are connected (federated) to allow users to exchange information.

Single Sign-On

Single Sign-On uses a central system to authenticate users across multiple applications.

For example, a user logs in to his computer via his Windows Active Directory password. He is then able to access the corporate intranet, procurement application, online library, payroll, and e-mail without having to re-enter a username or password.

Once logged in, the remaining applications understand that the user is already authenticated. In the background the applications receive authorization from the Active Directory server.

A user (and the organization) does not have to maintain separate usernames/passwords for each application.

If the single sign on system fails, then the user will not be able to access any of the applications.

Increasingly, social media sites such as Google and Facebook provide SSO services to other websites. For example, a user can use their Facebook account to log in to another site. Using Facebook for Single Sign On is a bad idea because Facebook will collect data about your visits to other websites and the websites will collect data from your Facebook account.

Transitive Trust

A **Transitive Trust** is a relationship between two Microsoft Active Directory domains. In Active Directory, there is a main domain (known as the parent domain). A user can create a child domain underneath the parent. The child domain can contain child domains of its own.

In the transitive trust, the parent domain trusts the child domain and everything that the child domain trusts. A member of a child domain receives the same privileges as a member of a parent domain. A transitive trust may be one-way or two-way.

When an application is authenticated by a domain, all the other domains that have a trust relationship with that domain will also authenticate the application.

4.2 Given a scenario, install and configure identity and access services

- *LDAP*
- *Kerberos*
- *TACAS+*
- *CHAP*
- *PAP*
- *MSCHAP*
- *RADIUS*
- *SAML*
- *OpenID Connect*
- *OAUTH*
- *Shibboleth*
- *Secure Token*
- *NTLM*

LDAP

LDAP stands for **Lightweight Directory Access Protocol** or **LDAPS** (for secure access). LDAP is essentially an address book. LDAP is governed by the X.500 standard.

LDAP includes a server called a **Directory Server Agent**, which typically speaks on port 389 or 636 for LDAPS. A client connects to the server.

A client can do the following (a client may have permission to do only some of these)
- Add
- Delete
- Modify
- Search

For example, a photocopier with "scan to email" capabilities would connect to the LDAP server and obtain e-mail address entries for the various users in the office.

Kerberos

Kerberos is a protocol that allows clients and servers to authenticate with each other and prove their identities. The Kerberos protocol protects against eavesdropping and replay attacks. Kerberos uses UDP port 88. Kerberos provides encryption over an unsecure network.

Kerberos' current version is V5. It was developed by MIT and made available for free.

All versions of Windows including Windows 2000 and later use Kerberos for authentication by default (although other protocols can be used). Kerberos is used to join a client to a Windows domain.

Most common versions of UNIX also use Kerberos.

If a client wishes to connect, the following procedure is followed. The client calls the Authentication Server (AS) to obtain authentication. The authentication server takes the client's username and sends it to another server called the **Key Distribution Center** (**KDC**). The KDC runs a service known as the **Ticket-Granting Service** (**TGS**), which maintains a secret key. The KDC issues a ticket known as the **Ticket-Granting Ticket** (**TGT**) and encrypts it with the secret key. The encrypted key is sent back to the client.

- A user would like to log in to a Windows machine, with a username and password. Even on a corporate network, the password should not be sent to the server (domain controller) in plain text.
- The Windows machine encrypts/hashes the password
- The client sends the user ID to the authentication server (in plain text).
- The Authentication Server verifies that the client is in the database. The AS creates a secret key from the hash of the user's password and returns to the client the following messages
    o A TGS Session Key, which is encrypted with the newly created secret key (Message A)
    o A TGT, which includes an expiry date, the client's network address, all encrypted with the TGS's secret key (Message B)
- The client takes the TGS Session Key and decrypts it with the hash of the password entered earlier. If the client entered the wrong password, then the client will be unable to decrypt the TGS Session Key.
- The client uses the decrypted TGS Session Key to communicate with the TGS
- Requesting additional services
    o Client sends additional messages to TGS
        ▪ Message C is the TGT from Message B and the ID number for the requested service

- Message D is the authenticator (client ID and time stamp), encrypted with the Client/TGS
  - TGS obtains Message B from Message C and decrypts it (Only TGS has the encryption key for Message B). TGS uses this to decrypt Message D.
  - If the Client ID in Message C and Message D match, then the client is authenticated
  - TGS sends additional messages
    - Message E is the Client-to-Server Ticket, which includes the client ID, network address, and expiry, encrypted using the service's secret key
    - Message F is the Client/Server Session Key, encrypted with the Client/TGS Session Key
  - The client takes Message E and Message F and uses them to authenticate with the Service Server
  - The client sends
    - Message E from before
    - Message G, which is an authenticator, including the client ID, and timestamp
  - The SS decrypts Message E with its own secret key and obtains the Client/Server session Key. It uses this key to decrypt Message G. If they match, then the client is authenticated with the service
  - The SS sends Message H to the client, which includes the timestamp in Message E, encrypted with the Client/Server Session Key
  - The client decrypts Message H. If the timestamp on Message H is correct, then the client knows it can trust the server. A rogue agent could issue a fake message but would not be able to match the timestamp.

The encrypted key will expire, but if the user is logged in, the key will renew (the client will automatically contact the server and obtain an updated key).

To communicate with another node, the ticket is sent back to the service. The TGS verifies that the user is permitted to access the service and then sends the ticket to the Service Server (SS).

Kerberos has a single point of failure, which is the authentication server.

Kerberos also requires the clients, servers, and services to be responsive (since timestamps must match on all devices). That means that all devices must have synchronized clocks. If a client/server issues a ticket/message with a timestamp that doesn't match due to a clock that is out of sync, then the system will fail. Clocks must not be more than five minutes apart.

TACACS+

TACACS or **Terminal Access Controller Access-Control System** is a protocol for accessing/managing network devices. It was developed by UNIX.

TACACS+ was developed by Cisco and is a separate protocol from TACACS. Most systems use TACACS+ or RADIUS.

TACAS uses port 49 to communicate.

TACACS+ encrypts the full content of each packet while RADIUS encrypts only the user passwords. TACACS+ uses TCP, while RADIUS uses UDP (therefore RADIUS has more errors). Cisco continues to support RADIUS, but TACACS+ is recommended.

TACACS+ uses the AAA architecture, where each element is separate. Therefore, a system could use a different form of authentication (such as Kerberos) with TACACS+ authorization and accounting. Some forms of authentication

- Point-to-Point
- PAP
- CHAP
- EAP
- Kerberos

Authentication

- The client sends a START message to the server
- The server sends a REPLY message
- The client sends a CONTINUE message, if additional information is required for authentication
- Otherwise, authentication is complete

Authorization

- A default state of "unknown user" is created if the user's identity is unknown
- Otherwise, the TACAS+ server responds with a RESPONSE message, which contains the restrictions on the user

Accounting

- A START message records when the user started the connection
- A STOP message records when the user stopped the connection
- An UPDATE message says that a task is still being performed

TACACS+ allows an administrator to configure different privilege levels for each user (for example a user may not be permitted to modify an ACL on a router). RADIUS does not allow different privilege levels (all users are effectively superadmins).

CHAP

CHAP is **Challenge-Handshake Authentication Protocol**. It authenticates a network host with a server/ISP. CHAP protects against replay attacks.

CHAP uses PPP to validate the identity of each client through a three-way handshake.
- The link is established between the client and the server
- The authenticator sends a challenge message to the peer
- The peer combines the challenge message with its secret, and calculates a one-way hash, which it returns
- The authenticator calculates its own hash value, verifies that the hash sent by the peer matches
- If the hashes match, then the client is authenticated
- The authenticator will randomly send additional challenge messages to the peer while the connection is active. Each challenge will have a new ID.

CHAP requires a shared secret between the client and the server.

PPP (Point-to-Point Protocol) can only support CHAP and PAP.

PAP

PAP or **Password Authentication Protocol** is a protocol used to validate users. PAP is considered weak but supported by almost all network operating systems.

PAP sends usernames and passwords over plaintext.

PAP protocol
- Client sends the username/password to the server continually until a response is received
- Server returns either "ack" if the credentials are correct or "nak" if the credentials are incorrect

MSCHAP

MSCHAP is the Microsoft version of **Challenge-Handshake Authentication Protocol**. The latest version is MS-CHAPv2.

MS-CHAP allows an authenticator to control the password change mechanism and the retry mechanism (in the case of a failed login attempt).

MS-CHAP and MS-CHAPv2 can be broken through brute force methods and should not be used.

RADIUS

RADIUS, or **Remote Authentication Dial-In User Service**, is a server that has three components
- Protocol
- Server
- Client

The **Network Access Server** is a Client of the RADIUS Server. When a user attempts to log in to the client, the client sends user information to the RADIUS server. The client and server encrypt their data with a shared secret, but the communication between the user and the client are not encrypted.

The RADIUS server receives connection requests and authenticates the user. RADIUS does not allow different privilege levels (all users are effectively superadmins). A RADIUS server combines authentication and authorization.

Authentication
- Many methods are possible including PPP, PAP, and CHAP
- The client sends the RADIUS server the user's username and encrypted password
- The RADIUS server replies with
    - Accept – the user is authenticated
    - Reject – the user is rejected (credentials invalid)
    - Challenge – the user must provide additional information

Authorization
- Authorization tells the client what privileges to assign to the user

Accounting
- Accounting data is transmitted at the beginning and end of a session

SAML

Security Assertion Markup Language is a standard for exchanging authentication and authorization data.

SAML is typically used to allow a user to log in through a web-browser Single Sign On

SAML has three roles
- The Principal, also known as the user
- The identity provider (IdP). The IdP identifies the Principal.
- The Service Provider (SP). The SP provides a service to the Principal and requires proof of his identity.

The procedure works as follows
- The Principal requests a service from the SP. For example, a user attempts to log in to his online banking account.
- The SP sends the user back to the IdP. For example, the user's bank accepts identity verification from Gmail and several other sources. The bank sends the user to the Gmail website.
- The user requests a Single Sign On from the IdP. This may happen automatically. For example, the user is required to log in to Gmail and obtain the response.
- The IdP responds with an XHTML form. The form contains the IdP's response to the SSO request (which may be positive or negative).
- The SSO response is provided back to the SP. This is handled through a process called an Assertion Consumer Service.
- The user is redirected to the target resource. The user returns to the online banking website.
- This time, the target resource is provided to the user. The user is not redirected to the IdP again.

OpenID Connect

OpenID Connect is a service that works on top of **OAuth** and **OAuth 2.0**, which is a standard for allowing users to connect to websites without having to provide passwords.

For example, a user may log in to the New York Times website using their Google account or their Facebook account. The user does not have to provide the New York Times with their Facebook account password.

OAuth provides authorization, but not authentication. The OpenID Connect provides authentication, but not authorization. Thus, both are typically required. OAuth operates on top of OpenID.

Typically, the OAuth service provider requires the user to authenticate. As a result, OAuth should not be used for authentication, only for authorization.

The process

- The user requests the resource from a service provider
- The service provider requests authentication/authorization from the identity provider
- The identity provider authenticates/authorizes the user
- The user is redirected back to the service provider
- The service provider reads the response from the identity provider and determines if the user should be provided with access

OpenID obtains additional user data from the Identity Provider through a RESTful API. The data is provided in JSON format.

OAUTH

OAuth and OAuth 2.0 are services that allow a user to authenticate with a service provider. OAuth 2.0 is the current version and is not compatible with OAuth 1.0. OAuth is used with OpenID.

Shibboleth

Shibboleth is a system that allows a user to identify themselves to different online services with one user ID. It works like the other systems mentioned (OpenID). This system is commonly used by universities.

An Identity Provider (IdP) supplies user information to a Service Provider (SP) which provides a user with required services.

Shibboleth 2.0 is the current version. It allows the SP to request additional information from the IdP.

The process

- A user requests a service from the SP
- The SP sends the user a request (in a URL) that encodes the entityID, location, and page to return the user to
- The user is sent to their IdP, where they can sign in. The system that they are on will typically detect the user's home IdP. If not, the user might be prompted to identify where they are from.
- The user authenticates themselves
- The Shibboleth creates a temporary handle that is linked to the IdP request
- The user returns to the SP, which requests additional information about the user's identity from the IdP
- The IdP returns the requested data to the SP
- The SP uses the information to decide whether to provide access

For example, a user at the University of Alberta is issued a single user ID known as a Campus Compute ID. This ID provides the user with access to

- Beartracks (a course registration website)
- eClass (a website that contains course data such as notes, textbooks, and exams)
- Library website (access to databases, etc.)
- Finance website
- Many other websites, some of which may be internal, and some of which may be external. The University would like to restrict access to only members of its community.

The University of Alberta operates a central authentication service. This service allows the user to authenticate with their central service through Shibboleth, and then provide access to the other resources.

For example, a user visits the library website from a campus computer. The user is asked to log in to their University of Alberta account. In the background, the University's authentication service communicates with the library's website to identify the user who requires access. It is not enough to authorize the user; the library also needs to know the identity of the user. The library will want to inform the user of the books that he has checked out, holds, fines, etc..

Secure Token

A **Secure Token** is a piece of data that is issued by a server, so that a user does not need to keep logging in.

- User signs in with a username/password
- Secure Token Service validates the credentials and provides the user with a secure token
- User stores the token and returns a copy of the token with every HTTP or HTTPS request
- Service provider verifies the token and responds with the appropriate data

NTLM

NTLM or **New Technology LAN Manager** is a Microsoft system that allows users to authenticate with a server. It is like MS-CHAPv2.

The process
- The client connects to the server. The client sends the server a NEGOTIATE_MESSAGE message and states its capabilities.
- The server sends a CHALLENGE_MESSAGE, which seeks to identify the client.
- The client responds with an AUTHENTICATE_MESSAGE, to prove its identity. The server determines whether the client has provided the correct response.

The current version of NTLM is NTLMv2. The client sends the server two responses (each 24 bytes long). The responses contain
- A hash of the server CHALLENGE_MESSAGE
- A hash of the user's password
- A client challenge
  - The server uses the client challenge to verify the response

The use of NTLM is not recommended because it is not secure. It does not support modern encryption methods.

When a developer builds an application, they should not hardcode the requirement of using NTLM. They should instead use a security package (library) known as "Negotiate". Negotiate will select the most secure available security protocol. Currently, the most secure protocol is Kerberos, which will be selected unless it is not available.

NTLM is not used when
- Connecting to a server that is not part of a domain
  - When the client and the server are part of the same Windows HomeGroup, Public Key Cryptography based User to User Authentication is used, and not NTLM
- Connecting to a server that is part of a domain, but
  - the client is not part of a domain (or only the client's IP address is available)
  - the connection is blocked by a firewall (port 88 is blocked)
  - the client and the server are joined to different domains and there is no trust relationship between the domains

How to break NTLM

- A Pass the Hash attack can be used to hack a NTLM protocol. A hash can be stolen from one computer and used to provide a second computer with access to the server.
- Ability to predict the pseudo-random numbers, challenges, and responses generated by NTLM. This vulnerability has been fixed.
- Crack the NTLM hash (an 8-bit hash can be cracked in 2 hours). The server should have a mechanism to detect and stop brute force attacks.

4.3 Given a scenario, implement identity and access management controls

- *Access Control Models*
  - *MAC*
  - *DAC*
  - *ABAC*
  - *Role-Based Access Control*
  - *Rule-Based Access Control*
- *Physical Access Control*
  - *Proximity Cards*
  - *Smart Cards*
- *Biometric Factors*
  - *Fingerprint Scanner*
  - *Retinal Scanner*
  - *Iris Scanner*
  - *Voice Recognition*
  - *Facial Recognition*
  - *False Acceptance Rate*
  - *False Rejection Rate*
  - *Crossover Error Rate*
- *Tokens*
  - *Hardware*
  - *Software*
  - HOTP/TOTP
- *Certificate-Based Authentication*
  - *PIV/CAC/Smart card*
  - *IEEE 802.1X*
- *File System Security*
- *Database Security*

Access Control Models

There are different models for access control in an organization. The specific control chosen depends on the needs of the organization, the type of data being protected, and the type of users. An organization may implement multiple access control models.

Access Control permissions usually relate to being able to read, write, delete, and/or modify a file, and list contents of a folder. Additional, more extensive permissions, can apply to a database (such as the ability to read, write, delete, or modify entries in a database, create tables in a database, or create users in the database).

The permissions can apply to the entire system or gradually to specific files.

MAC – Mandatory Access Control
- Each user has certain permissions on the system
- The user cannot grant his permissions to other users
- For example, if a user has read access to a file, the user cannot grant another user with read access to the file
- The user cannot modify any of the permissions on the file

DAC – Discretionary Access Control
- A user has certain permissions
- The user can grant his permissions to other users
- For example, if a user has read access to a file, the user can grant another user with read access to the file
- An example of when DAC is better than MAC: a project manager has access to files related to his projects; the project manager grants access to other members of the team. The project manager does not have to contact an IT person to obtain access for members of his team.
- An example of when MAC is better than DAC: an intelligence analyst needs to grant a co-worker access to classified documents; the analyst should not be able to do so; the individual requesting access must have a need-to-know basis and appropriate security clearances, which need to be verified by a central authority

ABAC – Attribute-Based Access Control
- Each user has certain attributes (for example, the user's role in the organization, age, security clearance, department, etc.)
- Each resource has certain attributes (for example, the contents, department, owner, etc.)
- When the user attempts to access the resource, the system uses the user's attributes and the resource's attributes to determine whether to provide access.

- ABAC is more complicated because the system requires many rules to decide whether to permit/deny a user. If a rule does not exist, then the default action is to deny the access. It might take a substantial amount of work to set up all the rules.

Role-Based Access Control
- Permissions are not assigned to individual users or to objects
- Permissions are assigned to operations/actions (known as roles)
- A user can be assigned to a specific group (the user is given a role); the user inherits the permissions assigned to the role
- The organization can define the operations and actions that are relevant to their organization. For example:
    o Sales person (can access sales data)
    o Accountant (can enter data into the accounting system)
    o Accounts payable clerk (can approve invoices and issue payments)

Rule-Based Access Control
- Permissions are not assigned to individual users or objects
- Instead, a set of rules exist; the rules may permit or deny specific actions depending on the attributes
- Each time an action is attempted, the system evaluates the action against the set of rules
- The rules do not consider who is attempting the action, only what the action is

Physical Access Control

Physical access control permits users to access a building or service.

Items that can be controlled
- Doors
- Gates
- Garage Doors
- Vending machines/cubicles (industrial warehouses, hospitals, etc.)
- Photocopiers (secure document printing)

The ways that a physical access control can be implemented
- Magnetic swipe card (not recommended)
- Proximity card reader (more secure, but some older models can be hacked); some readers will work with credentials on a smart phone via NFC; combined with a user's smart card or identification card
- Physical control by a security guard (necessary on more high-risk sites such as airports and nuclear plants, where 100% positive ID verification is required)
- Numeric Keypad (not recommended because single code is shared by many people); keypads can be electronic or mechanical
- Combination of physical access card with biometric identification (fingerprint, retinal scan, etc.) for added security. This is necessary at sites like airports.

Granular approach to access control
- Only provide a user with the access that they need
- Each user can be assigned a specific role
- Limit the areas that a user can access based on their role (for example, only IT department employees will require access to the server room)
- Limit the time of day that a user can access the facility (can limit the access to only business hours)
- Ensure that lost or stolen cards are immediately deactivated
- Audit the records to ensure that all access attempts were legitimate; the system can identify uses where the person attempted to gain access to a door that they do not have access to
- Install cameras near each sensor to identify who accessed it

Biometric Factors

Physical access control can be combined with biometric factors to improve security. A physical card can be lost or stolen, in which case, an unauthorized user can gain access.

Biometrics include
- **Fingerprints**
    - A fingerprint scanner maps a person's fingerprint and converts it into a mathematical signature. This signature is stored.
    - It later compares new scans to the original mathematical signature.
    - Advanced fingerprint scanners can verify that a real finger has been scanned (as opposed to a mold of a finger)
    - Fingerprint scanners are cheaper than other biometric sensors
- **Retinal Scan**
    - A retinal scan uses a laser to examine the blood vessels in the back of the eye
    - Retinal scans are unpopular because they require a user to have a laser shined into his eye; the user must also put his eye up against the sensor
- **Iris**
    - An iris scan photographs the front of the eye from a distance
    - Iris scanners are more popular than retinal scanners
- **Voice Recognition**
    - Voice recognition is hard to implement
    - Voice recognition sensors have a high rate of false positives and false negatives
- **Facial Recognition**
    - Facial recognition scans features that are present on the user's face
    - Facial recognition systems work well

In general, biometric algorithms generate a mathematical model of the body part being scanned. The model is stored. When a user attempts to authenticate, the new scan is used to generate a model. The two models are compared. If they are similar, the user is authenticated. The two models do not have to be identical. It is known that every scan will be slightly different. The user might have a scratch on his face, the user might stand at a different angle, the user's hair might be different, etc.. Each of these factors results in a slightly different scan.

The biometrics may be stored on a central server or encrypted onto the user's smart card.

Biometrics have a failure rate
- False Acceptance Rate. A false acceptance is when an invalid user is authenticated. If the false acceptance rate is increased, all legitimate users will be accepted, but many unauthorized users will also be accepted.

- False Rejection Rate. A false rejection is when a valid user is rejected. If the false rejection rate is increased, all unauthorized users will be rejected, but many authorized users will also be rejected.
- Crossover Error Rate. The Crossover Error Rate is when the False Acceptance Rate and the False Rejection Rate are equal. An administrator can adjust the system's rejection threshold so that the two rates are equal. At the Crossover Error Rate, the system operates efficiently.

Tokens

A token generates a code that a user provides to log in to a computer. The user logs in to a server with a username and password combination. If the username/password is compromised, an unauthorized user can log in. To prevent this, the server also requires a "one-time" password, generated by a token. The user will have physical possession of the token.

There are many types of tokens

- RSA token. The token generates a one-time numeric key that the user must enter to log in. The token generates a new key each minute.
- Calculator. The application provides the user with a code. The user enters the code into the calculator and the calculator returns a response key, which the user must enter to log in.
- YubiKey. A USB key that automatically generates a one-time numeric key.
- SmartCard. The smart card is similar to the Yubikey but is in a Smart Card format. The device must have a smart card reader, or a USB smart card reader.
- Software token. The application can be installed on a computer or smartphone to generate keys. It should not be installed on the device that it is providing access to. The software token can generate keys for multiple accounts.

There are two ways to generate a token code

- **HOTP (HMAC-Based One Time Password)**
  - The token and the server have a shared secret key, known as a seed; the seed is used to generate token keys
  - The token and the server also have a counter
  - The server increments the counter when a user attempts to enter a token key and the token increments the counter when a new key is generated. If a user generates a key on the token and does not enter it into the server, then the counter on the server will be out of sync with the counter on the token. The server can be set to accept keys that are several "counts" away. If the counts are too far apart, the server and the token must be resynched.
  - A token key is valid until it is used
  - Both the server and the token can generate keys, so that the server can validate that the user has provided the correct key
- **TOTP (Time-Based One Time Password)**
  - The token and the server know about a secret key, known as a seed; the seed is used to generate token key
  - The token and the server also know what the current date and time is

- The token generates a new key every 30 or 60 seconds
- The key is only valid for 30 or 60 seconds
- The server can also generate keys, so that it can validate the correct key
- If date/time is not correct on either the server or the token, then the key will not be valid. The server will be expecting a different response. Since time is not perfectly synched, the server may be programmed to accept key that are a few minutes apart.

Certificate-Based Authentication

There are several methods for a user to verify his identity with a certificate, including PIV, CAC, and Smart Cards.

PIV

- **Personal Identity Verification Standard**
- Issued by the United States federal government to employees and contractors
- Described by FIPS (Federal Information Processing Standard) PUB 201-2
- Designed to provide a common standard for identity verification across the entire federal government
- Credential is issued to an individual only after
  - The individual's identity is verified (with at least two forms of identification; one form must be a government-issued photo identification)
  - The individual has completed a background check
  - A government agency has requested that the credential is issued
  - At least two individuals must authorize the issuing of the credential (so that a single corrupt government official cannot issue a fraudulent credential)
  - Fingerprints are collected
  - An iris scan may be collected and stored on the card
- When the card is created, a private (non-exportable) key is generated and stored on the card. The card can prove that it is legitimate.
- The card also contains additional keys such as card authentication keys
- The card also contains public keys corresponding to the private keys of the card issuer (United States government). When the card is presented to a reader, it can use the public keys to verify that the reader is legitimate.
- When a user attempts to access a resource
  - The card reader obtains the Card Authentication Certificate from the card
  - The card reader validates the certificate to ensure that it is valid, that it has not been revoked, and that it is from a trusted source
  - The cardholder must enter a PIN or biometric data if required
  - The card reader sends the card a challenge message
  - The card replies with a response
  - If the response is valid, then the system provides access

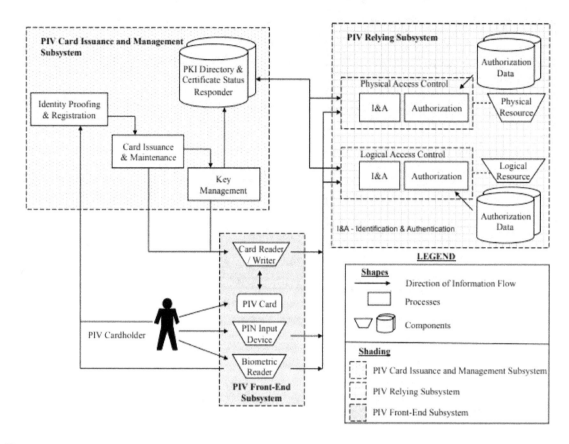

CAC

- **Common Access Card**
- Issued by the Department of Defense to military personnel, civilian employees, and contractors.
- The card serves as an identification card. It also allows a user to access military buildings (access control), and computer systems (smart card)
- The card contains the user's name, photograph, rank, blood type, and other information
- The user may be required to enter a PIN when accessing a secure site
- The card uses 2048-bit encryption
- Issuance is covered by Department of Defense Manual 1000.13

Smart Card

- A smart card is a plastic card with a microchip, known as an integrated circuit
- Uses of smart cards
  - NFC Payment. NFC technology is contactless. The card must be several inches from the reader. Most credit cards incorporate NFC technology for transactions of low dollar value (under $100). The card may store the funds in a cryptographically secure manner; in which case, the card/reader does not have to connect to a bank to verify that sufficient funds are present.

408

- o EMV Payment. The card must be inserted into a reader. Most credit cards incorporate EMV technology. The credit card reader validates that the credit card is valid. The information on the card may be secured by a PIN.
  - o Access control/Identification. A smart card can be used to access a computer. The card contains a certificate that validates its identity. The card can also contain encryption keys for BitLocker/VeraCrypt.
  - o Drivers Licenses. In Turkey, drivers' licenses incorporate smart card technology. Truck drivers must insert their drivers' licenses into a digital tachometer while operating their vehicles. The card records any speed violations and monitors the amount of time that a driver has been operating their vehicle.

    Many other governments issue smart card drivers' licenses.
  - o Other uses including school identification, public transit, and healthcare.
- Security Risks
  - o The smart cards are tamper-resistant and secure.
  - o A smart card's activity can be monitored through differential power analysis, which monitors the time and electric current used by the chip embedded into the card. This data can be used to determine the private key stored on the card. The success of this technique depends on the type of encryption algorithm implemented on the card.
  - o The best way to extract data from a smart card is to physically disassemble the chip, but this would physically damage the card.
  - o A user could also find ways to compromise the system that authenticates the smart card and bypass it altogether.

IEEE 802.1X

- IEEE 802.1X is a standard for Network Access Control. It allows a device to authenticate when connecting to a LAN or WAN.
- There are three devices
  - o The supplicant is the device that chooses to connect to the LAN/WAN. It could be a laptop, desktop, smartphone, tablet, or other computing device
  - o The authenticator is a network device that allows/denies access. It could be a switch, a router, a firewall, or a proxy server.
  - o The authentication server is a server that decides whether a device should be granted access
- The procedure
  - o The supplicant connects to the network
  - o The authenticator (switch) detects the new supplicant and automatically sets the port to an unauthenticated status. Only traffic related to 802.1X is permitted.
  - o The authenticator sends frames to the supplicant. These frames demand that the supplicant provide credentials such as a user ID. The frames are sent on the local

network segment to a specific address (01:80:C2:00:00:03). The supplicant listens for messages on this address.

- o The supplicant replies to the message with an EAP-Response Identity frame
- o The authenticator sends the supplicant's response to an authentication server
- o The authentication server and the supplicant negotiate an authentication method. The server and the supplicant may support different methods and must agree on one that both understand. The negotiation methods are transported through the authenticator.
- o The authentication server attempts to authenticate the suppliant. If successful, the authenticator changes the port status to authorized. If unsuccessful, the authenticator keeps the port status as unauthorized.
- o When the supplicant logs off or is disconnected, the authenticator changes the port status back to unauthorized. When the supplicant logs off, it sends an EAPOL-Logoff message to the authenticator.

- Security Risks
  - o A hacker can physically insert himself between the port and the authenticated computer; and then use the authenticated port
  - o A DDOS attack can take place. A hacker can create EAPOL-logoff messages with the MAC address of the supplicant and send them to the authenticator, forcing the port to go into an unauthorized state. This would force the supplicant to continually go offline.

File System Security

File System Security encompasses many strategies.

Access to a file system is handled logically with Windows Role-Based authentication or Attribute-Based authentication, as previously discussed.

On a logical/physical level, if a disk is not encrypted, then file system security is not truly possible. A hacker can physically remove the disk (or boot from an external drive) and access the files, regardless of the logical security that is in place.

In a Windows environment, security requires

- Encryption such as BitLocker or Encrypting File System to prevent a physical bypass of the security
- File system that allows user-level access control such as NTFS
- Access control policies such as MAC or DAC
- System to grant users access such as Active Directory or group policy

Database Security

Database security can be transactional or controlled by the underlying source code.

MySQL/MSSQL databases interact with an application and the application interacts with the users. Database credentials are typically hardcoded into the application. The application must determine what access a user has, but the application itself has full access.

Oracle databases are **transactional**. The user authenticates directly with the database. Users are created in, and managed by, the database server.

4.4 Given a scenario, differentiate common account management practices

- *Account Types*
  - *User Account*
  - *Shared and Generic Accounts/Credentials*
  - *Guest Accounts*
  - *Service Accounts*
  - *Privileged Accounts*
- *General Concepts*
  - *Least Privilege*
  - *Onboarding/Offboarding*
  - *Permission Auditing and Review*
  - *Usage Auditing and Review*
  - *Time-of-Day Restrictions*
  - *Recertification*
  - *Standard Naming Convention*
  - *Account Maintenance*
  - *Group-Based Access Control*
  - *Location-Based Policies*
- *Account Policy Enforcement*
  - *Credential Management*
  - *Group Policy*
  - *Password Complexity*
  - *Expiration*
  - *Recovery*
  - *Disablement*
  - *Lockout*
  - *Password History*
  - *Password Reuse*
  - *Password Length*

Account Types

In any system, there are several types of accounts.

- **User Account**. This is the standard account. There may be multiple types of user accounts with different levels of privileges and access.
  - An organization may grant administrative privileges to all user accounts, to some user accounts (based on business need) or to none of the user accounts. The organization must weigh the benefits of granting these privileges against the risk of damage.
  - A large organization can group different privileges and access into groups, and then assign the groups to accounts as required

- **Shared and Generic Accounts**.
  - A shared account is one that is used by multiple users. For example, a shared mailbox can be used by multiple helpdesk agents.
  - It is better to allow each user to log in with their own account, and then delegate access to them. They will be able to access the same information, but their activities can be accounted for.
  - A generic account is one that may be used by a device such as multi-function printer/scanner or conference room phone. This device must connect to the corporate network and access specific resources. Generic account credentials usually do not change.
  - A generic account is risky. For example, a photocopier may store the generic account username and password in plain text. The organization must take precautions to ensure that only the device in question can authenticate with that account or use other methods to allow devices to access the network.
  - The generic account should be assigned the least amount of privileges required for it to perform its tasks.

- **Guest Account**. A guest account is granted to visitors and contractors. The guest account typically has limited privileges. Guest accounts should be locked out when not required.

- **Service Account**. A service account is used for maintenance. For example, a software application running on a server may require a service account to download/install updates. The service account may not be permitted to log in to a computer.

- **Privileged Account**. A privileged account is also known as an admin account or an elevated account. The privileged account will have more access than the user account. In a large organization, there can be different levels of privilege/access, or groups of privilege/access (for example, domain administrator, email administrator, etc.)

General Concepts

Some account security concepts

- **Least Privilege**. The user account should be granted only the least privileges/access required for the user to perform his/her job (or function in the case of a generic account).

- **Onboarding/Offboarding**.
  - o User accounts should be tied to an HR management, vendor management, or asset management application. That is, every account should be accounted for.
  - o When the user is first contracted/hired, the organization should identify his role and create an account that provides the necessary privileges. When an asset is purchased, the account should be created to provide it with access.
  - o When the user is terminated or when the asset is disposed of, the account should be locked or deleted. The account should be locked prior to the user being terminated (this would prevent an angry user from causing damage after learning that he will be fired)

- **Permission Auditing and Review**
  - o User accounts should be audited to ensure that users are not granted permission to objects that they do not require
  - o Auditing should be conducted on a regular basis

- **Usage Auditing and Review**
  - o No system is perfect; therefore, user accounts should be audited on a regular basis to ensure that all users are active
  - o Inactive accounts can be locked out

- **Time-of-Day Restrictions**
  - o An account can be restricted so that it can only access the system (or specific system resources) during specific times of day or specific days.
  - o Workers who operate on a fixed schedule should only be permitted to access the system when required to perform their job

- **Recertification**
  - o Recertification is the process of reactivating an account

- **Standard Naming Convention**
  - o User accounts should be given standard names so that there is no confusion
  - o Each organization can develop a naming convention based on their own needs

- The name can include one or a combination of the user's full name, department, job title, location, and employee ID number

- **Account Maintenance**
  - The system should regularly verify that all active accounts belong to active employees/contractors
  - Accounts belonging to terminated users should be deactivated

- **Group-Based Access Control**
  - In a large organization, assigning privileges to each account manually can be time consuming and lead to security vulnerabilities (when too many privileges are assigned) or disruption to the business (when not enough privileges are assigned)
  - Instead, groups can be created. A group is a role that a user plays in the organization. Each group can be assigned specific privileges consistent with that role. A user can be assigned to one or more groups. The user then inherits the privileges that were assigned to each group.
  - For example, an organization may create an "engineers" group. The engineers group is given the privilege of accessing AutoCAD files. When a new engineer is hired, he is added to the engineers group. He now has access to AutoCAD files.

- **Location-Based Policies**
  - A location-based policy is one that provides a user with privileges based on his physical location at the time of log in, or based on his office location
  - When accessing the network through a mobile device, the user's GPS location may be used to determine the appropriate policy

Account Policy Enforcement

Account Policies can be enforced through several methods

- **Credential Management**, which requires users to use specific login methods such as smart cards

- **Group Policy**
  - o Windows system that enforces policies across different users and devices
  - o Group policy is controlled by a central server

- **Password Complexity**
  - o A password policy may require a user to have capital letters, numbers, special symbols and/or lowercase letters in their password
  - o A user cannot repeat a character
  - o A user cannot use a dictionary word or their name in the password
  - o The password must have a minimum length
  - o Passwords that are easy to guess represent security risks

- **Expiration**
  - o An account can be set to expire (for example, a contract employee with a known termination date should have an account that expires on his termination date)
  - o A password can expire after a specific time. The user would be required to change his password once it expires. A typical expiry time is three months

- **Recovery**
  - o If a user forgets his password, he must have a method for resetting it
  - o There are several methods
    - ▪ Self-service password reset, where the user is authenticated through another method such as answering security questions or receiving an automated phone call/text message. The self-service password reset is cost-effective because it allows a user to reset his password without involving an administrator.
      - • The danger is that a hacker could reset the user's password by spoofing/intercepting the phone call or guessing the answers to the security questions.
      - • A user may not have set up the self-service password recovery options.
    - ▪ An administrator can reset the user's password after verifying his identity. If an administrator resets the user's password, the user should be required to change the password at the next log in. An administrator should not need to know any user's password. There is a risk that by communicating the

password electronically or in person, the password could be intercepted.

- **Disablement**
  - The user account can be disabled when a threat is detected or when the user is terminated
  - If the account was logged in from the wrong location, then an administrator may need to review the security logs
  - For example, if a user based in New York logs in to his account in Los Angeles, then there might be a problem

- **Lockout**
  - The user account can be locked after too many incorrect logins
  - The lockout period can be temporary or permanent (for example 15 minutes)
  - The user may have a self-service option to unlock the account, may need to contact the administrator, or may need to wait

- **Password History**
  - The system keeps track of every password used by a user
  - A password expires after a period (for example, 3 months)
  - Once the password expires, the user must choose a new password
  - The system verifies that the new password does not match any of the previous passwords
    - Passwords used in the last number of days (for example 450 days)
    - The last number of passwords (for example the last six passwords)
  - An intruder/eavesdropper may have guessed/seen the password and then used it to log in and steal resources. By changing the password often, the risk that the intruder continues to have access is mitigated.

- **Password Reuse**
  - Passwords should not be reused, not even in combination
  - For example, if the user's password is 'Apple1', they might be tempted to choose 'Apple2' as the next password
  - This is a bad idea
  - It is difficult to enforce if the system stores one-way hashes of passwords. The hash of 'Apple1' may be quite different than 'Apple2'. It can be mitigated by implementing a multi-factor authentication policy.

- **Password Length**
  - The length of the password should be at least eight characters to reduce the risk of a brute force attack

Part F: SY0-501 5.0 Risk Management

5.1 Explain the importance of policies, plans and procedures related to organizational security

- *Standard Operating Procedure*
- *Agreement Types*
  - *BPA*
  - *SLA*
  - *ISA*
  - *MOU/MOA*
- *Personnel Management*
  - *Mandatory Vacations*
  - *Job Rotation*
  - *Separation of Duties*
  - *Clean Desk*
  - *Background Checks*
  - *Exit Interviews*
  - *Role-Based Awareness Training*
    - *Data Owner*
    - *System Administrator*
    - *System Owner*
    - *User*
    - *Privileged User*
    - *Executive User*
    - *NDA*
    - *Onboarding*
    - *Continuing Education*
    - *Acceptable Use Policy/Rules of Behavior*
    - *Adverse Actions*
  - *General Security Policies*
    - *Social Media Networks/Applications*
    - *Personal Email*

Standard Operating Procedure

A **Standard Operating Procedure** a set of instructions for common tasks that an organization performs. Employees, vendors, and contractors are required to follow standard operating procedures when those procedures exist. A standard operating procedure is designed to reduce risk, reduce uncertainty, and improve safety

IT Standard Operating Procedures can exist for
- Creating new user accounts
- Disabling terminated user accounts
- Acquiring software and hardware

Standard Operating Procedures are based on laws and security practices. An organization will revise the procedures when they acquire new information about risks.

Agreement Types

There are many types of agreements. An agreement is a legally enforceable document that sets out the responsibly of each party.

- **BPA – Business Partners Agreement or Business Partnership Agreement**. This agreement outlines the relationship between two organizations or individuals. The organizations may be engaging in a joint venture or may have a vendor/purchaser relationship. The agreement could include
  - The responsibilities of each party
  - The revenue share in the event of a joint venture
  - The cost that one partner may pay to the other
  - The cost of goods or services being acquired
  - The payment terms
  - The type of goods and services being acquired
  - The length of time that the agreement will last
  - How the agreement will be enforced (which jurisdiction is the agreement subject to). For greater certainty, the parties may choose to have disputes heard in a court of law local to them or may choose to have disputes enforced by an arbitrator.

- **SLA – Service Level Agreement**. A Service Level Agreement details the required level of performance and penalties for not meeting those levels. For example, if an organization purchases web hosting services, the hosting company may guarantee that services will operate 99.99% of the time. If the web hosting is available less than 99.99% of the time, the organization may be entitled to a refund. The SLA holds the service provider accountable because downtime costs the organization money. SLA could include
  - Response time for different issues, depending on their impact and priority. For example, two business day response for non-critical issues, one-hour response time for critical issues
  - Uptime guarantee for web hosting, servers, internet connections, and other services
  - Geographical location where the SLA applies. For example, urban locations may have a two-hour response time, while rural/remote locations could have a two-day response time
  - Penalty for not meeting the response time or uptime guarantee. The penalty could be structured as
    - A refund of 10%, 25%, or 100% of the monthly fee paid for a service outage exceeding 1%, 2%, or 5%. This structure is common for web hosting and cloud compute service providers.
    - A penalty for each violation. The service provider could be required to pay a penalty for each violation.
    - The service provider could be required to reimburse the customer for actual damages caused by the outage. This not a typical structure because most

agreements prohibit indirect or consequential damages. The service provider's liability is typically limited to the fees paid by the customer.

- **ISA – Interconnection Security Agreement**. The ISA details how two IT systems will connect to each other. Two organizations may connect their systems to share data. For example, two banks may connect their systems so that they can engage in financial transactions with each other. The ISA might include
  - The types of systems that will connect
  - Specific technical details about how the systems will connect
  - The purpose of the connection
  - The type of data that will be shared
  - The obligations that each party must undertake to keep their data confidential
  - The cost of connecting the systems and how the costs will be shared

- **MOU/MOA – Memorandum of Understanding/Memorandum of Association**
  - An MOU is a general document that outlines the reasons that two parties have for pursuing an agreement (i.e. how each party will benefit from the agreement).
  - The MOU provides a framework for further negotiations
  - Once the MOU is in place, then the parties can negotiate more detailed terms.
  - In the event of a dispute in a formal agreement, a court may look at the original purpose outlined by the MOU/MOA, but an MOU is generally not legally binding

Personnel Management

The biggest threat that an organization faces is internal. It is impossible to prevent every internal attack. It is impossible to predict which employee is a thief, especially when given an opportunity to steal. It is better to trust nobody.

Some ways to prevent internal theft
- **Mandatory Vacations.** An employee who is a weasel will be able to cover his tracks if he is always at work. For example, a crooked bank manager who is writing bad loans to himself and then writing them off can cover up if he is at work. But if the manager is forced to take a vacation, then another employee can come in to review his work.

  The mandatory vacation policy does not create an environment of mistrust or singles out a specific employee.

- **Job Rotation.** Employees are forced to rotate through different positions at the organization. For example, an employee who is responsible for procurement or signing checks is forced to rotate with another employee. Each employee spends only a small amount of time at each role.

  This system allows the organization to train multiple employees in each role. If one is fired or quits, another employee can step in to perform his job.

  This system can be inefficient because
  - Employees must be trained often to understand new job roles
  - Employees may be frustrated, especially if they must learn new roles, and/or move to different offices physically

- **Separation of Duties.** No single employee can or should do everything. For example, an employee who approves invoices should not also be the one to create/sign the checks. If the employee who approves invoices submits a fraudulent invoice and attempts to pay themselves, they would be caught.

- **Clean Desk.** Each employee is literally required to have a clean desk when they leave work for the day. In some organizations, sensitive information should be locked, and only specific people can have access. The clean desk policy is in place at many organizations, but many employees do not respect it. Be wary of janitors and other contractors who may come into the building after hours and steal or copy anything that is not hidden.

- **Background Check.** A Background Check can consist of

- **A criminal record check**. In some states, an employee with a criminal record cannot legally be excluded from a job just because of their criminal record. There must be a threat to the employer. For example, an applicant convicted of fraud may not work at a bank. The employer should verify if the applicant has been rehabilitated and determine how long it has been since the crime took place. In some states, an employer may not consider criminal records that are more than seven or ten years old. A person with a clean record may actually be a hardened criminal, but hasn't been caught yet.

  A criminal record check may span multiple countries depending on where the person lived (or claimed to have lived).

  Due to many different court systems across the United States and other countries, criminal record information is not centralized or may be incomplete.

  An advanced criminal record check may query local court records in every jurisdiction that the candidate lived in.

- **A credit check**. An employee with poor credit can be susceptible to bribes or may be tempted to steal. Under Federal Law and under state law, the credit check cannot be used to exclude an applicant unless there is a legitimate reason. A person with excellent credit can also be greedy and susceptible to bribes or may hate their employer.

- **Immigration Check**. Verify that the employee has the legal right to work in the country that they are in.

- **License verification**. Verify that the employee has the legal right to work in the occupation that they are applying for (doctor, nurse, lawyer, pharmacist, accountant, etc. all require licensing from a relevant board).
    - Verify also that the candidate did not have any disciplinary action pending or adjudicated before their board (malpractice, unethical practice, incompetence, etc.)
    - Verify that the candidate is not facing any civil lawsuits regarding their practice

- **Drivers abstract**. For a candidate who will be required to operate a motor vehicle on behalf of the employer as a main part of their job or even casually, the employer must verify that the candidate has a clean driving record. This may be a legal requirement on behalf of the employer's insurance company.

- o **Education verification**. Verify that the employee's degrees, diplomas, and certifications are valid. It is easy to generate a fake degree parchment from a legitimate school. It is easy to pay a diploma mill to provide a legitimate looking degree or attend an online university that is not accredited (a school where the student learned absolutely nothing). There are thousands of universities and colleges in the United States, and even if an educational institution is licensed, it does not mean that it is producing out good graduates. The employer may be more concerned with the employee's knowledge and experience than with what the employee learned in school.

- o **Employment verification**. Verify that the employee worked at the places he said he worked. A former employer will confirm the dates that an employee was employed but may not be able to any further details, due to the risk of defamation lawsuits. In industries where "everybody knows everybody", such as on Wall Street, a former employer may provide negative information "off the record".

- o **Reference check**. The candidate may be required to provide references – people they have known personally or professionally. These references may be contacted, but it is likely that the candidate will provide names of people who are likely to provide a positive reference.

- o **Social media check**. Some people do stupid things on their days off. They must remember that they continue to represent the company when they go home for the day, especially if they are managers or executives. They will be seen by other employees, customers, regulators, and the public, and must portray the company positively. If they make poor choices and post inappropriate photos/videos online (drinking, committing crimes, etc.) they should be excluded.

- o **Background investigation**. A background investigation for a government position may be more in depth and would include interviews with neighbors, teachers, former employers, friends, and family members. It will go back at least ten years and identify every place that the candidate lived, worked, or studied.

- o It is important to
    - Obtain the employee's written consent before conducting any background check
    - Follow all relevant laws regarding obtaining and storing the data
    - Obtain additional consent from the different organizations that hold the data
    - Disclose to the candidate all information received, except where prohibited by law

- Provide the candidate with the opportunity to contest or correct any negative information obtained, and to not make adverse employment decisions unless required to do so

    o A background check can be conducted when an individual is first hired and during regular intervals or when an incident occurs. An employer may choose to hire an employee and conduct the background check later, if they need to fill a position quickly, or if a full background check will take a long time. In the United States, criminal record checks can be obtained online in a matter of hours.

- **Exit Interview**. An exit interview is an interview that is conducted when the employee or contractor is terminated. It is important to embody the obligations that remain after termination into the employment contract. At the exit interview, the employee is advised

    o Of the obligations of the employee to the employer such as safeguarding the trade secrets and other relevant data belonging to the employer

    o Of the obligations of the employer to the employee such as for how long the employer will retain records

    o Of how intellectual property developed by the employer or employee can be used in the future

    o Of what kind of reference the employer will provide to the employee's future employers

- **Role-Based Awareness Training**
    o Each user must be trained to protect the organization's data. The type of training depends on the user's role. All training must be documented.

    o **Data Owner**. The data owner is the person who created the data, or who oversees the people who created the data. In general, the data owner always has full access to the data (to read the data). An organization may choose to prohibit a data owner from modifying or deleting the data after it has been created.

    o **System Administrator**. The system administrator manages the system that holds the data. The system administrator has full access to the data (to read, modify, and delete the data). There must be safeguards in place to prevent a malicious system administrator from deleting data and causing harm to the organization. There must also be safeguards in place to monitor what a system administrator can access and ensure that the system administrator has appropriate security clearance.

Consider the case of Edward Snowden, and more recently Joshua Schulte, both of whom stole classified government data. A system administrator should not be able to remove data from a system, certainly not without authorization from another person. This goes back to having separation of duties.

- o **User**. A user is a person with access to some data. The user may be able to read or modify the data. The user is granted access based on his role in the organization, which can be controlled by group policy. The user must not be provided with more access than required.

- o **Privileged User**. A privileged user has additional rights above normal users. The privileged user may be able to grant other users with access.

- o **Executive User**. An executive user is a person like a CEO, COO, CFO, or CIO. This person may require access to all organizational data so that he can properly perform his job. In theory, this person has access to everything, but, he will not need access to everything. The executive is a high-value target, and his account should be tightly controlled so that it is not compromised.

- • **NDA. An NDA is a Non-Disclosure Agreement**. Each employee, contractor, or vendor with access to any sensitive data must read and sign the Non-Disclosure Agreement prior to being provided with access to any data. The NDA may be revised from time to time. The NDA contains the following features
    - o Prohibits employees from disclosing any sensitive data to any person outside the organization

    - o Identify how the organization marks sensitive data

    - o Describes how the employee should store sensitive data (encrypted USB, laptop, not taking data home, use of personal mobile devices)

    - o The NDA may have exceptions for legal reasons such as in response to a court order or other legal process

    - o Describes how an employee should report the inadvertent disclosure of sensitive data

    - o The obligations under the NDA do not stop when the employee leaves the organization

- **Onboarding**. Onboarding is the process when the employee is first hired. The employee is introduced to the policies of the organization and the consequences of not following those policies.
    - The onboarding process may last a few minutes or several weeks

    - The user account is created during the onboarding process

- **Continuing Education**. Employees should be educated about new security threats as they arise. Education can take place through webinars, in person, newsletters, posters, or meetings. The education can be tailored to each individual employee based on his role.

- **Acceptable Use Policy/Rules of Behavior**. The Acceptable Use Policy describes what the employee may do and what they may not do while on a company's system. In general, the employee should
    - Only use the employer's computing resources for purposes that benefit the employer

    - Not use the computing resources for illegal purposes

    - Not access games, social media, pornography, or racist content

    - An employer may allow an employee to use the devices for non-commercial purposes if the impact to the business is minimal (this is a work life balance choice that the employer may make)

    - The AUP must clearly state that the employer's systems are subject to monitoring and recording, and that the employee has no reasonable expectation of privacy. In the event the employee is terminated for violating the AUP, the employee will not be able to exclude evidence of wrongdoing in a wrongful termination lawsuit.

    - The employer's computer systems should clearly state that the system is subject to monitoring and recording.

- **Adverse Actions**. An adverse action is one that is taken when an employee violates a policy
    - **Zero Tolerance**. A Zero Tolerance policy means that an employee is terminated for his first violation, regardless of his position or performance.
        - A zero-tolerance policy is bad because it essentially forces the employer to "shoot itself in the foot" when having to fire a successful employee, especially one who cannot be easily replaced.

    - **Discretionary Action**. The HR department will decide what kind of action to take, which could include a written warning, a suspension, or termination.

- The discretionary action must be applied fairly. If the policy is applied inconsistency, then a terminated employee may have grounds to file a wrongful termination lawsuit.

- **General Security Policies**
  - The General Security Policies outline the security goals of the organization. These goals are implemented through more detailed security policies.

  - **Social Media Networks/Applications.** Social media policy is important to prevent people from posting inappropriate content on social media, such as
    - Trade secrets
    - An employee's personal opinions about the organization that do not reflect the views of the organization
    - Inappropriate content that could portray the organization negatively (employees represent the organization even when they are not at work)

    Amplify is an application that allows employees to post (or repost) pre-approved content about their employer.

  - **Personal Email.**
    - An employee must not use personal email to communicate with customers
    - Personal email service providers such as Hotmail and Gmail may store e-mail in other countries, and may not provide an acceptable level of security
    - Customers have the right to know where their data is stored and what kind of data is stored about them. The organization will not be able to fulfill this obligation if personal e-mail accounts are utilized.
    - In litigation, the organization may be required to disclose electronic documents including e-mails. E-mails stored at a personal service provider will not be disclosed, since the organization is unaware of their existence. This could violate the organization's discovery obligations and subject them to sanctions if the breach is later discovered.
    - Sending e-mails to a customer from a personal account appears unprofessional. A customer may suspect that e-mails from personal accounts are illegitimate.
    - When an employee uses a personal device to access corporate e-mail, they may see personal and corporate email on the same phone. They should be careful to make sure that they do not use the wrong e-mail address when corresponding with a client. Apps such as Outlook will prevent this issue.
    - An employee should not use a corporate e-mail for personal use. The employee should not expect to have any privacy with respect to their corporate e-mail account, which can be monitored or disclosed to third parties.

5.2 Summarize business impact analysis concepts

- *RTO/RPO*
- *MTBF*
- *MTTR*
- *Mission Essential Functions*
- *Identification of Critical Systems*
- *Single Point of Failure*
- *Impact*
  - *Life*
  - *Property*
  - *Safety*
  - *Finance*
  - *Reputation*
- *Privacy Impact Assessment*
- *Privacy Threshold Assessment*

In any business plan, operation, or agreement, a business must evaluate all risks that could occur. A risk could be positive or negative. The business must ask

- What are all the risks?
- For each risk, how likely is it to occur?
- If a risk occurs, what is the impact (on revenue, on health & safety, and on reputation)?
- What risks can the business tolerate and for how long?
- What risks is the business unable or unwilling to accept?
- How can the business mitigate or eliminate each risk? Can a risk's impact or likelihood be reduced?

RTP/RPO

RTO/RPO – RTO is the Recovery Time Objective and RPO is the Recovery Point Objective. The RPO is the maximum loss of data that a business could endure and survive. How many days worth of data can a business afford to lose? For example, a business could tolerate a data loss of up to one week worth of data. If data was backed up on Monday and data was lost on Thursday, then the business could survive. The RPO tells us how often we must back up our data.

RTO is the maximum time a business could survive while waiting for business operations to be restored. How fast does a business need to recover? For example, if business could tolerate disruption at its factory for four hours, and the factory shut down for three hours, the business could survive. If the factory shut down for six hours, the business would not survive. The RTO tells us how fast we need to react to restore the business.

The shorter the RTO and RPO, the more expensive a disaster recovery plan will be. RTO and RPO can vary from business to business and can vary within different units of the same business.

MTBF

MTBF is the Mean Time Between Failures. This is the average amount of time between failures of a device. Some devices can be repaired, and some devices cannot. For example, a hard disk drive that fails irreparably after 300,000 hours has a MTBF of 300,000 hours. A computer server that fails (but can be repaired) after 100,000 hours and then again after 300,000 hours has an MTBF of 200,000 hours (average of 100,000 and 300,000).

The MTBF of electronics and industrial equipment is usually measured in hours (since devices that are not in use are less likely to fail). Some devices have a failure rate that is measured in cycles or per use (for example airplanes are rated based on the number of times they take off and land, and not the amount of time they spend in the air – take offs and landing put more stress on the airplanes' components than the actual flying).

A manufacturer will should disclose the MTBF on each device that they manufacture so that customers can make informed purchasing decisions. If a device is inexpensive but has a high failure rate, then the long-term cost may be much higher.

If an organization purchases hard drives with a 300,000-hour MTBF, but they have deployed 100,000 hard drives, then they can expect that (on average) one hard drive will fail every three hours (or about eight per day).

Electronic devices usually fail on what is called a bathtub curve (high failure rate at the beginning and end of their life span, and low failure rate in the middle).

$$MTBF = \sum \frac{START\ OF\ DOWNTIME - START\ OF\ UPTIME}{NUMBER\ OF\ FAILURES}$$

MTTR

MTTR is the Mean Time to Repair. The mean time to repair is the average time a device is repaired. For example, if a server breaks down, how many hours or days will it take until it is restored?

The MTTR is the time to resolve to the issue, not the time to respond the issue. For example, if a server fails, and a repairman arrives within three hours, but it takes an additional hour to troubleshoot and repair the issue, then the repair time is four hours.

The shorter the MTTR, the more expensive it will be.

Different types and severities of incidents can have different response times. The organization must weigh the response time against the impact to the business. Critical incidents may require response times measured in hours while trivial issues may allow response times measured in days or even weeks.

$$MTBF = \sum \frac{TOTAL\ DOWNTIME}{NUMBER\ OF\ FAILURES}$$

The system's availability is the time that it is available.

$$AVAILABILITY = \sum \frac{MTBF}{MTBF + MTTR}$$

Mission Essential Functions

A **Mission Essential Function** is a component of a business that must always operate. It is fundamental to the existence of the business (the business will shut down without it).

A business must identify all its mission essential functions. A business should also identify vendors who are essential to its own functions. The business must protect all its mission essential functions and ensure that they remain operational in the event of a disaster, or that they can be quickly restored. Other non-essential functions can wait.

Examples of mission essential functions
- Hospital emergency room
- Manufacturing facility
- Security at a nuclear power plant
- Control room for a power grid

Examples of non-essential functions
- Janitorial staff
- Human resources
- Marketing

Identification of Critical Systems

The business must identify systems that are critical to its operation. These are systems that provide essential functions.

If a critical system fails, then the business will not be able to operate. A critical system may be spread across multiple offices or states.

Single Point of Failure

A **Single Point of Failure** is a component that, when it fails, will bring down an entire system. A Single Point of Failure can be a physical object or a process in an organization.

Example of a single point of failure
- Motherboard in a server; if the motherboard fails, the entire server stops functioning
- Router in a computer network; if the router fails, the entire network stops functioning
- Having only one accountant to approve accounts payable invoices; if the accountant is sick, the business will be unable to pay vendors

The organization should carefully identify single points of failure in its equipment and in its processes. It should replace each single point of failure with a redundant system, when possible.
- Redundant systems are more expensive than non-redundant systems
- Some systems cannot be made redundant, but there are usually workarounds
- The organization may choose to accept the risk associated with the single point of failure. The executives must understand the risk that they have accepted.

Examples of redundant systems
- Server with multiple power supplies (even in the event of the failure of a power supply or power source, the server continues to operate)
- Having two servers run in parallel with a load balancer; the failure of one server will not affect other servers or the application that they are running
- Having multiple individuals trained to cover specific roles, such as dispatchers, accounts payable clerks, system administration, and engineers. These individuals should be in geographically different areas, to protect from natural disasters.

Impact

The **impact** of a risk is how the risk will affect the business and to what extent. For example, a risk may only have a financial impact, but the financial impact is $1,000,000.

Areas where a risk can impact a business

- **Life**. A life impact is physical or psychological harm to a human being or animal. This could cause the individual to suffer or die. The life impact may be short term or long term. A life impact may be to an employee, to a vendor, or to third parties. Life impacts usually also cause financial impacts (the organization will be forced to compensate those who are harmed) and reputational impacts. For example, an explosion at a chemical plant could kill and injure employees and contractors who work at the plant. The resulting pollution would introduce harmful chemicals to the environment, which could cause long term cancer rates to increase in the surrounding population.

- **Property**. A property impact is damage to property such as a building, equipment, or property belonging to third parties. For example, an explosion would cause damage to the plant. A property impact is also a financial impact. It may take a long time to repair or replace the damaged property. Some property cannot be repaired (for example a historical building that burns down).

- **Safety**. Impact to safety is when there is a risk of personal injury. When a work environment is not safe, work must stop until the deficiency is corrected.

- **Finance**. A risk that causes a strictly financial impact is rare. Usually, the financial impact is the consequence of some other impact. For example, damage to property usually results in a financial impact when it is repaired or replaced. An example of a strictly financial impact is a bad investment.

- **Reputation**. The impact could also be reputational. If the organization was found to be negligent in creating a risk (that resulted in harm to people or damage to property), then its reputation is also impacted. If the organization's operations are disrupted, and it is no longer able to meet customer demands, then its reputation is also impacted.

Privacy Impact Assessment

A **Privacy Impact Assessment** is a review process that determines the impact of a data leak. Every organization should review its data controls to determine the impact that an inadvertent or deliberate release of information could cause.

The **PIA** analyses how **Personally Identifiable Information** travels through an organization. Who has access to it? Where is it stored? Where does it go? How was it collected?

The types of information that could be released include
- Proprietary corporate information regarding operations, trade secrets, and finance
- Personnel records
- Customer records (banking records, healthcare records, etc.)

The organization should know
- What kinds of information does the business store and where?
- Does the business share information with third parties, and how do they protect that information?
- How does the business protect sensitive information and how does it control/monitor access to this information? Do people have access to information that they do not require?
- How will the business respond to a data leak (how it will investigate the source of the leak)?
- What impact the leak will have on the business (fines, damage to reputation, etc.) and what impact it will have on its customers/employees?
- How will the business notify people who are affected by the leak?
- What can the business do to mitigate the impact of a leak?
- What can the business do to reduce the risk of a leak?

Privacy Threshold Assessment

The **Threshold Assessment** identifies the types of data being stored by the organization to determine their level of sensitivity. Information could be

- Confidential/proprietary
- Personally Identifying Information
- Personal Health Information
- Classified
- Law enforcement sensitive
- Information belonging to third parties

The way in which some forms of information are collected, stored, disclosed, or used may be subject to laws, regulations, or contractual obligations. For example, two organizations participating in a joint venture may have a contract to store shared trade secrets in a locked vault.

5.3 Explain risk management processes and concepts

- *Threat Assessment*
  - *Environmental*
  - *Manmade*
  - *Internal vs External*
- *Risk Assessment*
  - *SLE*
  - *ALE*
  - *ARO*
  - *Asset Value*
  - *Risk Register*
  - *Likelihood of Occurrence*
  - *Supply Chain Assessment*
  - *Impact*
  - *Quantitative*
  - *Qualitative*
  - *Testing*
    - *Penetration Testing Authorization*
    - *Vulnerability Testing Authorization*
    - *Risk Response Techniques*
      - *Accept*
      - *Transfer*
      - *Avoid*
      - *Mitigate*
  - *Change Management*

Threat Assessment

There are two types of threats: environmental and manmade

An environmental threat is one that is natural. It could include
- Fire
- Flood
- Natural disaster

A manmade threat is one that is created by humans. It could include
- Theft
- Fraud
- Illegal activity
- Accidents

An internal threat comes from within the organization. In theory, the organization has the right to control an internal threat. An external threat comes from outside the organization. The organization may be able to control the external threat.

In a threat assessment, an organization analyses its systems to determine all of the possible threats.

Risk Assessment

A Risk Assessment is a procedure that an organization implements to identify all the risks it faces. Not every risk can be identified. There are several tools for calculating risks.

- **An SLE is the Single-loss Expectancy.** It is the value of the asset after a risk has occurred. For example, if a building is worth $1,000,000 and a fire occurs, and the building loses $800,000 in value, then the SLE is $800,000.

  The new value of the asset is only 20%. This is known as the Exposure Factor.

- **An ALE is the Annualized Loss Expectancy.** The ALE is the SLE annualized. For example, if the building is worth $1,000,000 and loses $800,000 in value, then the loss is $800,000. The organization does not expect to have a fire every year, but instead perhaps once every ten years. If the risk of a fire is once every ten years, then the ALE is $800,000 / 10 = $80,000. It can be calculated as ALE = ARO x SLE, which is the Annual Rate of Occurrence.

  The organization would like to know how often the risk could occur in a year so that they can plan for it financially. For example, they could expect to lose $80,000 this year. An insurance company would use this calculation to determine what premium to charge.

- **An ARO is the Annual Rate of Occurrence**, or the percent chance that a risk will occur in a year. If the fire would happen once every ten years, then the ARO is 1/10, or 10%. There is a 10% chance that the fire would happen this year.

- **An Asset Value is what something is worth.** It is important to know what each asset is worth prior to a risk occurring.

- **A Risk Register is the list of risks.** The organization will list each risk in the register, along with the impact of the risk, and the person or group that is responsible for managing it. The organization will also record ways in which each risk can be mitigated. The Risk Register is updated from time to time because risks and their impacts are subject to change.

- **The Impact of the risk is the damage that it will cause.** The impact might be completely financial, or it may cause physical or reputational harm.

- **Likelihood of Occurrence is the percent chance that a risk could occur.** The organization must choose realistic likelihoods. Sometimes it is difficult to predict if a risk will occur especially if it has not occurred before and there is no real-world data. An organization can use insurance databases to predict risk.

- **Supply Chain Assessment** is where the organization examines its supply chain to see the impact a risk would have on its access to raw materials. The supply chain operates in two directions.
  - The supply of raw materials that the organization uses to manufacture products and deliver services
    - Disruption of supply of raw materials could cause damage to the organization because it would not be able to manufacture its product
    - Organization should be able to predict the disruption of any product and relay this information to its customers so that they too can adapt
    - For example, if the organization manufactures food and the raw materials are contaminated then the organization must halt production
    - An organization should have multiple sources of raw materials so that it can restore production without relying on one vendor
  - The distribution chain from the organization to the consumer/end user, which may include retail stores
    - The organization must ensure that the product's integrity is not breached from the factory to the end user
    - Damage to the product during transportation costs the organization money
    - Damage to a product such as a pharmaceutical or food/beverage could trigger a recall or cause reputational harm

- **A Quantitative Risk Assessment is the process of predicting the impact of a risk** by relying on mathematical modems and historical data. A quantitative risk assessment is objective but can be biased.

- **A Qualitative Risk Assessment is the process of predicting the impact of a risk** by relying on expert opinions and experience. A qualitative risk assessment is subjective.

Risk Testing

We should test each assumption to ensure it is valid. In performing the test, several techniques are used. We must obtain authorization from the organization.

- Penetration testing authorization.
- Vulnerability testing authorization.

The organization gives approval for this testing to take place. The organization must understand the techniques utilized by each tester.

Risk Response Techniques

As mentioned earlier, a risk could be positive or negative. Most people assume hat all risks are negative,

For example, if an organization is building a bridge with an estimated cost of $1,000,000 and time to complete of one year, a positive risk is that the bridge is built faster or cheaper. A negative risk is that the bridge takes longer to complete.

A risk is not guaranteed to occur. It may occur once, several times, or never. The organization must understand the impact of the risk and the likelihood that it will occur. That is, what happens to the organization if the risk occurs. How much money will they lose? Will people get hurt? Will the organization's reputation be harmed in the media or with its customers? The impact may be long term and difficult to quantify.

For example, if a construction site is unsafe and an employee gets hurt, the organization may be fined $100,000 under the occupational health law. The organization may assume that the risk is monetary and only $100,000. But, the long-term risk may be higher. For example, the accident could generate negative publicity and harm the organization's reputation. It would be harder to recruit new employees or gain customers. The organization's insurance premiums might increase.

Some risks are considered unacceptable risks. Most organizations consider the value of a human life to be so great that any risk of death is unacceptable. Most organizations also believe that any physical injury to an employee is a risk that can always be avoided. The responsibility for avoiding injury is shared by the employer and the employee. The employer provides a safe work environment, training, and protective equipment. The employee is obligated to follow the safety rules.

Risks do occur even when the organization does not want to accept them.

There are four ways to deal with a risk

- **Accept the risk**. The organization understands the impact of the risk is and its consequences. The organization chooses to do nothing because the cost of mitigating the risk may be higher than cost of the risk itself, and the risk is not considered unacceptable. For example, deploying a security guard to mitigate the risk of graffiti at an office building is more expensive than cleaning up the graffiti when it happens.

- **Transfer**. The organization transfers the risk to another organization. The risk could be transferred to an insurance company through an insurance policy, transferred to a joint venture, or moved to a subsidiary. Not all risks could be transferred. Car insurance is an example of a risk transfer strategy. The financial impact of the motor vehicle collision is transferred to the insurance company, but the physical risk to the vehicle operator cannot be.

- **Mitigate the risk** so that its impact is lower, or so that its likelihood is lower. The organization is willing to accept the risk. Wearing personal protective equipment is an example of a risk mitigation strategy. At a construction site it is impossible to avoid having things fall on your head, but if we teach people not to drop things, we reduce the likelihood that they will. And if you wear a hardhat, the chance that a falling cinderblock will hurt you is lowered. It will still hurt, but not as much.

- **Avoid**. The organization avoids the risk by not engaging the activity that will result in the risk. The organization may do this if they cannot mitigate or transfer the risk. For example, a construction company is building a bridge in an area that frequently experiences landslides. The organization cannot stop the landslides, so they choose to stop building the bridge instead.

Change Management

Change Management is the process for managing changes to assets and systems. Change management is also known as configuration management (configuration in the engineering sense, not configuration in the computer sense).

Consider a petrochemical refinery with one million valves, pipes, sensors, and wiring. Each item in the plant is documented so that if it fails or requires maintenance, the refinery knows exactly what it is they are replacing and where it is. Imagine if you had to drill into a pipeline and you didn't know what it was carrying? Imagine if somebody took a water pipeline and replaced it with a flammable gas pipeline but forgot to document the change? Another worker came along later to perform work on this pipeline, but didn't have the correct tools or safety equipment, because he assumed that the pipeline was full of water. This is an overly simplified example, of course, because pipelines are labeled with their contents. But people have drilled into pipelines that were full of steam or gas, even though the documentation said that those pipelines were empty.

In a large organization, a single employee cannot make a change. He must seek approval from a committee, known as the Change Control Board. The CCB decides whether a change is approved or denied. If it is approved, the CCB ensures that the employee who performs the change does so in accordance with the organization's policies. When the change is complete, the CCB documents the change.

In an IT environment, change management applies to network hardware configuration, switch configuration, security policies, the physical location of infrastructure, and many other items.

The PMP (Project Management Professional) Body of Knowledge covers Risk Management and Change Management in greater depth.

5.4 Given a scenario, follow incident response procedures

- *Incident Response Plan*
  - *Documented Incident Types/Category Definitions*
  - *Roles and Responsibilities*
  - *Reporting Requirements/Escalation*
  - *Cyber-Incident Response Teams*
  - *Exercise*
- *Incident Response Process*
  - *Preparation*
  - *Identification*
  - *Containment*
  - *Eradication*
  - *Recovery*
  - *Lessons Learned*

Incident Response Plan

An organization must maintain an Incident Response Plan that is reviewed and practiced regularly. The plan will include:

Documented Incident Types/Category Definitions
- The organization should maintain a list of different types of incidents and categorize them based on the business lines that they affect
- The plan should allow a user to determine the severity of an incident (Critical, Serious, Minor, etc.) based upon its impact to the business, human life, clients, etc.
- Each category and severity should have a standard response procedure
  - Who should we notify (executives, customers, government agencies, 911)?
  - What does each person do?
- Why do we do this? When an incident occurs (and incidents will occur!), we don't have to panic. We categorize the incident based on its severity and impact, and then we follow the appropriate procedure.

Roles and Responsibilities
- Each department is specifically tasked with a responsibility for each incident category
- When an incident occurs, a team composed of each departments' representatives is summoned. Each person on the team will have reviewed the plan and knows exactly what to do.

Reporting Requirements/Escalation
- Does the organization have to respond to the incident at all? Do they have to report the incident to a higher level in the organization (vice president, CEO, board of directors, shareholders, etc.)? This depends on
  - The severity of the incident
  - How long it takes to resolve the incident
  - The impact to the business and its customers
- Organization may have to report the incident to the government if it involves a
  - Data leak
  - Chemical spill
  - Public health matter
  - Contamination of a food product or pharmaceutical

Cyber-Incident Response **Teams**

- An organization may maintain a Cyber Incident Response Team that is dedicated to responding to a cyber incident. This team may travel to the physical of the incident or work remotely.
- Other third parties also have cyber response teams. The FBI has a cyber response team that can deploy to any cyber incident location within 48 hours.

Exercise

- It is impossible to know how a person will react to a real crisis until it happens. Nevertheless, the organization should practice its response to each type of incident on a regular basis. The more people practice, the better they will respond when the crisis occurs.
- No plan ever failed on paper. The exercise also allows an organization to identify errors that made it through the planning phase.
- After a real crisis, the organization should evaluate its response and modify the plan accordingly.

Incident Response Process

The incident response process starts with preparation. Preparation should take place well before any incident takes place. The organization may not be able to respond to an incident that takes place if they are not prepared. Preparation includes creating an incident response plan, training responsible individuals, and stockpiling tools and supplies necessary to respond.

Identification the process of identifying when a situation is not a normal operating condition (an incident). Is this incident worth responding to? To avoid false alarms and the unnecessary expenditure of resources, the organization may have a threshold for responding to an incident. For example, if a server is unreachable for 30 seconds, the organization may wait to see if it comes back up. If a server is unreachable for an hour, the organization will need to respond.

Containment is the process of preventing an incident from spreading. In many cases, that means disconnecting an infected system from the rest of the network. For example, if a computer is infected with a virus, it can be contained by disconnecting it from the network so that the virus does not spread to other machines.

Eradication is the process of removing the threat. Eradication may be a part of the containment process. For example, if the incident is a fire, putting out the fire is both the containment and eradication process. If the incident resolved itself, then eradication may not be necessary.

Recovery is the process of returning the organization to the state it was before the incident occurred. A full recovery is not always possible because the incident may have caused financial or reputational loss that cannot be restored. If the cause of the incident is covered by insurance, recovery can be obtained from the insurance company.

The Lessons Learned process allows the organization to document the incident so that it never happens again. It is literally as it sounds: what did we learn from this incident.

5.5 Summarize basic concepts of forensics

- *Order of Volatility*
- *Chain of Custody*
- *Legal Hold*
- *Data Acquisition*
    - *Capture System Image*
    - *Network Traffic and Logs*
    - *Capture Video*
    - *Record Time offset*
    - *Take Hashes*
    - *Screenshots*
    - *Witness Interviews*
- *Preservation*
- *Recovery*
- *Strategic Intelligence/Counterintelligence Gathering*
    - *Active Logging*
- *Track Man-Hours*

Order of Volatility

In computer forensics, data must be collected in the order of its volatility. The order of volatility is how long it will take until the data is erased or disappears. The order of volatility

- **Data in the RAM of a computer that has just been shut down.** This is data that is practically impossible to collect, except with specialized equipment that supercools the RAM (and even then, an investigator has only five minutes to collect the data). The purpose of collecting this data is to attempt to obtain the BitLocker (or FDE) encryption key, which is present in the RAM of a running computer.

- **Data in the RAM a computer that is powered on.** The forensics investigator must collect the data from the RAM without modifying the data on the computer and without allowing the computer to lock itself. Once the computer is encrypted, it may be impossible to collect the data. How to avoid this
  - A running computer can be transported to a lab with the mouse jiggler and the special tool known as a HotPlug Field Kit.
  - Sometimes catching the suspect in the act when he has the phone and/or computer unlocked is necessary; this requires coordination with multiple law enforcement officials
  - Introducing spyware into the computer or phone to capture data; this may be illegal and can be challenged in court later
    - Whether it is legal
    - Whether it was appropriate or if other measures where considered/attempted/exhausted
    - Whether the spyware modified the computer and/or produced accurate results
    - The defense may require a copy of the source code to challenge it; if the source code is sensitive then this could lead to a circumstance where the government is forced between dismissing the charges and disclosing the source code
  - Bugging the office where the suspect is located to capture the data on the screen or phone
    - This is the most extraordinary measure
    - The government must prove that the measures are necessary to obtain the evidence and that other measures have been tried and failed
    - This won't always be reliable to capture data on a computer screen or a phone screen; the surveillance device must be positioned correctly
    - The government must be able to enter the office without detection
  - Force the Defendant to provide the login credentials/encryption keys

- Violates the Fifth Amendment and Canadian Charter of Rights and Freedoms against self-incrimination.
- Courts have debated whether a password/encryption key is considered "evidence"
  - Consider a physical analogy. If incriminating documents were stored in a safe, the documents are evidence, and the safe combination is the password.
  - Even if the government cannot compel production of the safe's combination, they can break the safe and obtain the documents.
  - Some courts have held that an encrypted computer is like a safe (a container)
- The US government can compel production if the government can prove that the specific data exists on the device and is simply encrypted; that is, it cannot be a fishing expedition but must be clear that the evidence will be found
  - The government must describe the contents of the device with "reasonable particularity"
  - In re Boucher, the government can compel production of a password to decrypt a hard disk drive after the Defendant had already provided the government with access to some of the files
  - United States v. Fricosu held that the government can compel production under the All Writs Act.
  - Normal constitutional protections do not apply at the border
  - The Defendant can be held in contempt and jailed until he provides the password
  - Eleventh Circuit: if the government has shown by clear and convincing evidence that the Defendant can decrypt the devices is a foregone conclusion, then the Defendant can be compelled to decrypt the devices
- United Kingdom and Australia passed laws that require Defendants to decrypt encrypted devices
- R v. Shergill in Canada held that the government could not compel disclosure of a password, because the password was testimony. The password existed in the suspect's brain and compelling production would create a physical version of the password.
- In some cases, the courts have held that the Defendant can be forced to unlock the phone/device but cannot be forced to provide the password.
- In a civil case, the Defendant can be compelled by a court to disclose data during discovery process. The fifth amendment does not apply to a civil case.

- In an Anton Pillar Order, the Defendant can be compelled to disclose login credentials/encryption keys.
- A civil suit by a government agency (such as FTC or SEC) can occur concurrently with a criminal investigation that can exchange evidence. The government agency can share the data obtained during civil discovery with criminal investigators.
- Best method is to obtain the data some other way, because it is not clear how the court will rule
  - o Obtain the encryption key from a third party. BitLocker keys and other passcodes can be stored online through password-backup applications.

- **Data on a cell phone**. Remember that a cell phone can be wiped remotely. A cell phone that is locked can be encrypted. Most newer model phones are encrypted by default.
  - o If the phone cannot be unlocked and data downloaded, then it must be made offline, so that the data cannot be wiped remotely. A Faraday cage can be used.
  - o iPhone and Android phones are encrypted by default. Encryption can be broken on old phones but not new phones, although security vulnerabilities are always being found
  - o It is important to have a toolkit such as Cellebrite, MobilEdit, or Oxygen, which can unlock most of the phones
  - o Most phones back up their data to the cloud. iPhones back up to iCloud and Android phones back up to Google. Individual applications such as Facebook and Twitter back up data to their own sources. Even if the phone cannot be unlocked, a substantial portion of the data can be obtained from third parties.
  - o Compel production of the passcode if necessary, as previously discussed.
  - o Only a limited logical image can be obtained from more recent editions of the Apple iPhone, even when unlocked. A full logical image can be obtained from most rooted Android phones.
  - o The phone manufacturer may cooperate if they can. Apple has refused.
    - The Apple iPhone uses a hardware root of trust to authenticate the operating system prior to loading it. The iPhone will not load an operating unless it has been digitally signed by Apple.
    - The iPhone uses a "secure enclave" processor to store and process encrypted data. It is not possible to bypass the processor and directly access the storage medium on an iPhone.
    - It might be technically possible for Apple to create an update to the operating system that automatically unlocks the phone or that allows it to transfer data to a third-party server.
    - Apple has been compelled under the All Writs Act to create such an operating system or to otherwise bypass the encryption on their phone.

Apple has refused, and to date, Apple has not complied with any order.

- **Data on a computer**
  - Like a cell phone, a computer can be encrypted.
  - Check if the computer has a hidden/encrypted partition such as TrueCrypt. In the case, US vs Schulte the Defendant maintained multiple hidden partitions to store data.
  - If the computer is owned by an organization, the organization's IT professional may have admin rights to unlock the computer. It is possible that a rogue employee installed a second layer of encryption, that is not accessible by the organization.
  - Physically disassemble the computer to determine whether multiple physical storage devices are present.

- **Data in the cloud**. Data in the cloud can be erased (although a service provider can be ordered to retain the data).
  - This may be the first step in a criminal investigation
  - Compel production through a subpoena (for data) or search warrant (for e-mails) as previously discussed
  - Service provider can be required to preserve data
  - A service provider may notify the Defendant and give them an opportunity to quash the subpoena, or if illegal activity is detected, may terminate the defendant's access to the services. This warning may allow the Defendant to destroy evidence or escape.

- **Data stored on a USB drive, CD-ROM, DVD, or Flash memory** may last for years or decades. It can be taken off site and imaged later.
  - USB drives can be encrypted via software or hardware
  - Some USB drives have a self-destruct feature (example is the IronKey), which destroys all data after multiple incorrect password entries

To obtain any data, there must be a legal process. There are four scenarios: National Security, Criminal Investigation, Civil Suit, or Internal Investigation.

National Security

- Warrant from a FISA (Foreign Intelligence Surveillance Act) court, which is considered classified. In general, the service provider has no recourse is because the warrant is classified, and disclosure is not permitted. The service provider will not be able to challenge the warrant in court.
  - The court has permitted the collection of a large amount of telephone call metadata.

- National Security Letter. This is issued by the FBI and no warrant is required. The NSL requires a business to provide the FBI with records relevant to a national security investigation.
  - The recipient is not allowed to disclose the presence of the NSL or the records being sought. The FBI must prove that the gag order is necessary.

Criminal Investigation.

- **A letter or e-mail.** Many companies will provide basic data to law enforcement without any court order or notice of a criminal investigation. This could include subscriber contact and payment information.

- A prosecutor can issue a criminal **subpoena.** The service provider may disclose the subpoena or provide the subscriber with an opportunity to challenge the subpoena in court. The law enforcement agency may demand that the subpoena be kept secret, but there is no legal requirement to do so.

- **Search warrant** to recover email under the Stored Communications Act (18 USC § 2701 to 2713)
  - There are two types of service providers
    - A **Remote Computing Service**: "any service which provides to users thereof the ability to send or receive wire or electronic communications."
    - An **Electronic Communications Service**: "the provision to the public of computer storage or processing services by means of an electronic communications system"
  - Any e-mail in storage for 180 days or less is considered an electronic communication and may only be disclosed
    - In response to a search warrant.
    - To the government when urgent disclosure is necessary to prevent the death or serious injury of a human
  - Disclosing e-mail metadata (e-mail addresses, time/date sent/received, etc.) does not require a warrant
  - Disclosure of e-mail content is not permitted through a civil subpoena
  - Many companies (such as Facebook, Twitter, etc.) have classified themselves as "electronic communications services" instead of "remote computing services" and are refusing to provide most "content" data through civil subpoenas.

- **Search warrant.** A search warrant allows a law enforcement agency to physically enter a private property and seize objects. The warrant may be issued by a federal or state court.
  - The warrant must describe in particular the items to be seized
  - Exceptions to a warrant
    - The law enforcement official has observed illegal evidence "in plain view"
    - There is a legitimate emergency to protect human life

- The law enforcement official is in hot pursuit of a criminal suspect who has entered a building
- There is a risk of imminent destruction of evidence
  - The law enforcement must announce their presence before they can enter the premises (an exception known as a "no knock" warrant exists)

- **Delayed Notice Warrant.**
  - This warrant is obtained when law enforcement wish to enter a premises and inspect the property and/or collect evidence without informing the suspect
  - This is also known as a "sneak and peak" warrant

- **Pen** Register
  - A pen register warrant allows law enforcement to record metadata related to telephone calls, which could include date/time telephone call was placed, duration, and numbers dialed
  - Pen register does not allow collection of telephone call content

- **Telephone Wire Tap**
  - Covered by Communications Assistance for Law Enforcement Act (18 USC § 2510)
  - Requires telephone companies to implement systems that allow them to readily assist law enforcement
  - Requires a phone company to provide contents of wire communication in response to a warrant
  - Prior to obtaining a wire tap, the government must prove that all other options for obtaining evidence have been exhausted
  - The warrant typically expires after thirty days unless renewed
  - The government must take steps to minimize the collection of privileged or irrelevant communications. The monitoring agent should only disclose communications that are criminal in nature to the investigative team.

- **Warrants in general**
  - The government must show "probable cause" that a crime has been committed and that evidence is likely to be found
  - Special considerations must be made for searching the office of a lawyer because of the presence of legally privileged information

Civil Suit
- The evidence standard for a civil lawsuit is lower than that of a criminal case.
- The lawsuit must be filed in a court with jurisdiction over the subject matter and parties

- The lawsuit must allege specific facts that show how the Defendant harmed the Plaintiff. Specific evidence may be in possession of the Defendant or may be a matter of public record.
- The Defendant is expected to provide evidence through discovery. Parties are expected to exchange evidence in good faith prior to trial.
  - Deposition (relevant witnesses are interviewed)
  - Discovery (each party is obligated to disclose evidence)
  - Interrogatories (each party may pose a set of questions to the other party)
  - Subpoena (each party may subpoena relevant data held by third parties)

- Rules of civil procedure may limit the amount of discovery that can take place. Parties may ask the court for increases to the limits in unusual cases.

- A party in a civil suit does not have the right to
  - Obtain or execute a search warrant
  - Obtain stored communications (e-mails) from a service provider

- In special circumstances, a party may apply for an Anton Pillar Order (in Canada or the UK). This order allows a Plaintiff to search the premises of a Defendant. An APO is like a criminal search warrant, except that the party executing the APO may not use force. Prior to obtaining an Anton Pillar Order, the party must prove that
  - Evidence will be destroyed
  - The plaintiff will be irreparably harmed
  - The defendant has evidence in his possession

- In the United States, a Plaintiff may obtain an impoundment order to sieze items that infringe his copyright under the Copyright Act.

Internal Investigation
- In an internal investigation, an organization can obtain data held on their own systems/property. Data could include computer and cell phone devices issued to employees and held by third parties.

- An employee may have an expectation of privacy, even on an employer-owned device. The employer must ensure that the employee has agreed to the monitoring.

Chain of Custody

The **chain of custody** is a legal process that shows where the evidence was held. Consider that evidence must be seized from a location and stored somewhere. Later this evidence is analyzed and then put back in storage. In the end, the evidence is presented in court. The Plaintiff must prove that the evidence has not been modified since it was seized. That requires that the Plaintiff know exactly where the evidence was stored.

When the evidence is seized, there should be two witnesses to document the time, date, and location. Be as specific as possible. Do not say "seized from house", instead say "seized from living room coffee table". The people who seized it must document their observations.

The evidence must be stored in a secure vault or evidence locker. Access to the evidence locker must be secured. A second person should document who entered or left the evidence locker, and when. The evidence locker must be climate controlled so that the devices are not damaged.

When working with evidence, there must be an original. From the original, make one master copy. Make multiple copies of the master copy and work with them. When additional copies are required, make more copies from the master copy. That way, the original evidence stays secure and the risk of modifying it is limited.

When working with digital evidence, a device known as a "write blocker" is used. The write blocker prevents inadvertent modification of the evidence by a connected computer system.

Legal Hold

A **Legal Hold** is a process where an organization preserves evidence in response to an external request.

Under the rules of Civil Procedure, an organization or individual is legally obligated to preserve any data that is subject to a lawsuit. This obligation begins when an organization is notified of or threatened with a lawsuit, even if it has not been served with a complaint or subpoena. The obligation applies when the organization

- Is a Plaintiff in a lawsuit
- Is a Defendant in a lawsuit
- Is presented with a third-party civil subpoena or criminal subpoena/warrant

Wilful or negligent destruction of evidence is illegal.

The organization must have a method for searching for and preserving data. Many commercial applications such as Office 365 have built in tools for preserving data.

Under the Corporate and Auditing Accountability, Responsibility, and Transparency Act (also known as Sarbox, Sarbanes-Oxley, or SOX), public corporations and their accounting firms have a legal obligation to preserve certain types of data for at least seven years.

Data Acquisition

Data Acquisition has several steps. How do we collect evidence?

- **Capture a System Image**
  - This is a full copy of the system's raw data including deleted and hidden data. A complete system image can be analysed later.
  - Hardware-Based: physically remove the drives and put them into a duplicator that copies to an identical drive. Use a write blocker. Hardware based data collection is best.
    - If the drive is physically broken, it may need to be sent to a specialized laboratory where it can be repaired.
    - Always physically disassemble the computer to determine if it contains more than one physical drive.
  - Software-Based: a software-based imaging application such as Recon can be used
  - Some devices (such as an iPhone) cannot be physically or logically imaged. These devices can be connected to a forensics suite and imaged manually. Software include Axiom, Oxygen, and Cellebrite.

- **Network Traffic & Logs**
  - Capture all network traffic and logs from network devices
  - Capture all configurations
  - Cisco devices may have a SD card with the configuration and IOS; other devices may not

- **Capture Video**
  - Video surveillance should be captured
  - Video can be stored on an NVR/DVR, on each physical camera, or in the cloud

- **Record Time Offset**
  - The time that a file is created or the time stamp that is on a video may be different from the actual time
  - If a device does not update its time from NTP (network time server) then there will be an offset that can be challenged in court. The defense will ask why there is a time difference.
  - If there is proof of the offset, then the correct time can be obtained

- **Take Hashes**
  - Hash all the data to prove that none of it has been modified from when it was collected

- **Screenshots**

- Screenshots are useful in high stakes scenario where the device is found running or when it could risk being encrypted ·
- Take a screenshot with a digital camera
- If you take a screenshot through the computer (such as with the snipping tool) then the evidence will be modified – there is no clear case law and the risk is minimal, but this risk should be avoided

- **Witness Interviews**
  - Interview all people associated with the site
  - Unless ordered by a court, a witness is generally not required to submit to an interview
  - Remind the witness that lying to a law enforcement officer is illegal; lying during an investigation could lead to civil liability
  - In a professional investigation – law, engineering, etc., a professional may have a legal obligation to comply with an investigation established by their board

For evidence to be admissible in a court, it must comply with the relevant rules established in that court's jurisdiction. For example, US Federal courts accept evidence that is admissible under the Federal Rules of Evidence.

- Under the "best evidence rules" if original version of a document is available, then only the original is admissible, and not a copy
- Admissible evidence must be relevant
- Evidence that is prejudicial (likely to bias the jury) may be inadmissible even if it is relevant
- Evidence must be competent. The person introducing the evidence may be required to prove that it is authentic.
  - The person who collected the evidence may be called to testify as a material or expert witness.
  - If called as an expert witness, the witness must prove that he is qualified to provide the expert opinion. This is known as the Daubert standard.
- Hearsay rule
  - A person cannot testify about something he heard somebody else say
  - Hearsay is inadmissible because the person who was heard is not available to testify under oath or be cross-examined
  - Business Records Exception: records created in the ordinary course of business are admissible because they are made on a regular basis. The records are admissible even when the person who created them is unable to testify as to their authenticity.
  - There are other exceptions to the hearsay rule
- The rules of evidence do not apply to some proceedings such as bail hearings
- The rules of evidence are lengthy and beyond the scope of this book. Every jurisdiction has its own set of rules, and further standards established by case law.

Preservation

Preservation is the process maintaining the data. When the case gets to trial, how can we prove that the data we are presenting is the same as the data we collected

- We took care to document the crime scene
- We took a hash of the data that was collected
- We stored the evidence in a secure location and documented each person who had access to the evidence. We maintained the chain of custody
- We only worked on copies of the data
- We performed our work on computers that were air-gapped and through a write blocker
- We used forensically sound software and techniques to analyse the data
- We hashed the final data and verified that the hashes matched the hash of the original data

Recovery

Recovery is the attempt to obtain missing or deleted data. There are several ways to recover data.

A recovery attempt should not be made on the live evidence unless it is a last resort, and no other method is possible. A recovery attempt on a live system will modify the system, damage the evidence, and delete parts of the deleted data.

A recovery attempt should be made on a physical copy of the evidence collected. Recall that deleted data can be deleted at the logical level but preserved at the physical level – data is stored as 0's and 1's on a physical hard disk drive. A group of 0's and 1's makes a file. Details about the file are stored logically in the file system. When the file is deleted, details are removed from the file system, but the original physical data may be maintained until it is overwritten.

If a physical copy is not available, then recover attempts should be made on the logical copy. The logical copy will not contain deleted data but may contain artifacts of deleted files such as thumbnails, log files, and history.

Databases are a special type of file. A database - when viewed in a standard database viewer – will not display any deleted data. When a user deletes an entry (a record) from a database, the database software will mark it for deletion, but it may not be removed from the file. A special database analysis tool can be used to locate deleted data.

Data can be recovered as complete files or as file fragments. Once a file fragment is recovered, a tool can be used to determine the type of file that it was. This tool looks for patterns in the file. A file may contain clues about its type in the beginning or end. Once the file type is known, then more specialized tools can be used to analyse the fragment.

If a file was encrypted and then deleted, it may be impossible to recover the original data.

Strategic Intelligence/Counterintelligence Gathering

A large organization may engage in counterintelligence gathering. Organizations face several threats:

- **Malicious Competitors**. A competitor may attempt to steal trade secrets or sabotage the organization's systems. The competitor may install rogue employees to spy on processes or intentionally damage systems. Finding out who they are is important.
- **Competitors**. A competitor may be engaging in competitive behavior that is not illegal. The organization should (legally) gather information so that they can remain competitive.
- **Fraud**. Rogue employees or contractors may engage in fraud or steal data from the organization's systems.
- Actbivists. Political or environmental activists may engage in fraud or damage to hurt the organization if they do not agree with its activities.
- **Foreign Governments**. A foreign government may attempt to harm an organization to hurt the host country politically or to gain a competitive advantage in its own industry.
- **Hackers/malicious users**. External hackers may attempt to hurt the organization, either for "street credit" or to harm the organization.

The organization may need to seek the help of external law enforcement agents to help with a threat.

- A private individual/organization does not have the same power as law enforcement. They cannot seek a subpoena, search warrant, wire tap or pen register to gather data.
- The organization may not have the resources or experience to monitor or detect a large threat.

Track Man-Hours

Tracking the number of hours spent on an investigation is important for billing purposes. In a successful civil case, the Defendant may be required to pay the Plaintiff for costs incurred. The organization will be able to recover its costs when there are accurate billing records.

5.6 Explain disaster recovery and continuity of operation concepts

- *Recovery Sites*
    - *Hot Site*
    - *Warm Site*
    - *Cold Site*
- *Order of Restoration*
- *Backup Concepts*
    - *Differential*
    - *Incremental*
    - *Snapshots*
    - *Full*
- *Geographic Considerations*
    - *Off-Site Backups*
    - *Distance*
    - *Location Selection*
    - *Legal Implications*
    - *Data Sovereignty*
- *Continuity of Operation Planning*
    - *Exercises/Tabletop*
    - *After-Action Reports*
    - *Failover*
    - *Alternative Processing Sites*
    - *Alternate Business Practices*

Disaster Recovery is a process where an organization can resume normal operations in the event of a disaster (natural disaster, strike, data loss, fire, war, ransomware attack, or protest). An organization must

- Plan out a cost-effective disaster recovery plan considering all the different causes of disruption. For example, an organization located in Florida should consider hurricanes, but an organization in Wyoming should not.

- Identify the amount of downtime the organization can accept before having to resume normal operations. An organization such as an insurance company may not accept any disruption to its operations. A retail store may accept a disruption of one or two weeks. The shorter the disruption, the more expensive the recovery plan.

- The organization should practice the disaster recovery plan, holding regular drills with the key responders.

- The organization should review and revise the disaster recovery plan to take advantage of new technologies and consider new threats.

- The more effective the disaster recovery plan, the more it will cost. The disaster recovery plan may cost the organization, even when no disaster has taken place. For example, maintaining a second office for emergency use may cost the organization tens of thousands of dollars per month. Is the potential harm caused by the disaster (multiplied by its likelihood) more expensive than the cost of maintaining the office?

Recovery Sites

A **Recovery Site** is a location that a company can use to resume operations. The recovery site might be an office, a factory, or a data center. It contains all the technology and equipment that the company requires to resume operations should their existing facilities be damaged or inaccessible.

An organization must weigh the cost and benefit of the type of recovery site they will operate. A hot site allows an organization to resume operations immediately (without a cost to its business) but is more expensive. A cold site forces an organization to wait to resume operations (at a substantial cost) but is much cheaper.

There are three types of recovery sites

- A **hot site** is a site that is continually running. With the use of a hot site, an organization has multiple locations that are operating and staffed. For example, an insurance company may have a call center in New Jersey, a call center in Florida, and a call center in California. The insurance company staffs all three centers 24/7. If the California call center is affected by an earthquake, the insurance company diverts calls to New Jersey and Florida, and operations are not disrupted.

  in the case of a data center, the organization will maintain data centers in multiple geographic locations. These data centers are connected to each other over WAN links. Data is replicated across multiple data centers, so that damage to one data center does not compromise the data. For example, an insurance company stores customer data in data centers at California, Utah, and Virginia. The Virginia data center is hit by a tornado, but all the data has been replicated to the other two centers. The organization and its customers can continue accessing their data.

  A hot site is expensive to maintain. In the example of the insurance company, they can staff the three sites cost-effectively. A smaller organization (such as a restaurant or warehouse) that operates out of a single location may not find it cost-effective to operate a second site.

- A **cold site** is a location that does not contain staff or equipment. An organization hit with a disaster must send employees to the cold site, bring in supplies, and configure equipment. The cold site does not contain any data; the organization must restore its data from back up.

  A cold site is cheaper to operate than a hot site. In the event of a disaster, the cold site can be used to operate the business. The cold site may be an empty office, an abandoned warehouse or a trailer.

  Companies such as Regus provide immediate short-term office space in the event of a disaster.

- A **warm site** is a compromise between a cold site and a hot site. A warm site may contain some hardware and preconfigured equipment. The organization may need to bring in staff and/or specialized equipment for the warm site to become operational. The warm site may contain copies of data, but they will not be current.

Order of Restoration

What do we restore first? Second? Last? The organization must rank each system based on how critical it is for the organization's goals. Factors include

- Is the system critical for life safety such as a fire alarm, security system, electrical generator, etc.?
- Do other systems interconnect with or rely on this system? For example, the organization cannot restore any servers until the power is first restored.
- How profitable is each system? Systems belonging to profitable business units should be restored first.
- What is the demand for each system? Systems belonging to business units that provide high-demand products or services should be restored first.

Order of Restoration commonly applies to data loss. Copying data from a physical back up to a production system represents a bottleneck. It may take hours (or days or weeks) to copy all the data. During the back up process, the organization must separate the data based on its criticality, so that more important data can be identified and copied first during the restore process.

If all the data was stored as a "blob" in the back up, then it would be impossible to restore critical data first.

Backup Concepts

There are four main types of back ups: Full, Differential, Incremental, and Snapshots. The type of back up affects the way that data is backed up and the way that data is restored.

A **Full backup** is a backup of the entire set of data. The first time a back up is performed, a full back up must be performed. An organization may perform a full back up once per week or once per month. A Bare Metal back up is a full backup of a logical drive, which includes the server operating system. It can be used to restore the server's operating system and applications, whereas a full back up may contain only user-generated data.

A **Differential Backup** is a backup of the data that has changed since the last full backup. The organization must be careful to ensure that it is able to accurately keep track of data that has changed.

An **Incremental Backup** is a backup of the data that has changed since the last Full Backup or Incremental Backup. Why use Incremental or Differential backups? Which is better?

Consider an organization that performs Full and Differential backups. If the organization performed
- A full back up on Monday (all the data is backed up)
- A differential back up on Tuesday (the data that was changed between Monday and Tuesday is backed up)
- A differential back up on Wednesday (the data that was changed between Monday and Wednesday is backed up)
- A differential back up on Thursday it performs a differential backup (the data that was changed between Monday and Thursday is backed up)

Consider an organization that performs Full and Incremental backups. If the organization performed
- A full back up on Monday (all the data is backed up)
- An incremental back up on Tuesday it (the data that was changed between Monday and Tuesday is backed up)
- An incremental back up on Wednesday (the data that was changed between Tuesday and Wednesday is backed up)
- An incremental back up on Thursday it performs an incremental backup (the data that was changed between Wednesday and Thursday is backed up)

An incremental backup generates less data than a differential backup, but it is faster to restore data from a differential backup. If the organization uses differential backups and experiences data loss on Thursday

- It must restore the data that from Monday's full back up
- Then it must restore the data from Thursday's differential back up

If the organization uses incremental backups and experiences data loss on Thursday

- It must restore the data that from Monday's full back up
- Then it must restore the data from Tuesday's incremental back up
- Then it must restore the data from Wednesday's incremental back up
- Then it must restore the data from Thursday's incremental back up

Notice that in every process, the full backup must first be restored. In the case of a differential backup, the most recent differential backup must then be restored. In the event of an incremental backup, all the incremental backups created after the full backup must be restored. A incremental backup takes less time to create than a differential backup, but takes longer to restore.

If the organization creates a full backup each week, then the organization would (at most) restore six incremental backups. If the organization creates a full backup each month, then they would have to restore up to thirty incremental backups.

Why use a combination of full and incremental back ups? Why not perform a full back up every day? A full back up may take a long time to run and take up a large amount of space. What if the full back up takes 28 hours to run? What if the organization maintains 10,000TB of data, but only changes approximately 100TB per week? Should the organization generate 70,000TB of data back ups every week?

A **snapshot** is an image of a virtual machine or a disk. A snapshot allows an organization to restore a server or application to a previous state in the event of a hardware failure or corruption of the software. The benefits of a snapshot

- A server can be restored to an exact state, which could include its operating system, applications, configuration, and data.
- It would otherwise take hours or days to restore a server to its original state, especially if the application installers are no longer available, or if the installation process was not documented
- If a user makes changes to the system that cause damage or undesired operation, the system can be restored to a working state

It may not always be possible to take a snapshot. A hypervisor can take a snapshot of a live system, it may not be possible to image a physical system without shutting it down (which could affect operations).

How often does an organization need to perform a back up? The organization must weigh the cost of the back up against the cost of the potential data loss, and the time that it will take to restore the data.

- If the back up is performed daily, the organization could risk losing a day's worth of data.
- If the back up is performed weekly (say on a Monday), and data loss occurs on a Friday, the organization could lose all the data generated between Monday and Friday.
- If the back up is performed in real time (i.e. replicated to another site), then the organization will not lose any data, but replication is expensive and requires a dedicated internet connection.

Questions that should be asked
- How much is the data worth?
- How much revenue will the organization lose if the data is lost?
- How much does the back up cost?
- How much time will it take to restore the data from a back up? How much revenue will the organization lose while waiting for the data to be restored?

Geographic Considerations

Where should backed up data be stored? Consider an organization that backs up its data to removable tapes or hard disk drive cartridges. Should they store the tapes in their office? Of course not. If the office burns down, the servers will be destroyed, and the tapes will also be destroyed.

The tapes should be stored "off site". There are several options
- Storage service such as Iron Mountain
- Another office location (where the organization has multiple offices)
- At a bank safe deposit box

How far away should the data be stored? If there is a data loss, the organization must retrieve the back up, bring it back to the office, connect it to their equipment, and restore the data. The further the data, the longer it will take to return to the office, and the longer the organization will be without its data.

If the data is stored too close, there is a risk that a natural disaster will destroy (or make inaccessible) both the office and the data. Therefore, the organization may choose to store their data in another state. For example, an organization with an office in Miami, Florida may send their data to an office in New York, New York. If they kept their data in Miami, both the office and the data could be affected by a hurricane.

If the data can be backed up over a fast, dedicated internet connection, then the time it would take to retrieve the data is no longer relevant. An electronic back up may be more advantageous than a physical back up. Examples of electronic back up services include Amazon Glacier and Carbonite.

If the data is sent to a storage service, then the organization must consider
- How much will it cost to store the data?
- How long will it take to retrieve the data? One hour? One day? One week?
- Can the storage service be trusted with the data, or does the data need to be encrypted? Data should always be encrypted before being sent to a third party and this question should not even be asked.

Consider that an organization in Florida sends its data to New York or California. Florida does not have strong privacy laws, but California and New York do. The organization must be aware that its data will be subject to the laws of the jurisdiction where it stores its data
- Data must be stored in accordance with the privacy laws of the state that it is stored in
- Data could be subject to disclosure (for example, a state court in California could demand production of the data in response to a civil or criminal subpoena, which would have no effect if the data remained in Florida)

- The organization may be required to seek consent from the users whose data is moved to another country

It is difficult enough to move data from one state or province to another, but it is even more difficult (or even legally impossible) to move data from one country to another.

Data sovereignty is an idea that data should be subject to the laws of the country in which it is stored, and that people should have the right to determine where their data is stored.

Microsoft Corp. v. United States (In the Matter of a Warrant to Search a Certain E-Mail Account Controlled and Maintained by Microsoft Corporation) before the United States Court of Appeals for Second Circuit was an important case regarding data sovereignty:

- When a user signs up for a Microsoft service, such as Outlook e-mail, Microsoft creates an account
- Microsoft stores the user's basic data (username, password, billing information, etc.) on a server in the United States
- However, Microsoft stores the bulk of the user's data (e-mails, photographs, etc.) on a server geographically closest to the user (this server could be in Canada, the United States, Ireland, etc.). By storing the data in a geographic location closest to the user, network latency is reduced.
- In this case, a user who was suspected of drug trafficking signed up for an e-mail account, and Microsoft's servers automatically chose to store the data in Ireland.
- A United States Magistrate Judge in the Southern District of New York issued a search warrant ordering Microsoft to hand over the e-mails for this user.
  - Recall from earlier that e-mails must not be disclosed in response to a subpoena (only a search warrant under the Stored Communications Act).
  - In practice, search warrants issued under the SCA are not executed by force. An investigating agency serves the warrant on the service provider via hand delivery or fax. The service provider then electronically disclosed the e-mails requested through the warrant.
  - Search warrants are required because e-mails are considered highly private and not subject to disclosure through a subpoena.
- Microsoft refused to comply with the subpoena
  - Microsoft said that the e-mails were stored in Ireland and therefore, a search warrant could not be used to obtain the e-mails (since the government could not physically enforce a search warrant outside of the United States)
  - The court disagreed, considering that the SCA warrant was "subpoena like" in practice, and that Microsoft technically had control over the e-mails stored in Ireland
- Microsoft appealed to the Circuit Court of Appeals

- The court agreed with Microsoft that e-mails stored outside the United States cannot be disclosed due to a warrant under the SCA
- The court said that laws, in general, apply only inside the territory of the United States and that the focus of the SCA was to protect the privacy of users
- The government of Ireland stated that it could provide the e-mails to the United States Department of Justice through a request under MLAT (Mutual Legal Assistance Treaty) and that the e-mails should only be disclosed to the government of Ireland

- The case was appealed to the Supreme Court
  - During the appeal, the **Clarifying Lawful Overseas Use of Data Act or CLOUD Act** was passed
  - The CLOUD Act amended the SCA to require the production of e-mails stored overseas but under the control of US-based companies
  - The CLOUD Act allows the executive branch to enter into data sharing agreements with other countries
  - Since the CLOUD Act rendered the appeal moot, the case was dismissed by the Supreme Court

Continuity of Operation Planning

If there is a disaster, how can the business restore operations? How fast can it restore operations? It is not enough just to restore data. Questions to ask

- What does the organization do? What products or services does it provide?

- What equipment is required to manufacture the products or provide the services? Where can this equipment be sourced or does the organization have spares? What does it require to operate?

- Where can the organization operate from? Does it have a secondary location? Can employees work from home?

- Who are the key leaders? What kinds of skills are required to restore the organization's operations and which employees, or contractors possess those skills?

- How can the organization communicate with its customers and employees? Does the organization maintain a back up forms of communication in case the normal communications systems are disrupted?

Exercises/Tabletop

Remember that no plan ever failed on paper. The organization must test out the plan. A tabletop exercise is a gathering of the organization's senior leadership; a gathering where the leaders act out potential disasters and the organization's response.

Employees who are trained to respond to disasters must have clearly defined roles (i.e. incident commander, communications, technical support, medical, etc.)

The exercise will not produce accurate results, because the participants know that they are not facing a real situation. The stress level is much lower than in a real disaster. Nevertheless, it produces more accurate results than not having an exercise.

A better method is a "drill" where the organization creates real (but controlled) disasters and forces employees to respond. When employees have no prior knowledge, their responses will be more accurate. A drill may be illegal because it may cause physical or emotional harm to employees. For example, if the organization creates a real fire, but people are harmed while trying to escape, the drill would be counterproductive.

The exercise must be repeated on a regular basis, and when the disaster recovery plan changes.

After-Action Reports

After a disaster, a report must be made, documenting the following
- A description of the disaster
- How the organization responded to the disaster
- How the disaster was corrected, and how long it took to correct
- The damage caused by the disaster
- The causes of the disaster

The organization can use this to learn from their mistakes.

Failover Testing

Failover is a system that takes over for another system (the first system "fails over" to the second system). When a system is designed with no single point of failure, how does an organization know that it will work when required?

Consider a classic example. The organization has a router with two internet connections: a primary and a secondary. Traffic flows through the primary connection. If the primary connection fails, the system "fails over" to the secondary connection. But how does the organization know that the secondary connection will work when required? They must test it. They must unplug the primary connection and see if the system switches over to the secondary. That only proves that the connections are working at the time of the test, not that they will continue to function when they are needed.

A better approach would be to route half of the traffic over the primary and half over the secondary, and continually monitor both connections. If one connection were to fail, corrective action would be taken immediately.

Alternative Processing Sites

An **alternative processing site** is one that a business can use when their primary site experiences a disaster.

The site may be identical to the primary site, or it may have limited resources, depending on what the organization needs (and can afford). The site may have multiple primary sites in different geographical locations, all of which are operational. The organization can close one or more sites in a disaster and continue to operate from the remaining sites.

Can employees can work from home? What do they require?
- Computer/laptop
- Phone
- VPN
- Skype
- Microsoft Teams
- Data storage consideration (access to sensitive/classified information from home may not be permitted)

Alternative Business Practices

An **alternative business practice** is one that can be used when the primary business practice is unavailable due to the unavailability of something
- Key system offline
- Key employee unavailable
- Factory unable to produce product (supply chain disruption or equipment malfunction)

The organization must plan a response. It is not always possible to have a cost-effective alternative business practice. Organizations that source raw materials cannot always resume operations. Examples include oil wells, mines, and farms.

How to make ensure that alternative business practices are successful
- Train multiple employees with the same skillset. All business processes should be documented and backed up on paper and electronically. The knowledge and experience should not reside in the brain of one person. People die, get sick, and quit all the time. If a key person is unavailable, somebody else should be able to take over.

- There should be a succession plan at all levels of management, such as the CEO, CFO, and middle management. In the event of an unavailable manager or executive, the organization should be ready to appoint another qualified person.

- There must be a supply chain of raw materials and component products. Raw materials should be sourced from multiple vendors where possible. For example, a car company should be able to source steel from different metal suppliers (ideally in different geographic locations). If one is unavailable, then the other company should be able to supply. An organization should work with its vendors to ensure that they have the capacity to supply the required quantity of raw materials or components.

  if an organization becomes the largest (or sole) customer of one of its vendors, it should consider acquiring ownership of that vendor. This eliminates the risk of a vendor going out of business and disrupting the organization's supply. For example, Amazon purchased Kiva, a company that supplied its warehouses with robots and conveyor belts.
- Vendors and contractors. The organization should maintain relationships with multiple vendors and contractors in each geographic area. The organization should document the role of each vendor or contractor so that it can take over when necessary.

  The vendor should be available to provide coverage when the organization's regular staff are unavailable or overwhelmed.

  For example, if the organization outsources its logistics, it should maintain relationships with two or three logistics vendors (such as FedEx and UPS). If UPS is unavailable, the other FedEx should have enough spare capacity to deliver their packages.

- Distribution network. The organization should have multiple ways to get its product to the marketplace. That means maintaining relationships with distributors, transportation companies, and retail outlets. The organization should be able to sell the product direct to consumers through the mail and internet.

5.7 Compare and contrast various types of controls

- *Deterrent*
- *Preventative*
- *Detective*
- *Corrective*
- *Compensating*
- *Technical*
- *Administrative*
- *Physical*

A control is a mechanism that is used to prevent a behavior. There are different types of controls.

Controls prevent unsafe, illegal, or undesired behaviors. From a safety perspective, the best control is one that physically removes the hazard.

All controls can be bypassed. There should always be an administrative control, which provides legal consequences for violating or damaging a Technical or Physical control. Undesired behavior is a risk, and the use of a control reduces the organization's risk.

NIST Special Publication 800-53 revision 4 lists 600 controls in 18 categories and is an excellent reference. We will not cover these controls in detail.

Deterrent

A **deterrent control** is a method that discourages a behavior. For example, a user could be fired for sharing sensitive data. The deterrent control does not prevent the user from engaging in the activity, but it makes the consequences of that activity discouraging. The organization should consider the benefit that an undesired behavior will bring to the perpetrator and implement consequences that are greater than the benefit. Deterrents do not work well by themselves because there are always people who do not expect to get caught.

Preventative

A **preventative control** is one that stops a user from engaging in a specific behavior. For example, elevator doors close and lock when the car is moving so that people do not fall into the shaft. It is physically impossible to open an elevator door while it is moving (take my word for it). Encryption prevents an eavesdropper from reading your confidential conversation.

People will try to break preventative controls. People try to pick locks and break windows all the time. The cost of the preventative control must be weighed against the asset that it is supposed to protect. A more expensive control takes more effort to bypass.

Preventative controls can be installed in layers. For example, a locked server room, inside a locked building, behind fence with a locked gate has three layers of preventative controls. Even if one layer fails (the thief breaks the gate or the administrator leaves the server room unlocked, for example), the other layers will continue to protect the asset.

Detective

A **Detective control** only detects undesired behavior. It does not deter or prevent the behavior. It is useful when the organization wants to monitor behaviors. A detective control allows an organization to respond to undesired behavior.

The organization may follow up with individuals who engaged in the undesired behavior. The organization may have many violators and may want to monitor trends to better address the problem.

For example, the city installs a camera at an intersection to catch speeding motorists, who are later fined. Drivers who speed too often lose their licenses. The camera does not stop people from speeding. The fine could also be considered a deterrent control.

An alarm with a siren and a motion is a better example of a detective control. If an intruder passes by the motion sensor, the alarm is triggered. The alarm does not prevent the intruder from trespassing, but it may alert a security guard of the violation so that he can respond and apprehend the individual.

If the intruder knew about the presence of the alarm, he may be reluctant to trespass. Thus, an alarm could also be a deterrent. Most detective controls are also deterrents.

Corrective

A **corrective control** is one that reverses a behavior. For example, a door with a spring-loaded hinge is a corrective control. If a user leaves the door open, the hinge will automatically close it.

A corrective control may reverse the behavior quickly or slowly. A backup of a storage appliance is a corrective control. If the storage appliance fails, the data can be restored from backup.

Compensating

A **compensating control** counteracts a behavior. If the actual control is not available, or if the organization is not able to implement the original control because of a legitimate technical or business restriction, then the organization will implement a compensating control, which

- Meets the original intent of the requirement
- Provides similar levels of control as the original requirement
- Does not cause additional risk to the organization

If the organization is unable to implement a valid control, then they may need to stop the activity.

A fire suppression system is an example of a compensating control. It won't deter, prevent, or detect the fire, but it will reduce the damage that the fire causes (and create a flood in the process).

Another example is a rescue plan for a person working in a confined space. Confined spaces are dangerous because there is a potential for high levels of toxic gas build up, a lack of oxygen, and/or an explosion. Confined spaces exist in manholes, sewers, oil wells, mines, and many other places. Sometimes work must be performed in these places. By law, when an organization sends a person into a confined space, a dedicated rescue team must be standing by to pull him out should the conditions warrant it. The organization could not prevent the risky conditions, so they created a compensating control. If they could not assemble a rescue team (the control), they would not be able to send a worker into the confined space.

Technical

A **technical control** is also known as a logical control. The technical control does not physically prevent a person engaging in a behavior, but it might technically prevent him.

A technical control can be bypassed if it contains a security vulnerability. It should be backed up by an administrative control. When a technical control is operating correctly, it can be as strong as, or stronger than a physical control. If you store sensitive data on a hard drive, and then encrypt that hard drive with BitLocker or the RSA algorithm, and then store the hard drive in a safe, you have used a physical control and a technical control. A thief might be able to break the safe, but he won't be able to defeat the algorithm.

Technical controls include access control system, a firewall, an access control list, or a malware detector.

Administrative

An **administrative control** is one that is established in policy. It is not physical.

For example, an employee could be fired if they violate a policy.

Physical

A **physical control** physically prevents a user from engaging in a behavior. For example, storing sensitive data in a locked filing cabinet would prevent a user from accessing or sharing sensitive data stored within.

A physical control can be bypassed if there is enough brute force. The physical control should be backed up by an administrative control so that there are consequences.

5.8 Given a scenario, carry out data security and privacy practices

- *Data Destruction and Media Sanitization*
    - *Burning*
    - *Shredding*
    - *Pulping*
    - *Pulverizing*
    - *Degaussing*
    - *Purging*
    - *Wiping*
- *Data Sensitivity Labeling and Handling*
    - *Confidential*
    - *Private*
    - *Public*
    - *Proprietary*
    - *PII*
    - *PHI*
- *Data Roles*
    - *Owner*
    - *Steward/Custodian*
    - *Privacy Officer*
- *Data Retention*
- *Legal and Compliance*

Data Destruction and Media Sanitization

It is important to destroy sensitive data. The best method depends on the medium in which the data is stored, and whether the organization needs to reuse the media.

- **Burning**. Burning is good for paper records but can be dangerous and present environmental concerns. Burning destroys material through fire.
- **Shredding**. Shredding works for paper documents, CDs, DVDs, and disk drives. Shredding tears the material into small pieces.
    - Special scanners and software scanners can put shredded documents back together if the pieces are large enough.
- **Pulping**. Pulping is a process where the paper is broken down into its fibers and the ink is removed. This is completed after shredding. The shreds are placed into a detergent. Pulping is better than shredding because paper can be put back together.
- **Pulverizing**. Pulverizing is a term used for destroying hard disk drives and solid-state drives. Pulverizing is like shredding. It is the best way to erase a drive, but then the drive cannot be reused.
- **Degaussing**. Degaussing only works for hard disk drives. It uses a strong magnet that damages the data on the drive. It does not work on solid state drives, CDs, DVDs, or flash memory.
- **Purging**. Purging is a process to erase sensitive data from the storage media. It cannot be completed on read-only media such as CDs and DVDs.
- **Wiping**. Wiping is another term for erasing storage media. Wiping and purging involve writing data on top of the old data. These methods are considered logical and do not necessarily work well on solid state drives due to wear leveling. A wiped device can be reused.

Data Sensitivity Labeling and Handling

Data should be labelled so that unauthorized disclosure does not take place. Each page of a confidential document should be labelled with its privacy level. A single document, or a single page in a document may contain information at multiple privacy levels.

The document must be redacted before being disclosed. When redacting a document, it is important to state why it is being redacted.

- **Confidential**. The information contained in the document is secret and should only be viewed by people who need it to perform their jobs. Disclosure of confidential data can cause serious harm.

- **Private**. Private data is like secret data but belonging to individuals. The disclosure of private data can cause harm (but potentially less harm than the disclosure of confidential data).

- **Public**. Data that is available to the general public. But consider that the information may have been private and made public through accidental or deliberate disclosure. For example, a rogue employee posted confidential data on WikiLeaks. The organization may still consider the information to be private and take measures to protect it. The organization may refuse to confirm or deny the authenticity of the leaked information.

- **Proprietary**. Private data such as a trade secret. The organization may have different ways of storing proprietary data depending on contractual obligations with the party that provided it.

- **PII. Personally Identifying Information**. This may be protected by law and includes the names, addresses, SSN/SIN numbers, and banking information of the organization's customers or employees.

- **PHI. Protected Health Information**. This may be protected by law and includes healthcare records, diagnostic information, and billing information.

The law may require that information to be stored in a specific way. Each province and state has a privacy commissioner who may establish regulations governing how personal information is handled. A violation is subject to a fine and possible criminal charges.

The federal governments may also have different regulations.

An organization may be required by law to provide subjects with copies of all records it stores about them. Individuals typically have a right to know about the data that organizations store about them. They also have a right to request that inaccurate information be corrected. They may also have the right to request that the information be deleted.

There may be exceptions

- Sensitive law enforcement information should not be disclosed
- Information that could cause harm or death should not be disclosed
- An individual does not have the right to request that their credit store be deleted
- An organization may need to retain data to protect itself and its customers from fraud

Data Roles

There are different roles for managing the data.

- **Owner** – The owner created the data or is the subject of the data. The owner may create policies regarding the use of the data.
- **Steward/Custodian** – Manages the data and maintains custody of the data and released data. The custodian enforces policies set by the owner and privacy officer.
- **Privacy Officer** – Creates policies in accordance with applicable law. The privacy officer must be familiar with the privacy laws in each jurisdiction where the organization operates. The privacy officer may respond to subpoenas and Freedom of Information Act requests.

Data Retention

How long should an organization store data for? The short answer is for as long as necessary, and no longer. Storing more data than necessary can increase the risk that data is inadvertently disclosed.

- When an organization collects personal information from a customer it should tell the customer how long it will store the data for. It should also tell that customer why it is collecting the data, how it will be used, and who it will be provided to.

- An organization may be required by law to retain data for a minimum period. For example, SOX requires an organization that is publicly traded to keep data for at least seven years.

- Some jurisdictions have laws prohibit an organization from storing data for a long time.

- Some professional organizations (engineers, lawyers, pharmacists) may require their members to store client records for many years or decades. For example, if an engineer designed a bridge, the records may need to be stored for the lifetime of the bridge (100 years). A doctor or lawyer may need to store data for at least ten years.

- When a professional (doctor, lawyer, engineer, accountant, pharmacist) stops practicing, there is a procedure for the disposition of those records. The guidelines are issued by the professional's organization. The clients have a right to those records.

Legal and Compliance

Legal and Compliance are important consideration when storing data. The organization must ask

- What data does the organization need to collect and from where?
  - Data that is a matter of public record, such as social media. This data may not be accurate because on the internet, anybody can write anything about anyone. The source of the data may not permit aggregate collection of the data, or any collection of the data. The organization should not make decisions based solely on public data.
  - Data voluntarily provided by customers.
    - Have the customers consented to the data collection?
    - Are the customers informed about the type of data collected, how it will be used, how long it will be stored, and who will have access to it?
    - Is there a mechanism for the customers to view and correct the data stored by the organization?
  - Data provided by third parties
    - This could include criminal record checks and credit checks
    - The organization should obtain consent from the customer before accessing this data

- Is the organization permitted to collect the data by law?
  - Which laws apply?
  - Do multiple overlapping laws apply? Such as state and federal law? Or regulations by multiple state and federal agencies?
  - If the data is collected in one country and stored in another country, do the laws of multiple countries apply?
  - How can the data be stored?
  - Who can access the data?
  - How long can the date be stored (minimum and maximum)?
  - What rights do customers have over their own data?

The organization may need to disclose the data to a court, government agency, or third party, without the consent of the customer. The circumstances:

- Disclosure to a third party without the consent of the customer is rare. It may be provided if
  - The third party is engaged in litigation against the customer
  - The third party has obtained a valid subpoena or court order (such as an Anton Pillar order) that permits the disclosure of the data
  - The data custodian should still verify that the subpoena or court order is valid (and not a forgery), and that the court that issued the order has jurisdiction over the custodian. For example, if the data is stored in California and a court in New York issued the order, the custodian should deny the request.

- o The custodian should still not disclose the data even after confirming that the order is valid and that the court has jurisdiction. The custodian should provide the details of the order to the customer (unless prohibited by the order – and this is extremely rare) and provide the customer with an opportunity to contest the order or quash the subpoena.

- Disclosure to a government agency
  - o The organization may be required by law to disclose information to a government agency.
  - o Examples include
    - An employer must disclose tax/income information to Revenue Canada or the IRS
    - A hospital or doctor must disclose diagnosis of a communicable disease to a public health authority
    - An organization may disclose cases of fraud to the government
    - Disclosure of limited information to a law enforcement agency where there is a risk of physical harm or death to a person. The organization must verify that the threat is credible, and that the law enforcement agency is legitimate.
  - o The organization must be sure that it is disclosing the minimum amount of information to the agency, and that the information is disclosed securely.
  - o The organization must advise the customer of the disclosure, unless prohibited by law.
  - o The organization should include in its terms of service language that permits it to disclose cases of fraud to the law enforcement agencies without prior consent. The organization should be able to protect itself from legal liability and fraud at the same time.

- Disclosure to a court
  - o The organization must provide information to a court in a criminal case, if
    - Required by lawful order of that court
    - The court has jurisdiction over the custodian of the data
  - o The organization should provide the customer with an opportunity to contest the order if legally able to do so
  - o Examples of court disclosure
    - Criminal subpoena from a state or federal court. The criminal subpoena is typically issued by a prosecutor or grand jury, is not signed by a judge and is in response to an ongoing criminal investigation. Many criminal subpoenas contain language that advise the recipient not to disclose the contents of the subpoena to the defendant, although adhering to this is not generally required. Disclosure may compromise the investigation.

A Defendant on trial may also issue a subpoena to obtain information that is relevant to his defense.

If an organization does not respond to a subpoena, the prosecutor may need to obtain a motion to compel from the judge.

The organization may not respond to the subpoena if it is issued by a court that does not have jurisdiction over it. But the issuer may take the subpoena to another court (one that does have jurisdiction) and ask them to enforce it.

- Search warrant. The organization will not have an opportunity to respond to a search warrant because they are obtained ex parte and mandatorily enforced. The exception is for a search warrant obtained under the Electronic Communications Privacy Act.

- **FISA**. Orders issued by the FISA Court (**Foreign Intelligence Surveillance Court**) must typically be complied with. The orders are obtained in secret and are considered classified, and therefore cannot be provided to the customers.

  The organization can choose to contest an order issued by the FISA court but will not have access to the underlying classified data used to obtain it. As a result, it will be practically impossible to quash.

  An organization will not be able to disclose the fact that it even received an order (although it may release numbers in aggregate).

- **NSL**. A **National Security Letter**, or NSL. An NSL is issued by the FBI to obtain Toll Records (phone numbers dialed, and calls received, email addresses sent and received, billing records), Financial Records, and Credit Information.

  An NSL is not obtained through a court and is considered classified. The recipient is not permitted to disclose the contents of the NSL.
- Foreign court order. An organization should not comply with an order from a foreign court, but a foreign prosecutor can use a diplomatic channel to ask a local court to enforce the order. For example, the United States and Canada have an MLAT (Mutual Legal Assistance Treaty)
  - The MLAT allows Canada or the United States to request legal assistance. This process might be slow. Law enforcement will

informally share information outside the scope of this act, but the information will not be admissible.

Laws relevant to data privacy

- **HIPPA (Health Information Portability and Protection Act)** protects health information.
  - It covers information about
    - An individual's past, present or future physical or mental health or condition,
    - The provision of healthcare to the individual
    - Payment for healthcare
  - PHI may not be disclosed except
    - To the government (to investigate fraud, for compliance, etc.)
    - To law enforcement if it will prevent the death or serious injury of a person
    - In response to a court order
    - To the patient's healthcare provider
    - To the patient or patient's authorized representatives
  - The organization must
  - Designate a privacy officer who is responsible for maintaining privacy policies
  - Install data safeguards
  - Implement a mitigation plan for disclosure of protected data
  - Accept complaints from individuals regarding the storage of data
  - Train all employees to protect PHI

- **The Right to Financial Privacy Act (RFPA)**, 12 USC § 3414.
  - In 1976, the Supreme Court found in United States v. Miller that financial institution customers had no legal right to privacy with respect to their financial records
  - As a result, the RFPA was passed
  - The law states that "no Government authority may have access to or obtain copies of, or the information contained in the financial records of any customer from a financial institution unless the financial records are reasonably described"
  - The government must provide the customer with advanced notice prior to obtaining the records, so that the customer can challenge the disclosure in court
  - Exceptions
    - Disclosure of records that do not identify a specific customer
    - Disclosures to the IRS
    - Emergency disclosures
    - Disclosures in the interest of national security
    - Disclosures in response to civil litigation
  - A financial institution could be any organization that issues credit, including
    - Depository institution (banks, thrifts, credit unions)

- Money services business
- Money order issuers, sellers and redeemers
- Travelers check issuers, sellers and redeemers
- U.S. Postal Service
- Securities and futures industries
- Futures commission merchants
- Commodity trading advisor
- Casino and card clubs
  - A financial institution has the legal obligation to disclose the following
    - Any kind of insider abuse of a financial institution
    - Federal crimes against, or involving transactions conducted through, a financial institution that the financial institution detects and that involve at least $5,000 if a suspect can be identified, or at least $25,000 regardless of whether a suspect can be identified
    - Transactions of at least $5,000 that the institution knows, suspects, or has reason to suspect involve funds from illegal activities or are structured to attempt to hide those funds
    - Transactions of at least $5,000 that the institution knows, suspects, or has reason to suspect have no business or apparent lawful purpose or are not the sort in which the particular customer would normally be expected to engage and for which the institution knows of no reasonable explanation after due investigation

- The **Electronic Communications Privacy Act (ECPA)**, 18 USC § 2709. This act is made up of three smaller acts
  - The Wiretap Act
    - Defines the types of communications that can be lawfully intercepted (public radio communications, emergency communications, satellite communications, etc. can be intercepted)
    - Illegal to sell or advertise a device that can intercept a wire communication
    - A wiretap must be authorized by a federal judge; an application made to a federal judge must be approved by a Deputy Assistant Attorney General or higher
    - The application must state
      - A description of the offense that has been committed, a description of the person whose communications are being intercepted, and a description of the communications that are being intercepted
      - That other investigative procedures have been attempted and failed or that they are too dangerous
      - The length of time that the interception must take place

- A list of all other applications for interceptions that have been filed and whether they were approved or denied
  - The application will be approved if
    - There is probable cause to show that an offense has been committed or will be committed
    - Evidence of the offense can be obtained through the interception
    - Normal investigative procedures have failed or are too dangerous
  - A wiretap order expires after thirty days
  - The interception must be conducted in a method that minimizes the interception of irrelevant communications. Courts have created different methods for minimization.
    - Law enforcement can listen to all conversations, but can only record or keep communications that are relevant
    - Law enforcement can listen to the first part of each conversation, but can only continue listening or recording the conversation if the first part contains signs of criminal activity
    - Patterns of telephone use that indicate criminal activity
    - Use of code or cryptic language in the conversation may indicate the presence of criminal activity.
- The **Stored Communications Act**
  - There are two types of service providers
    - A Remote Computing Service: "any service which provides to users thereof the ability to send or receive wire or electronic communications."
    - An Electronic Communications Service: "the provision to the public of computer storage or processing services by means of an electronic communications system"
  - Any e-mail in storage for 180 days or less is considered an electronic communication and may only be disclosed
    - In response to a search warrant.
    - To the government when urgent disclosure is necessary to prevent the death or serious injury of a human
  - Disclosing e-mail metadata (e-mail addresses, time/date sent/received, etc.) does not require a warrant
  - Disclosure of e-mail content is not permitted through a civil subpoena
  - Many companies (such as Facebook, Twitter, etc.) have classified themselves as "electronic communications services" instead of "remote computing services" and are refusing to provide most "content" data through civil subpoenas.
- The **Pen Register and Trap and Trace Devices Statute**

- A pen register records phone numbers dialed
- A law enforcement officer can apply to a court for a pen register if they can certify that the information to be obtained is relevant to a criminal investigation
- A law enforcement officer can install and maintain a pen register without a court order if an emergency exists, but only for up to 48 hours, and must then apply for an order after the fact

- The **Fair Credit Reporting Act (FCRA)**, 15 USC § 1681
  - A consumer reporting agency (credit bureau) can only provide a credit report
    - To the consumer it relates to
    - In response to a court order
    - To a person who is evaluating a transaction with a consumer, to the consumer's employer, to the consumer's insurer, to the consumer's investor, or for another legitimate business requirement
    - To determine child support payments
    - To the federal government if it relates to national security
  - An employer may not take any adverse action that relies on the report without first providing the consumer with a copy of the report
  - A consumer has the right to obtain a copy of his report at no cost

- **Freedom of Information Act**
  - Information held by federal government agencies is subject to public inspection in an electronic format
  - A person may apply to a government agency for access to records. The agency must then search for the records. The person may request specific records or request that the agency search for records that match specific keywords or circumstances.
  - The government does not disclose
    - Classified information
    - Trade secrets and financial information
    - Personnel and medical files
    - Law enforcement data that is considered private, that could hurt a Defendant's right to a fair trial, that could compromise the identity of an informant, that could endanger a person, or that could disclose specific law enforcement techniques
    - Geological data
  - The federal government of Canada and some provinces in Canada have similar acts with similar names

- **Gramm-Leach-Bliley Act**
  - A financial institution must safeguard the privacy of its customers

- Financial institutions include companies that are engaged in
  - Lending, exchanging, transferring, investing for others, or safeguarding money or securities
  - Providing financial, investment or economic advisory services
  - Brokering loans
  - Servicing loans
  - Debt collecting
  - Providing real estate settlement services
  - Career counseling
- Any information that is personally identifiable financial information is protected unless it is publicly available
- A financial institution must provide each customer with a Privacy Notice
- The notice contains
  - Categories of information collected
  - Categories of information disclosed
  - Categories of affiliates and non-affiliated third parties to whom the information is disclosed
  - Categories of information disclosed and to whom under the joint marketing/ service provider exception in section 313.13 of the Privacy Rule (see "Exceptions").
  - Any disclosures required by the Fair Credit Reporting Act
  - Policies and practices for protecting the confidentiality and security of information
  - An "opt-out" notice explaining the individual's right to not have their information shared; a reasonable way to opt out; and, a reasonable amount of time to opt out before the information is disclosed
- The organization must safeguard data by
  - Designating an employee to maintain information security
  - Identify risks to security, confidentiality, and integrity of the information
  - Perform a risk assessment, which includes employee training, information systems, detecting intrusions
  - Install safeguards to prevent risks that were identified in the risk assessment and test or monitor those safeguards to ensure that they are functional

Part G: SYO-501 6.0 Cryptography and PKI

6.1 Compare and contrast basic concepts of cryptography
- *Symmetric Algorithms*
- *Modes of Operation*
- *Asymmetric Algorithms*
- *Hashing*
- *Salt, IV, Nonce*
- *Elliptic Curve*
- *Weak/Deprecated Algorithms*
- *Key Exchange*
- *Digital Signature*
- *Diffusion*
- *Confusion*
- *Collision*
- *Steganography*
- *Obfuscation*
- *Stream vs Block*
- *Key Strength*
- *Session Keys*
- *Ephemeral Key*
- *Secret Algorithm*
- *Data-In-Transit*
- *Data-At-Rest*
- *Data-In-Use*
- *Random/Pseudo-Random Number Generation*
- *Key Stretching*
- *Implementation vs Algorithm Selection*
  - *Crypto Service Provider*
  - *Crypto Modules*
- *Perfect Forward Secrecy*
- *Security Through Obscurity*
- *Common Use Cases*
  - *Low Power Devices*
  - *Low Latency*
  - *High Resiliency*
  - *Supporting Confidentiality*

- *Supporting Integrity*
- *Supporting Obfuscation*
- *Supporting Authentication*
- *Supporting Non-Repudiation*
- *Resource vs Security Constraints*

Consider two parties, Alice and Bob, who need to communicate privately. Carol also needs to communicate privately with Bob. Eve is attempting to spy on them.

The plaintext is the information that has not been encrypted. The ciphertext is information that has been encrypted.

An encryption algorithm works in conjunction with a key. Think of an algorithm like a lock on a door. There are many models of locks. Even if you and your neighbor have the same model lock, you will have different keys.

Vulnerabilities

- The key is too short. In encryption, somebody can guess the key and decrypt the text. In the real world, somebody can guess the key and 3D print a new one to open the lock.
- The lock is too weak. In encryption, somebody can break the algorithm even without knowing the key. In the real world, somebody can pick the lock.
- There is a backdoor. In encryption, the system has a security vulnerability unrelated to the lock. For example, a person installed a keylogger on the computer where the encryption takes place. In the real world, somebody left a back door or window unlocked.

Symmetric Algorithms

A **symmetric algorithm** is one that uses the same cryptographic key to encrypt and decrypt text. The keys may be identical or easily transformed from an encryption key to a decryption key and represent a shared secret between the two parties attempting to communicate.

A symmetric algorithm is less convenient than an asymmetric algorithm (public key cryptography) because both parties must have access to the same key.

Alice and Bob need to communicate. Alice and Bob agree on a shared secret (the key), but how can Alice share the key with Bob without anybody seeing it? She must put it on a USB drive and physically give it to Bob, or she must send it over the internet. If Alice encrypts the key with another key, then she would have to share that key as well.

If Carol needs to communicate with Bob, but Carol is thousands of miles away, and has never met Bob, then both Carol and Bob must exchange their shared secret over the internet.

Bob must use a different key with Carol than he did with Alice. If not, then Alice could intercept and decrypt a message between Carol and Bob. If Bob needs to communicate with many people, then Bob needs many keys.

Thus, the symmetric algorithm can be compromised regardless of the length of the key or the strength of the algorithm. On the internet, it is difficult to distribute a symmetric key with another party.

Modes of Operation

If the plaintext contains repeating patterns, then the ciphertext will also contain repeating patterns. The presence of these patterns makes decryption easy. Several algorithms prevent this

- **Electronic Code Book**
- **Cipher Block Chaining**
- **Cipher Feedback Mode**
- **Output Feedback Mode**
- **Counter Mode**

These algorithms will be covered in more detail.

Asymmetric Algorithms

An **asymmetric algorithm** is also known as **public-key cryptography**. It involves two keys: a public key and a private key. The public key is used to encrypt data and the private key is used to decrypt data. Only the private key must be kept private.

Bob generates a private key. He uses the private key to generate a public key. He publishes the public key on the internet. Alice needs to send Bob a message. She finds Bob's public key. She uses Bob's public key to encrypt a message. She sends the message to Bob and Bob uses his private key to decrypt the message.

There are many asymmetric algorithms, including RSA, Diffie-Hellman, and DSA.

The algorithm can be compromised by a man-in-the-middle attack (as discussed earlier).

- If the communication is encrypted and uses public key cryptography (such as Apple iMessage), a man-in-the-middle attack is more difficult. Users encrypt messages with public keys (which they obtain from a central directory). If Alice wants to send a message to Bob, she obtains Bob's public key from Apple, encrypts the message, and sends it to Bob. Bob uses his private key (which only he knows) to decrypt the message. Eve can intercept the message
  - She generates her own public and private keys
  - She hacks into the central directory and changes Bob's public key to her own. She copies Bob's public key
  - When Alice queries the directory, she receives what she thinks is Bob's public key (but is in fact Eve's public key)
  - Alice encrypts the message with Eve's public key and sends the message to Eve (thinking that she is sending it to Bob)
  - Eve decrypts the message, reads it, and then encrypts it with Bob's public key
  - Eve sends the message to Bob
  - Bob receives the message, thinking it came from Alice and decrypts it with his own private key
  - Eve does the same thing with Alice's public key so that she can intercept messages that Bob is sending to Alice

Hashing

A **Hash function** converts a piece of data from one format into another. A Hash function is typically one-way. The goal of the hash function

- Convert a piece of data from a variable length to a fixed length. An encryption algorithm may require an input of a fixed length. For example, an encryption algorithm may require a key that is 32-bits long, but users can select passwords of different lengths. The user's password can be converted into a hash that fits into the algorithm.

- Hide the original data. Original, plaintext passwords should not be stored. A user password can be converted into a hash that can be stored. If the hash is compromised, then the password will not be compromised. Many website databases are compromised, but if the user passwords are hashed, then the original passwords are not determined. This only applies to a non-reversible hash.

Since the hash is not reversible, then multiple inputs may result in the same hash.

There are many hash functions. Attributes of a good hash function

- Consider the mathematical space of the hash output. A 32-bit hash for example is 32 characters long. If the hash is only letters and numbers, then the hash would have 32^{66} possible values.

The number of possible password input combinations is always infinite.

A hash should be continuous along the entire space, and there should be an equal probability of generating each output value.

- Be impractical to guess two inputs that produce the same output. Given an input m_1, it should be difficult to find a different input m_2 such that **hash(m_1) = hash(m_2)**. This is known as weak collision resistance.

It should be difficult to find two different messages m_1 and m_2 such that **hash(m_1) = hash(m_2)**. This is known as strong collision resistance.

- A hash should be efficient. There is a trade-off between how fast a hash can be searched and how much disk storage space it occupies. A large hash index can be searched quickly but occupies more space on the disk.

It is better to have a faster hash function over a slow one.

- Deterministic. The hash must always return the same output for a given input.

- Not practical to be able to predict the input that created a given output. Given a hash value **h** it should be difficult to find any message **m** such that **h = hash(m)**. This is known as pre-image resistance.

- A small change to the input should result in a large change to the output. It can be assumed if two strings appear similar and have the same hash output, then they are identical.

- A hash should be difficult
  - Mathematically speaking, difficult means that it is not solvable in asymptotic polynomial time
  - Cryptographically speaking, difficult means that it is secure against any person for as long as the system must be operational

The use of the hash

- **Message integrity**. When a message is first sent, a hash of the message is computed by the sender. The hash is shared with the recipient. The recipient can calculate the hash on the message received. If the calculated hash matches the original hash, the recipient knows that the message did not changed during transmission.

- **Digital Signature**. A hash is calculated over the entire message that needs to be signed. The hash is then signed. A calculation to produce a digital signature is complicated, and it would save computing power to calculate the signature on the hash instead of on the entire message.

- **Password**. Passwords are stored as hashes instead of plain text. As discussed earlier, when a user account is created, the password is hashed, and the hash is stored. During a log in attempt, the hash of the entered password is calculated and compared to the original hash. If they are the same, then the user is authenticated. A hash allows a service provider to avoid storing the password in plaintext.

- **Proof-of-work**. Proof-of-work is a system that is used to prevent denial of service attacks and to prevent automated systems from accessing websites. The system that is attempting to access a resource is presented with a difficult mathematical equation that involves calculating a hash. If the hash is correct, then the system is provided access. The equation must be difficult to calculate but easy to verify.

  The machine requiring access is forced to use some of its computing resources before gaining access. If the machine is operated by a legitimate human user, then the calculation represents a minor inconvenience of a few seconds. If the machine is a bot making thousands of requests, the calculation would consume its resources.

Proof-of-work is also used by Bitcoin mining.

- File identifier. A hash of a file can be calculated to uniquely identify the file. In a file system with millions of files, each file can be retrieved by providing its hash. File hashing is used by online file sharing systems.

The hash functions that are commonly used
- **MD5**
    o Produces a 128-bit hash
    o MD5 was used to calculate checksums for files that have been transferred over the internet. It would verify that the file that was sent was also the one that was received. MD5 was also used to store passwords.
    o MD5 is not secure because it is easy to find a collision and should not be used.

- **SHA-1**
    o Produces a 160-bit hash
    o Used by the government to protect sensitive, unclassified material
    o Computing power to find a collision can be obtained for less than $100,000
    o In the process of being replaced by SHA-2

- **SHA-2**
    o Produces a 256-bit or 512-bit hash
    o Used by Bitcoin
    o SHA-2 is still in use and considered secure

- **SHA-3**
    o Produces a 256-bit or 512-bit hash
    o SHA-3 is not designed to replace SHA-2 as SHA-2 is still considered secure
    o Instead, SHA-3 is designed as an alternative that is available should SHA-2 be compromised in the future (and it will be!)
    o SHA-3 uses a sponge construction. Data is absorbed, transformed, and then pushed out.

- **Blake, Blake2**, and **Blake3**
    o Blake functions were developed in various cryptographic competitions
    o Blake2 is faster and more secure than SHA-2. It is faster and similarly secure to SHA-3.

Salt, IV, Nonce

Recall that it is bad security practice to store passwords in plain text. Passwords are typically hashed, and the hash is stored (the hash is not reversible).

But a hacker could generate a dictionary of passwords (common and uncommon) and calculate the corresponding hash for each one. This is known as a rainbow table. The hacker could then steal a hash and look up the corresponding password for each one.

Rainbow tables are readily available on the internet for passwords up to eight characters (every possible combination!) and rainbow tables of even longer passwords can be computed.

To prevent the use of rainbow table attacks, modern password hash functions incorporate a '**salt**'. The salt is a random set of characters appended to the end of each password before the hash is calculated. The hash and the salt are stored in plain text. If the hash database is compromised, the hacker would have to regenerate each rainbow table incorporating the salt into every password to make any sense of it.

A **Nonce** is a bit of data added to a cryptographic algorithm to prevent replay attacks.

Consider that Alice is communicating with Bob
- Bob wants to verify Alice's identity
- Bob requests Alice's password
- Alice provides her password, but may hash it first
- Eve intercepts the password or the hash
- Eve wants to impersonate Alice, so she sends the intercepted password or the hash to Bob later
- This is known as a replay attack

If Alice adds a nonce to the password and sends it to Bob, then when Even intercepts and attempts to resend the same data, Bob will notice that the nonce is the same and will not accept the message. Eve would need to somehow intercept Alice's message and send it to Bob in a way that is faster than Alice's method so that Bob receives Eve's message before he receives Alice's.

A nonce should not be reused or not reused often (the nonce should be much larger than the number of times it is expected to be reused).

A nonce can be randomly generated or sequential.
- A sequential nonce guarantees that it will not be reused.
- A sequential nonce prevents replay attacks when it is verified that the nonce is incrementing

- The best nonce has a random portion and a sequential portion

An Initialization Vector is like a nonce, except that it cannot be sequential. The Initialization Vector is not good for replay attacks because it could be faked.

Elliptic Curve

An **elliptic curve** is a curve on a plane (2-dimensional) over a specific field, with a single point at infinity. In summary, if you pick two points on an elliptic curve and add them together, the result will be a third point that is on the curve. Elliptic curve cryptography does not consume much computing power; therefore, it is well suited for mobile devices.

The curve is defined by the equation $y^2 = x^3 + ax + b$

There are many algorithms that use elliptic curves

- The Elliptic Curve Diffie–Hellman (ECDH) key agreement scheme
- The Elliptic Curve Integrated Encryption Scheme (ECIES), also known as Elliptic Curve Augmented Encryption Scheme or simply the Elliptic Curve Encryption Scheme,
- The Elliptic Curve Digital Signature Algorithm (ECDSA)
- The Edwards-curve Digital Signature Algorithm (EdDSA)

To implement the curve
- The users must agree on the domain (the shape of the curve). In general, the requirement is to select several points on the curve
    - **P**, the field size
    - **a** and **b**, which define the equation
    - **G**, the base of the curve
    - **n**, such that **nG = O**, where **n** is the **O** is the point at infinity of the curve
    - **h** where $h = \left(\frac{1}{n}\right)|E(F_p)|$, and where **h** is an integer between **1** and **4**
- The users can choose a random elliptic curve and calculate the above points, choose the points randomly and then generate a curve, or use a standard curve. It is faster to use a standard curve because calculations are complicated and time-consuming
    - FIPS PUB 186-4 lists several standard curves for use by government encryption methods
- Key size
    - The field should be twice the size of the encryption key size. A 256-bit key requires a curve that is 2^{512}
- Some curves can be calculated faster than others
    - Projective coordinates can be used to add different points on a curve without using inversion
    - Fast reduction can be accomplished if **p** is a pseudo-Mersenne prime, where **p** is approximately 2^d, or p = d² -1

Security risks

- **Side channel attack**
  - In Elliptic Curve Cryptography, a different operation is used to calculate addition and multiplication, each of which uses different amounts of power. A hacker could monitor the processor to detect the power consumption and timing to determine the curve parameters.
  - A side channel attack can be prevented by using an Edwards curve. The Edwards curve allows addition and multiplication in the same operation.

- **Backdoor**
  - Some have alleged backdoors are present in some of the number generators used to create elliptic curves
  - It may be better to generate your own curve, if you can verify that it is secure

Weak/Deprecated Algorithms

A **Weak Algorithm** should never be used. A Weak Algorithm is one that can easily be broken. A software developer should take careful to encode algorithms in a way that allows for their quick replacement when security vulnerabilities are discovered. In fact, an algorithm should be changed before they are deprecated (once new, stronger, proven algorithms are available).

A deprecated algorithm is one that has been officially replaced with a newer one.

Examples of weak algorithms
- MD5
- SHA-1
- 1024-bit RSA
- 160-bit elliptic curves
- DES
- Various homemade encryption algorithms. Do not make your own algorithm.

Key Exchange

A **Key Exchange** is a way for two people to exchange keys. Alice and Bob want to talk securely. Alice and Bob need to exchange encryption keys over the internet, but the internet is not secure. How can Alice and Bob securely exchange their keys, so that the further communication between them is encrypted? How can they be sure that the key is not stolen or intercepted?

There are several algorithms

- **Diffie-Helman Key Exchange**. This allows two people to exchange keys even when there is an eavesdropper who sees all their communications.
- **Public Key Infrastructure**. A certification authority holds the public keys for all users. A limitation of PKI is that there is no way to verify that the central authority has provided the key corresponding to the user with whom you want to speak to (a malicious authority could substitute their own key so that they can intercept your communications).
- **Web of Trust or PGP**. PGP allows two users to directly exchange keys without the use of a CA.
- **Quantum Key Exchange**. Quantum Key Exchange uses the quantum theory that an observation/measurement of an object in a quantum state modifies the object. If an eavesdropper observes the key exchange, the key will be modified, and the parties exchanging the key will be notified.

Digital Signature

A **digital signature** proves that a specific person signed a specific message. A valid signature proves that the message was created by the signer and that it was not modified in transit.

An electronic signature is not legally accepted in all countries. Some documents or transactions may require a "wet signature" in ink.

A digital signature has the following
- A key generation algorithm
- A signing algorithm
- A verification algorithm

As before, Alice would like to provide Bob with a signed document.
- Alice selects a private key
- Alice uses the private key to create a public key, which is published and available
- Alice uses the private key to sign the document
- For the key to be valid, it must be impossible to generate a signature without knowing the private key
- Alice sends the signed document to Bob
- Bob retrieves Alice's public key and uses it to verify her signature

Typically, Alice will not sign the entire document. She will generate a hash of the document and then sign the hash.
- It is more efficient to calculate a signature on a hash than on the entire document
- The document may be too large to sign, in which case it must be broken into separate portions, each of which must be signed separately
- The signature algorithm may not be able to sign/perform calculations on the entire content of the document, especially if it contains attachments, photographs, or other types of data. Some signature algorithms only work on text.

How to forge a digital signature
- Choose a random signature
- Use the verification algorithm to generate a different message that could correspond to the signature (or the hash that could correspond to the signature) – a collision. This is practically impossible when the users are using a strong hash.
- There are three types of forgery
  - Existential forgery
    - Create a message and signature pair that was not created by the legitimate signer

- This is considered the weakest hacking method. An algorithm that prevents existential forgery is practically unforgeable.
  - Selective forgery
    - Create a message and signature pair for a pre-selected message
  - Universal forgery
    - Create a valid signature for any message
    - This is the strongest hacking method

Other ways to forge a digital signature – What You See is What You Sign
- The security of the computing platform is more important than the security of the key
- A user is signing what he sees on the screen, but an untrusted application can display a different document than what is saved
- Therefore, the user's signature can be applied to a fake document
- The user is not actually inspecting the bits that are signed (or may not inspect the document after it has been saved)

Benefits of a digital signature
- A user can prove that the document was signed by the person who claimed to sign it
- A user can prove that the document was not changed during transmission
- The signer cannot later deny that they signed the document

The digital signature algorithm
- The algorithm must be secure
- The users must properly use their signatures
- The private key must be kept private
  - Place the key on a smart card
  - Only use your digital signature with trusted applications
- The owner of the public key must be verifiable

There are many laws related to signatures. Originally, a facsimile of a signed document was accepted like the original, but an e-mailed/scanned document was not. Governments have passed laws requiring the acceptance of digital/electronic signature.

For example, Title 21 CFR Part 11 requires the government to accept electronic signatures.

An electronic signature could be a printed name or an image of a signature. It is not necessarily a digital signature, nor is it necessarily cryptographically secure.

The Electronic Signatures in Global and National Commerce Act or ESIGN Act allows electronic signatures to be used for transactions that affect interstate or foreign commerce. Consumers have the right to opt out of an electronic signature requirement.

Diffusion

Consider a text that needs to be encrypted with a cryptographic key. The result is a cyphertext. It should be difficult for the ciphertext to be reversed into plaintext by an eavesdropper.

In **diffusion**, the relationship between the plaintext and the cyphertext is not clear or cannot be determined easily. If a single bit in the plaintext is changed, then on average, half of the bits in the cyphertext should change. If a single bit in the cyphertext is changed, then on average, half of the bits in the plaintext should change.

Confusion

In **confusion**, the key and the text are not related, or at least, do not appear to be related. It is difficult to determine the key from the cyphertext. If a bit in the key is changed, most of the cyphertext is changed.

Collision

As mentioned previously, a **collision** is when two input values produce the same hash value. For any given hash value, there is a limited set of outputs but an infinite set of inputs. Therefore, mathematically, there are an infinite set of inputs that can result in each output.

By definition, a collision is when plaintexts m_1 and m_2 exist such that **hash(m_1) = hash(m_2).**

Consider that Alice created a document and plans to send it to Bob. Alice previously hashed the document and signed the hash. Mallory wants to trick Bob. Mallory will create a different document, which has an identical hash to Alice's document and attach Alice's signature to it, and then send it to Bob.

It would be difficult to create a meaningful document that also has the same hash as the original. Mallory may need to try millions or billions of different combinations of documents until she finds one that matches Alice's hash. If the hash function was weak (if diffusion or confusion did not apply), Mallory would be able to tweak the document until it matched the hash.

Modifications to a collision attack
- Birthday Attack
    - Mallory wants Bob to sign Document B (the fraudulent contract)
    - She first creates Document A (the legitimate contract)
    - Mallory creates different versions of Document A, all of which look like the original, but are slightly different. The changes may include white space, commas, and other hidden formatting.
    - Mallory then creates different versions of Document B
    - She calculates the hash for each version of Document A and Document B until she finds a version of Document A that has the same hash as a version of Document B
    - She presents this version of Document A for Bob to sign
    - She then copies Bob's signature onto the version of Document B with the same hash
    - Bob can protect himself by
        - Keeping a copy of the document he signed
        - Making random changes to the document before he signs it
        - Using a large enough signature algorithm such that the hash calculations become impossible
- Chosen Prefix Collision
    - A hacker would append two prefixes, p_1, p_2 to the documents m_1 and m_2 (which have different hashes), such that the resulting documents have the same hash
    - Mathematically speaking, such that **hash($p_1 \parallel m_1$) = hash($p_2 \parallel m_2$)**
- Conditional Formatting

o Word and PDF documents can employ conditional formatting where certain text can display or not display depending on the location of the file, the date/time, or other attributes
o A hacker can insert hidden content into the document
o The victim would sign the document while the text is hidden, and then in the future, the hidden text would appear

Steganography

As mentioned previously, Encryption converts plaintext data so that it can appear in the open without being read.

A **Steganography Tool** does not encrypt data but hides it instead. If an eavesdropper located the hidden data, he or she would be able to read it. For added security, the hidden data should also be encrypted.

Steganography is used when encryption or encryption alone cannot protect the data. For example, a user is in a country where transmitting encrypted data is illegal or would raise suspicions but needs to send a secure message.

The steganography carrier
- The carrier is the medium carrying the hidden message. It could be a phone call, an e-mail, or a file transmission. The carrier is modified to carry the hidden message. It is important that
  - The carrier is much larger than the message. If the message increases the size of the carrier substantially, then eavesdroppers will notice that the carrier has been modified.
  - The carrier must be unique. If the carrier is publicly available, then the modified carrier can be compared against the original.
- Data can be split among multiple carriers
- Carrier engine. A carrier engine uses an algorithm to inject hidden data into legitimate data. The types of algorithms include adaptive substitution, frequency space manipulation, injection, generation, and metadata substitution.

Obfuscation

Obfuscation is the method of hiding data so that it cannot be read by humans.

In programming, machine code is not readable by humans and any code complied into machine code (such as C++) is automatically obfuscated.

Code which require interpreters (such as JavaScript, HTML, and Perl) must be obfuscated through various built in functions. Obfuscated code can quickly be reverse-engineered.

Stream vs Block

A Stream Cipher uses two algorithms
- An encryption algorithm
- A decryption algorithm

When presented with a plaintext, the algorithm encrypts or decrypts the plaintext one bit at a time. The encryption algorithm and decryption algorithms must be in sync. Some stream ciphers can automatically resync.

Consider that the key flows in a stream, and the plaintext flows in a stream, and these two streams combine to result in a ciphertext. A stream cipher is necessary when the length of the plaintext is not known, such as a Wi-Fi connection or a live video.

For the Stream to be secure
- The stream cipher must not reuse keys. If two ciphertexts are sent, which are encrypted with the same key, then the two messages can be compared to identify the key.

  $E(A)$ xor $E(B)$ = (A xor C) xor (B xor C) = A xor B xor C xor C = A xor B
- The keystream must have a large enough period (non-repeating portion)
- It must not be possible to identify the key from the keystream
- The key stream must not be distinguishable from random noise

A Block Cipher uses two algorithms
- An encryption algorithm
- A decryption algorithm

A block cipher encrypts plaintext of a specific length (the length of the block). If the plaintext is longer than the block, it must be broken into fragments that are the length of the block. The algorithm is then applied to each fragment. If the last portion plaintext is shorter than the block, then it must be padded.

There are a number of block ciphers
- Iterated Block Cipher
- Substitution-Permutation Network
- Feistel Cipher
- Lai-Massey Cipher

Security risks

- Brute-force Attack. By obtaining multiple blocks of ciphertexts and comparing them, the key can be determined. The larger the block, the harder it is to determine the key. But the larger the block, the more inefficient the algorithm.
- Integral Cryptanalysis. Integral Cryptanalysis compares multiple sets of plaintext blocks, where most of the value of the blocks are identical.
- Linear Cryptanalysis. In Linear Cryptanalysis, equations of plaintext, cyphertext, and key bits are created. These equations are used with pairs of plaintext/ciphertext to obtain the key bits.
- Differential Cryptanalysis. Differential Cryptanalysis is where the hacker obtains sets of plaintexts and ciphertexts. The hacker then compares the plaintext and ciphertext to determine the key.

The list of known algorithms
- Lucifer
- IDEA
- RC5
- AES
  - Advanced Encryption Standard
  - Used worldwide by many organizations and the United States government
  - 192, and 256-bit keys can be used to protect Top Secret data
  - There are several side-channel attacks that can be used to break AES
- Blowfish.
  - Blowfish is a public domain algorithm
  - Blowfish is still secure in most applications, but it is recommended to switch to Twofish.
- Twofish
  - Twofish is a public domain algorithm

Key Strength

The **key strength** is related to the key length. How hard is it to discover the key?

The longer the key, the stronger the encryption. Very long keys are not always practical, because they can require a large amount of computing power necessary to encrypt or decrypt the data.

As computing power increases, longer keys are required to protect the same data.

Session Keys

Consider that Alice and Bob want to have regular conversations. They should not use the same key to encrypt their messages each time. When an eavesdropper collects encrypted data, he can subject it to cryptanalysis. The more data he has (that is encrypted with a single key) the more likely he will be able to detect a pattern and decrypt it. The larger the quantity of data that is encrypted with a single key, the more likely it is that it can be decrypted.

Alice and Bob could use an asymmetric key, but this would require a substantial amount of computing power. Therefore, instead, they can choose a master key, which is asymmetric. They use the master key to generate a symmetric key.

Each time Alice and Bob communicate, they generate a new symmetric key. The symmetric key is known as the **session key**, and it uses less computing power than the asymmetric key.

The Session Key must be chosen randomly, so that it cannot be guessed.

Ephemeral Key

An **ephemeral key** is one that is used for a short period of time. The key may be used only once or multiple times within a session. When used only once, an ephemeral key provides Perfect Forward Secrecy.

Secret Algorithm

A **Secret Algorithm** is symmetric. The key that is used to encrypt the data is the same as the key that is used to decrypt the data.

A secret algorithm can be used only when all the parties can be trusted.

Consider that Alice and Bob need to communicate.
- Alice and Bob agree on a key
- Alice must be able to transmit the key to Bob; she must do so in person, because sending it over the internet would not be secure
- Alice uses the key to encrypt messages, and sends them to Bob
- Bob uses the same key to decrypt the messages
- If Eve intercepts a message, she would not be able to view the plaintext unless she had the key
- Consider now that Alice would like to communicate with Carol. Alice and Carol should agree on a different key than the one that Alice and Bob agreed upon. If they were to use the same key, then Bob could intercept the messages and view them (which Alice and Carol do not want)

Prior to using an encryption algorithm, an organization must be able to verify its internal functions. If they cannot understand or test the algorithm, they will not be able to verify that it is secure or that it does not contain a backdoor.

Data-In-Transit

Data-In-Transit is data that is being transported. It is also known as Data in Motion or Data in Flight. Data in transit must always be encrypted, because it travels over a public network. Data-In-Transit can be secured through TLS (Transport Layer Security).

Data-At-Rest

Data-at-Rest is data that is stored. It might be on a server, laptop computer, mobile phone, or other computing device.

Data-at-Rest should be encrypted in case the computing device is lost or stolen. Physical security measures should also protect the computing device. Encrypting data at rest will consume additional computing power.

- Protect data with multiple layers of encryption
- Encrypt databases and then encrypt the underlying database files if possible

Data can also be tokenized

- Consider a system that needs to process sensitive data
- Sensitive data such as credit card numbers, passwords, and birth dates can be replaced with non-sensitive substitutes
- The type and length of the data does not change, so that algorithms and databases that are sensitive to type and length are not affected
- Tokenization uses less computing power than encryption

Data-In-Use

Data-In-Use is data that is currently being processed. Data in use is typically stored in the RAM of a computing device.

It is possible to obtain the contents of memory through a cold boot attack. Some computing devices can provide full memory encryption, but it is not common. Virtual servers can provide full memory encryption, because the virtual machine file itself can be encrypted.

Consider however, that data in use can be compromised through the analog hole. Malware, unauthorized users, and rogue employees can expose the data to unauthorized individuals regardless of the type of encryption in place. Encryption does not stop a person from taking a photograph of a computer monitor.

Most processor manufacturers incorporate features that protect data in use. Examples include
- Intel Software Guard Extensions (SGX)
- AMD Secure Encrypted Virtualization

Random/Pseudo-Random Number Generation

A true **Random Number Generator** does not exist, because computers are logical devices. However, random number generation is important for encryption algorithms. If a hacker were able to predict the number generated, he could compromise the algorithm.

A true Random Number Generator can be created by measuring physical/natural processes, such as thermal noise, radio noise, or radioactivity. The observation of quantum data is considered the best way to collect random data. This may be known as a Hardware Random Number Generator, but the hardware device that observes the random data may introduce bias into the collection method.

A Pseudorandom number generator (PRNG) is a computing algorithm that generates random numbers. The numbers are not truly random because they are generated from a seed value. Many PRNGs have failed.

A **cryptographically secure pseudorandom number generator (CSPRNG) or cryptographic pseudorandom number generator (CPRNG)** is one that can be used in cryptography. To be a valid CSPRNG

- The CSPRNG should pass the "next-bit test". Given any number of bits of a randomly generated sequence, there should not be an algorithm that can predict the next bit (or any other future bit) with a success rate of at least 50%
- If the CSPRNG's current state is compromised, it should be impossible to predict any future or previous states.

Most PRNGs will fail the above tests. Even though a PRNG appears to be random, reverse-engineering and statistical analysis will be able to crack it.

Some papers reported that the NSA placed a kleptographic backdoor in the Dual_EC_DRBG PRNG, which was published as NIST SP 800-90A. RSA received a $10 million payment from the NSA to continue using the Dual_EC_DRBG PRNG.

There are several good CPRNGs
- Yarrow algorithm
- ChaCha20 algorithm
- Fortuna algorithm
- Microsoft's CrytpGenRandom function

The CPRNGs that have been standardized are
- *NIST SP 800-90A Rev.1 (Dual_EC_DRBG PRNG)*
- *ANSI X9.17-1985 Appendix C*

- ***ANSI X9.62-2005, Annex D***

It is likely that backdoors have been introduced into many other PRNGs and CSPRNG. Therefore, the most secure approach is to create a CSPRNG that observes a random, natural process.

Key Stretching

Key Stretching is a technique to make a weak key stronger. A human might choose a short password. The hacker would use a brute force attack to break the password.

The key is made longer by being inserted into an algorithm. The algorithm outputs a stretched key (known as the enhanced key). The enhanced key cannot be broken via brute force.

The hacker would have to attempt to brute force the enhanced key. The hacker would not be able to brute force the original password because he would have to calculate the enhanced key from each one first, which would consume more computing power than he has.

Implementation vs Algorithm Selection

The type of algorithm selected must be based on

- The types of data being encrypted
- **The crypto service provider**
  - A software library that provides cryptographic functions
  - Instead of manually writing code to implement a cryptographic function in an application (which may introduce security vulnerabilities), a developer can incorporate a pre-existing library
  - The library takes a plaintext input and outputs a ciphertext output or vice versa. The developer does not need to worry about the internal function of the library.
  - The library can be replaced when newer or more secure libraries are made available
- **Crypto module**
  - A crypto module is a physical device that performs encryption and decryption
  - The module may have specially designed hardware that is specifically suited to perform the encryption and decryption functions
  - An example is an AES engine in the Apple iPhone. This engine is a physical processor that performs encryption and decryption, and no other function. It is specially designed to remove encryption and decryption workloads from the iPhone's main processor.

Perfect Forward Secrecy

In **perfect forward secrecy**, a session key will not be compromised, even if the server private key is compromised.

Recall that the private key is used to generate additional session keys. A new key is created for each session. If a session key is compromised, only the data secured by that session key is compromised.

With forward secrecy, if a future key is compromised, then data secured in previous sessions is not compromised.

Consider Alice and Bob
- Alice and Bob generate an asymmetric public and private key pair as mentioned before
- They exchange the keys
- Alice and Bob generate a session key from the asymmetric key
- Alice symmetrically encrypts a message using the session key
- Bob decrypts Alice's message with the session key
- Each time Alice and Bob need to send a new message, they create a new session key
- If a session key is compromised, only the message encrypted by that message is compromised. Previous messages and future messages cannot be decrypted with the compromised session key.

Security Through Obscurity

Security through obscurity is a concept where the security architecture is hidden or camouflaged.

Security through obscurity is not a good security mechanism. It is like hiding a key under a doormat. The underlying system components were built by humans, and those humans may leave the organization with knowledge of how it works and can later compromise the system.

Common Use Cases

Common use cases of encryption

- **Low Power Devices**
  - Phones and other mobile devices have limited computing power. Computing power consumes battery life. By creating more efficient encryption algorithms, these devices can be secured without consuming substantial system resources or slowing them down.

- **Low Latency**
  - A low latency application is one where the data must be transmitted and received in almost real time. An example is a live two-way video stream. If the encryption and decryption processes take a substantial amount of time, the video stream will experience latency and the user experience will suffer.
  - A stream cipher can encrypt and decrypt a low latency application.

- **High Resiliency**
  - A high resiliency system continues to function after experiencing a disruption
  - Algorithms must be capable of operating even with parts of the ciphertext are lost

- **Supporting Confidentiality**
  - Confidentiality is where the data that is sent is only seen by the sender and the recipient

- **Supporting Integrity**
  - Integrity ensures that the data is not modified while in transit
  - A hash function protects data integrity

- **Supporting Obfuscation**
  - An obfuscated object is one that is hidden so that it is not readily visible
  - Obfuscation is not a secure method of protecting data but may be used when other options are limited

- **Supporting Authentication**
  - Authentication verifies that the person who claimed to send the message is the person who sent the message; that is, that the identity of the sender can be verified

- **Supporting Non-Repudiation**
  - Non-repudiation ensures that the sender cannot later deny sending the message
  - If a message is digitally signed, it is assumed that it was sent by the signer

- A user should not rely on a message that does not support non-repudiation

- **Resource vs Security Constraints**
  - The organization must weigh the resource requirements of each available algorithm against its benefits
  - In general, the more secure the algorithm, the longer it will take to encrypt and decrypt the data
  - We want to encrypt data in a way that protects it for a long time, but we also don't want to impact the user experience, and we do not want to spend money on expensive encryption hardware. We must find a balance.

6.2 Explain cryptography algorithms and their basic characteristics

- *Symmetric Algorithms*
  - *AES*
  - *DES*
  - *3DES*
  - *RC4*
  - *Blowfish/Twofish*
- *Cipher Modes*
  - *CBC*
  - *GCM*
  - *ECB*
  - *CTR*
  - *Streams vs Block*
- *Asymmetric Algorithms*
  - *RSA*
  - *DSA*
  - *Diffie-Hellman*
    - *Groups*
    - *DHE*
    - *ECDHE*
  - *Elliptic Curve*
  - *PGP/GPG*
- *Hashing Algorithms*
  - *MD5*
  - *SHA*
  - *HMAC*
  - *RIPEMD*
- *Key Stretching Algorithms*
  - *BCRYPT*
  - *PBKDF2*
- *Obfuscation*
  - *XOR*
  - *ROT13*
  - *Substitution Ciphers*

Symmetric Algorithms

There are many symmetric algorithms in use, as mentioned previously.

- **AES**
  - **Advanced Encryption Standard**
  - Used worldwide by many organizations and by the United States government
  - 192 and 256-bit keys can be used to protect Top Secret data
  - Replaced DES
  - The algorithm uses 10, 12, or 14 rounds of encryption to convert the plaintext to ciphertext
  - The algorithm uses a 2D matrix which shifts the rows and columns to generate the ciphertext
  - There are several side-channel attacks that can be used to break AES, but no known ways to cryptographically break AES

- **DES**
  - **Data Encryption Standard**
  - The algorithm is a block cipher
  - The key length is 56 bits (64 bits with 8 bits for parity)
  - DES uses a mathematical function known as the Feistel function, which uses expansions and permutations
  - Can be broken
    - Brute force attacks on a 56-bit key length can be broken in 48 hours with a set of computers that cost less than $10,000
    - Differential cryptanalysis
    - Linear cryptanalysis can be used if some plaintexts are known

- **3DES**
  - **Triple Data Encryption Algorithm**
  - There are three options
    - 3DES uses three independent keys. Each key is 56-bits, but the effective key size is 112-bits.
    - 3DES uses two independent keys. Key One and Key Two are independent, and Key Three is the same as Key One. The effective key size is 112-bits.
    - 3DES uses one key. The three keys are identical. This option is no longer considered secure.
  - 3DES can be broken with a Meet in the Middle Attack.
    - Consider that the method for encrypting a file is to operate an encryption algorithm with a key

- For added security, the encryption algorithm can be run multiple times, each time with a different key
- The number of attempts required to break the algorithm would increase exponentially
- If intermediate results of the encryption method are stored, then a Meet in the Middle Attack can be used to find keys that match a forward function from the plaintext to the intermediate and from the ciphertext to the intermediate

- **RC4**
  - RC4 or **Rivest Cipher 4** was a stream cipher
  - It was simple and fast
  - RC1, RC2, RC3, RC5, and RC6 were also created
  - The RC4 cipher should not be used because of the many security vulnerabilities
    - The RC4 produces a biased output; since the distribution of the output is not uniform, with enough ciphertext the original text can be determined
    - Fluhrer, Mantin and Shamir found that the first few bytes of the ciphertext are not random. An analysis of many messages can be used to find the key.

- **Blowfish**.
  - Blowfish is a public domain algorithm
  - Blowfish was a block cipher with a key length that could range from 32-bits to 448-bits
  - Blowfish used a 64-bit block size, which could be broken in a birthday attack
  - Blowfish is still secure in most applications, but it is recommended to switch to Twofish.

- **Twofish**
  - Twofish is a public domain algorithm that succeeded Blowfish
  - Twofish used 128-bit block sizes
  - It has not been broken, but then again, it is not widely used, so very few efforts have been made to break it

Cipher Modes

Since no random generator is truly random, biases are introduced into the encrypted data. The cipher mode attempts to hide the biases. Cipher modes apply to block ciphers.

There are several modes, but the two that are recommended are CBC and CTR.

- **ECB – Electronic Code Book**. With ECB, the plaintext is cut into blocks. Each block is encrypted separately and decrypted separately. This is the weakest form of encryption because repeating patterns are introduced into the blocks.

- **CBC – Cipher Block Chaining**. The plaintext is cut into blocks. An initialization vector is added to the first block. Each plaintext block is XORed with the previous ciphertext blocks before being encrypted. Therefore, each block depends upon the value of all the previous blocks,.

  CBC is the most common method. It is slow because encryption and decryption must take place sequentially. If there is a large amount of plaintext or ciphertext, it cannot be encrypted/decrypted in parallel with a powerful processor.

- **PCBC – Propagating Cipher Block Chaining**. PCBC is the same as CBC except that each plaintext block is XORed with the previous plaintext block and ciphertext block before being encrypted.

- **CFB – Cipher Feedback**. In CFB, the block cipher is converted into a self-synchronizing stream cipher. A single byte must be encrypted at a time.

- **OFB – Output Feedback**. In OFB, a block cipher is converted into a stream cipher. The keystream blocks are XORed with the plaintext blocks to obtain ciphertext.

- **CTR – Counter Mode**. In CTR, the block cipher is converted into a stream cipher. Each keystream block is generated by encrypting the value of a counter. Blocks can be encrypted in parallel.

Asymmetric Algorithms

There are multiple asymmetric algorithms in place

- **RSA**
  - Also known as **Rivest–Shamir–Adleman**
  - $(m^e)^d = m \pmod n$
  - How the RSA key is generated
    - Choose two prime numbers **p** and **q**. These prime numbers are private
    - Compute **n = pq,** where **n** becomes the modulus. **n** is the part of the public key
    - Calculate $\lambda(n)$, which is kept secret.
    - Choose an integer e such that $1 < e < \lambda(n)$ and $\gcd(e, \lambda(n)) = 1$, **e** becomes part of the public key
    - Calculate **d** as $d \equiv e-1 \pmod{\lambda(n)}$, where **d** is kept private
    - Thus, **n** and **e** are public, and **p, q**, and **d** are private
    - The effect is that it is easy to multiply two prime numbers (private key) but difficult to factor them (public key)
    - The public key can be distributed, and the private key is kept secret.
  - Alice wants to send a message to Bob. Bob publishes his public key. Alice uses Bob's public key to encrypt messages to Bob. Bob uses his private key to decrypt messages.
  - RSA Security Risks
    - The RSA key can be cracked if the prime numbers **p** and **q** are small
    - RSA can be cracked if a message is sent to multiple recipients who have the same **e**, but different **p, q**, and **n** values. The Chinese Remainder Theorem can be used.
    - The multiplicative property applies. $m_1^e m_2^e \equiv (m_1 m_2)^e \pmod n$. A hacker can ask a private key holder to decrypt a ciphertext where $c' = cr^e \pmod n$. The hacker can use it to determine the value of $c = m^e \pmod n$.
    - Coppersmith's attack on RSA
    - Faulty Key Generation. If **d** is not large enough, and **p** is between **q** and **2q**, then **d** can be calculated from the public key
    - Random Number Generation. If the **p** and **q** are not selected at random, then the **p** and **q** can be guessed. Many embedded applications have the values of **p** and **q** hardcoded.

- **DSA**
  - **Digital Signature Algorithm**
  - DSA uses a public key and a private key. The private key is used to generate a digital signature.

- o The key is generated from several parameters
  - Cryptographic Hash Function, **H** (typically SHA-1 or SHA-2)
  - Key Length **L**
  - Modulus length **N** such that **N < L** and **N < |H|**
  - N-bit prime **q** and L-bit prime **p**, such that **p-1** is some multiple of **q**
  - Random integer **h** from {2 to p -2}
  - Calculate **g** from $g = h^{\frac{p-1}{q}}$
  - The result is **p**, **q**, and **g**. All users of the system receive these parameters.
  - For each user, choose integer **x** from the set {1 to q – 1}
  - Calculate **y = g^x mod p**
  - **X** becomes the private key and **y** is the public key
- o A user can sign their message with **x** by calculating
  - **R = g^k mod p**
  - **s := (k^{-1}(H(m) + xr)) mod q**
  - The signature is **(r, s)**
- o A user can verify that the signature is valid by using **y**
  - Verify that **0 < r < q** and **0 < s < q**
  - Calculate **w := s^{-1} mod q**
  - Calculate **u$_1$:= H(m) w mod q**
  - Calculate **u$_2$:= r w mod q**
  - Calculate **v := (g^{u1} y^{u2} mod p) mod q**
  - If **v = r**, then the signature is valid

- **Diffie-Hellman Groups**
  - o Diffie-Hellman is an algorithm for exchanging keys
  - o How it works
    - Alice and Bob select a modulus and base
    - Alice chooses a secret integer **a**, and calculates **A = g^a mod p**, which she sends to Bob
    - Bob chooses a secret integer **b**, and calculates **B = g^b mod p**, which he sends to Alice
    - Alice calculates **s = B^a mod p**
    - Bob calculates **s = A^b mod p**
    - Alice and Bob have the same result, which is the shared secret, but neither of them had to share their secret.
  - o Diffie-Hellman can work with more than two parties
  - o Diffie-Hellman is secure against eavesdroppers
  - o Ephemeral Diffie-Hellman (DHE) can also be used
    - If Eve sat in between Alice and Bob, she could perform a Man in the Middle attack during the key generation

- Eve would intercept the values that Alice and Bob sent to each other and change them. In other words, Eve pretends that she is Bob to Alice and Alice to Bob. Bob thinks he is speaking with Alice, but he is talking to Eve, and Alice thinks she is talking to Bob, but she is talking to Eve.
        - Eve could cause Alice and Bob to generate different secrets
        - Then Eve would decrypt and encrypt the messages that are sent
        - To prevent this, a different key is generated for each session
        - Each time Alice and Bob connect, they generate a new set of keys. This is known as Ephemeral Diffie-Hellman
    - Elliptic-Curve Diffie-Hellman (ECDH) is another key generation method
        - ECDH works with elliptic curve keys

- **Elliptic Curve**
    - Mentioned earlier
    - More efficient than other methods

- **PGP/GPG**
    - PGP or **Pretty Good Privacy**
    - PGP uses a web of trust
    - Key features
        - Fingerprint. A public key can be shortened to a short fingerprint. A user can publish a fingerprint of their key.
        - Compatibility. As PGP changes, new features are added. Users who communicate over PGP must ensure that they are using the same version.
        - Confidentiality. PGP can be used to send confidential messages.
            - The sender generates a one-time symmetric key, known as the session key
            - The sender sends the message and the session key to the recipient
            - To protect the session key, the sender encrypts it with the recipient's public key
        - Digital Signature
            - PGP can be used to prove that a message has not been modified
            - PGP can be used to prove that a specific person sent the message
            - Like other functions, PGP calculates a hash of the message and then digitally signs the hash
        - Certificates
            - Public keys must be distributed in a way so that it is possible to verify that a given public key belongs to a specific individual. This is known as the web of trust.

- A public key may be digitally signed by a third party to confirm that it belongs to a specific person
- A trust signature can be used to create a certification authority. The trust signature belongs to a person who can sign other keys.
- A certificate can be revoked if it becomes compromised. A certificate can also contain an expiry date
- Security Quality
  - There is currently no known method of breaking PGP
  - PGP is subject to regular updates, but none of the algorithms in use have been broken
- History
  - PGP was developed by Phil Zimmermann in 1991
  - Exporting munitions without a license is illegal
  - Encryption technology with keys greater than 40 bits was considered a munition
  - Therefore, by putting the PGP source code on the internet, Phil Zimmermann exported a weapon without a license
  - He was never charged, but he was subject to a three-year criminal investigation
  - In Junger v. Daley, the United States Circuit Court of Appeals for the Sixth Circuit ruled that software source code was protected by the first amendment. In other words, code is speech.
  - In Bernstein v. United States, the United States Circuit Court of Appeals for the Ninth Circuit ruled that software source code was protected by the first amendment. The opinion was withdrawn, and the case was dismissed due to a technicality.
- PGP Itself is not easy to implement. PGP software applications for enterprise are sold by the PGP Corporation, which produces products such as PGP Desktop, PGP E-mail, and PGP Whole Disk Encryption.
- An Open Source PGP JavaScript library is available to implement in web applications
- GPG or GNU Privacy Guard is an application that uses PGP
  - RSA, ElGamal, DSA, 3DES, IDEA, Blowfish, Twofish, AES, MD5, and SHA-1 are all supported algorithms

Hashing Algorithms

There are many hash functions
- **MD5**
  - **Message Digest 5**
  - This hash function has serious security vulnerabilities and should not be used, but continues to be used
  - MD5 is subject to collision attacks. It is easy to find two different inputs that generate the same output.
  - Used to prove that a file transmission occurred successfully. Prior to sending a file, the MD5 hash is calculated. The file is sent along with the MD5 hash. The recipient calculates the MD5 hash on the received file. If the hash value received from the sender matches the hash value that the recipient calculated, then the recipient knows that the file was received correctly.
  - MD5 is also used to store passwords in a way that cannot be reversed
  - MD5 converts inputs of different lengths into hashes that are 128 bits long
  - The hashed value is also known as a message digest

- **SHA**
  - SHA or **SHA-1** is a **Secure Hash Algorithm**
  - SHA-1 is used by TLS, SSL, PGP, SSH, and IPSec. It has replaced MD5
  - SHA-1
    - Produces a 160-bit hash
    - Used by the government to protect sensitive, unclassified material
    - Computing power to find a collision can be obtained for less than $100,000
    - In the process of being replaced by SHA-2
  - SHA-2
    - Produces a 256-bit or 512-bit hash
    - Used by Bitcoin
    - SHA-2 is still in use and considered secure
  - SHA-3
    - Produces a 256-bit or 512-bit hash
    - SHA-3 is not designed to replace SHA-2 as SHA-2 is still considered secure
    - Instead, SHA-3 is designed as an alternative that is available should SHA-2 be compromised in the future (and it will be!)
    - SHA-3 uses a sponge construction. Data is absorbed, transformed, and then pushed out.

- **HMAC**
  - HMAC is also known as hash-based message authentication code

- HMAC is a framework, not an encryption algorithm; any hash function can be used (such as SHA-1)
- It is used to authenticate a message and verify its integrity. It does not encrypt a message.
- Procedure
  - A secret key is obtained and used to generate two keys, an inner key and an outer key
  - The message is broken into blocks which are hashed
  - The first hash produces an inner hash using the message and the inner key
  - The second hash produces a final HMAC code from the first hash and the second key
  - The message is sent along with the hash
  - A recipient will calculate the hash again using the secret key and compare it with the hash that was received. If the hashes match, then the recipient can confirm that the correct message was received.

- **RIPEMD**
  - RIPEMD stands for Race Integrity Primitives Evaluation Message Digest
  - RIPE Message Digest is a family of hash functions (RIPEMD, RIPEMD-128, RIPEMD-160, RIPEMD-256, and RIPEMD-320), each of which produces a different hash length
  - The original RIPEMD produced a 128-bit hash but was affected by collisions
  - RIPEMD-160 is the most common

Key Stretching Algorithms

There are several key stretching (password hashing) algorithms

- **BCRYPT**
    - Used by many Linux distributions
    - The password is converted to a 184-bit value
    - The function iterates thousands or even millions of times
    - BCRYPT adds a 128-bit salt

- **PDKDF2**
    - **Password-Based Key Derivation Function 2**
    - Superseded PBDKF1, which could produce keys up to 160 bits long
    - The function iterates multiple times, between 1000 and 100,000 times
    - PDKF2 is easier to brute force than BCRYPT because it uses very little RAM; a specific processor or GPU can be tuned to brute force a PDFK2

In the forward mode, running an algorithm millions of cycles to stretch a password does not occupy much computing power (a few seconds). When attempting to brute force the algorithm in reverse, a hacker's computer is slowed down by a factor of 1000 to 1,000,000 and will not be successful.

Obfuscation

Recall that an obfuscation algorithm does not actually encrypt the plaintext, it merely hides it. There are several obfuscation algorithms in place, but an obfuscation algorithm should never be used by itself.

- **XOR**. XOR is a cipher that is also known as modulus 2 addition.
    - XOR produces a ciphertext by adding a value to each bit in the plaintext string. To decrypt the ciphertext, the XOR must be reversed.
    - XOR does not require much computing power
    - XOR can be easy to break if part of the plaintext message can be guessed. Then frequency analysis can be applied to the remainder of the ciphertext.
    - If the key is random and at least as long as the plaintext, then it would be impossible to reverse with cryptanalysis. This key would be considered a one-time pad.

- **ROT13**
    - ROT13 is a substitution cipher, where each letter is replaced by a letter that is 13 characters away
    - For example, the letter A would be replaced by the letter N
    - ROT13 was used in online forums to hide offensive text but certainly cannot be expected to provide any security

- **Substitution Ciphers**
    - A substitution cipher is one where a letter or character is substituted with another letter or character
    - A table exists that maps the plaintext letter with the ciphertext letter
    - The table can be used to reverse the cipher
    - An eavesdropper can attempt to recreate the table through frequency analysis

6.3 Given a scenario, install and configure wireless security settings
- *Cryptographic Protocols*
  - *WPA*
  - *WPA2*
  - *CCMP*
  - *TKIP*
- *Authentication Protocols*
  - *EAP*
  - *PEAP*
  - *EAP-FAST*
  - *EAP-TLS*
  - *EAP-TTLS*
  - *IEEE 802.1X*
  - *RADIUS Federation*
- *Methods*
  - *PSK vs Enterprise vs Open*
  - *WPS*
  - *Captive Portals*

Cryptographic Protocols

There are several Wi-Fi encryption protocols in use

- **WEP (Wired Equivalent Privacy)** encryption uses a password to authenticate the host with the access point.
  - A packet sniffer can intercept packets and easily crack the password.
  - WEP has been known to be insecure since 2005 but is still in use today.
  - WPA keys were 64-bits long.

- **WPA (Wi-Fi Protected Access)** and **WPA2** use a password to create a handshake (which creates a unique one-time password) between the host and the access point.
  - A packet sniffer can intercept packets during the handshake process and identify the password.
  - WPA uses 256-bit keys
  - WPA2 uses AES encryption algorithms and has replaced WPA

- **WPA Enterprise** uses a RADIUS server to authenticate the identity of the host attempting to connect. The host will typically present a digitally signed certificate to the RADIUS server (i.e. the host computer must have a certificate installed to connect to the network). Another option is for the host to sign in to the wireless network by entering a username and password. Certificate-based WPA Enterprise is difficult to break, provided that the certificates are digitally signed using a strong algorithm and that there are no other flaws in the access point or RADIUS server. Username/password based WPA Enterprise can be broken if the username/password are intercepted. An attacker could set up a rogue access point broadcasting the same SSID and then intercept usernames/passwords.

- **WPA3** is under development but is expected to replace WPA2.

- **CCMP**, or **Counter Mode Cipher Block Chaining Message Authentication Code Protocol (Counter Mode CBC-MAC Protocol)** is the encryption protocol used by WPA
  - Uses Counter CTR mode ciphers to secure the data being transmitted (a block cipher)
  - Uses CBC-MAC to verify that the message has not been modified in transmission
  - The CCMP Data Unit contains
    - MAC header with source and destination
    - CCMP header
    - Data being transmitted
    - Message Integrity Code
    - Frame Check Sequence
  - CCMP ensures
    - Data confidentiality
    - Authentication (validates the identity of the user)

- Access control for Wi-Fi networks
  - CCMP can be attacked with a Meet in the Middle attack

- **TKIP** was a standard that was introduced to temporarily replace WEP.
  - WEP had been broken and the Wi-Fi alliance needed a quick solution to replace it without forcing customers to replace physical hardware
  - TKIP is no longer considered secure
  - TKIP uses the same functions as WEP, except that it
    - Adds an initialization vector to the secret key
    - Uses a sequence counter to prevent replay attacks
    - Uses a 64-bit Message Integrity Check
    - Encrypts every data packet with a unique encryption key

Authentication Protocols

There are many authentication protocols for wireless technology

- **EAP**
  - **Extensible Authentication Protocol.**
  - EAP is a framework for providing authentication, but there are more than 40 possible methods that can be used
  - RFC 5247.has defined EAP
  - Each vendor may have more specific requirements and new protocols are being developed all the time

- **LEAP**
  - **Lightweight Extensible Authentication Protocol**
  - Developed by Cisco
  - LEAP is not supported by Windows but is supported by many third-party applications
  - Cisco does not recommend using LEAP anymore because it does not protect user credentials

- **PEAP**
  - **Protected Extensible Authentication Protocol**
  - Originally, EAP assumed that communications would be secure; therefore, it did not provide a mechanism to secure the data being transmitted.
  - PEAP corrects this by providing a secure TLS tunnel
  - A server-side certificate is used to create a PKI tunnel

- **EAP-NOOB**
  - **Nimble out-of-band authentication for EAP**
  - Used by devices that do not have preloaded authentication information such as Internet of Things devices
  - The user must assist the device in connecting via an out of band channel
  - There are different connection options including QR codes and NFC
  - Ephemeral Elliptic Curve Diffie-Hellman (ECDHE) exchange takes place over the in-band EAP channel. The user then provides the out-of-band channel message from the server to the device or from the device to the server, depending on what is required.

- **EAP-FAST**
  - **Flexible Authentication via Secure Tunneling**
  - Designed by Cisco to replace LEAP
  - Three parts

- In band provisioning via Diffie-Hellman. The client is provided with a shared secret.
- Tunnel establishment. A tunnel is established between the server and the client.
- Authentication. The user is authenticated

- **EAP-TLS.**
  - **EAP – Transport Layer Security**
  - Uses TLS (Transport Layer Security) as its protocol.
  - All wireless manufacturers support EAP-TLS
  - Considered very secure
  - EAP-TLS requires a client-side certificate. When a system is authenticated with a certificate, a password is not required. Even if a hacker obtained the username/password, without a certificate, the hacker would not be able to connect to the Wi-Fi.
  - EAP is not implemented as widely as it should be because it requires the certificate

- **EAP-TTLS**
  - **EAP Tunneled Transport Layer Security**
  - Extends TLS so that the client does not require a certificate. Instead, the server creates a tunnel with the client. The client can then authenticate to the server using a legacy password or other authentication method. The tunnel protects the client from eavesdropping.

- **IEEE 802.1X**
  - IEEE 802.1X is a standard for Network Access Control. It allows a device to authenticate when connecting to a LAN or WAN.
  - There are three devices
    - The supplicant is the device that chooses to connect to the LAN/WAN. It could be a laptop, desktop, smartphone, tablet, or other computing device
    - The authenticator is a network device that allows/denies access. It could be a switch, a router, a firewall, or a proxy server.
    - The authentication server is a server that decides whether a particular device should be granted access
  - The procedure
    - The supplicant connects to the network
    - The authenticator (switch) detects the new supplicant and automatically sets the port to an unauthenticated state. Only traffic related to 802.1X is permitted.
    - The authenticator sends frames to the supplicant. These frames demand that the supplicant provide credentials such as a user ID. The frames are sent on

the local network segment to a specific address (01:80:C2:00:00:03). The supplicant listens for messages on this address.

- The supplicant replies to the message with an EAP-Response Identity frame
- The authenticator sends the supplicant's response to an authentication server
- The authentication server and the supplicant negotiate an authentication method. The server and the supplicant may support different methods and must agree on one. The negotiation methods are transported through the authenticator.
- The authentication server attempts to authenticate the suppliant. If successful, the authenticator changes the port status to authorized. If unsuccessful, the authenticator keeps the port as unauthorized.
- When the supplicant logs off or is disconnected, the authenticator changes the port status back to unauthorized. When the supplicant logs off, it sends an EAPOL-Logoff message to the authenticator.

  o Security Risks
    - A hacker can physically insert himself between the port and the authenticated computer, and then use the authenticated port
    - A DDOS attack can take place. A hacker can create EAPOL-logoff messages with the MAC address of the supplicant and send them to the authenticator, forcing the port to go into an unauthorized state. This would force the supplicant to go offline.

- **RADIUS Federation**
  o RADIUS provides network access
  o A user requests access from a Network Access Server. The request may contain a username, password, and/or certificate
  o The Network Access Server requests access from the RADIUS server
  o The RADIUS server verifies the user's identity. This could come from a database file stored locally, or from a connection to another service such as LDAP, Active Directory, or Kerberos
  o The RADIUS server can issue one of three responses
    - Access Deny
    - Access Accept. The RADIUS server performs further checks to ensure that the user is provided access to only the services that he is entitled to. RADIUS allows an administrator to provide granular access control.
    - Access Challenge. The RADIUS server requests additional information from the user, such as a PIN or smart card. The user and the RADIUS server may establish a secure tunnel to exchange the additional authentication data, in a way that shields it from the Network Access Server.

- When access is granted, a "Start" record is created. The Network Access Server sends a "start" command to the RADIUS server, which indicates that the user can begin access. When access is terminated, a "Stop" command is sent.
- Roaming
  - A RADIUS user can roam on multiple networks with the same RADIUS credentials
  - Each network is known as a realm (like a domain)
  - Each user is assigned to a specific realm (the realm may be appended to the username)
  - If a user attempts to connect to a network outside his realm
    - The user connects to the RADIUS server and provides his username and realm
    - The RADIUS server checks to see if it is configured to accept users from that realm
    - The RADIUS server sends the request to the RADIUS server belonging to the user's realm via a proxy. RADIUS servers should be configured to connect via a secure tunnel, because the default MD5 encryption of user credentials is weak.
- Source Code
  - RADIUS is open source
  - A specific vendor can implement a customized version of RADIUS, which may contain Vendor Specific Attributes

Methods

There are several methods for implementing Wi-Fi (WPA2) security.

- **PSK – Pre-Shared Key**
  - The server and the client agree on a pre-shard key
  - They use the key to establish a stronger session key
  - If the Pre-Shared Key is compromised, a hacker can use it to connect to the network
  - A Pre-Shared key could be compromised by a rogue employee, a shoulder surfer, or by brute force. WPA3 will reduce the risk of brute force attacks.

- Enterprise
  - WPA2 enterprise uses a RADIUS server to authenticate each user
  - There are several methods of authentication available through RADIUS
  - Each device creates a tunnel between itself and a network
  - WPA2 Enterprise authenticates the user with the server (that is, the server verifies the identity of the user). WPA3 Enterprise will also require the user to verify the identity of the server. The server's certificate will need to be installed on the user's device.

- **Open**
  - An open network is one where anybody can connect, and there is no security
  - An open network is never a good idea unless it incorporates a Captive Portal

WPS

- WPS, or Wireless Protected Setup, was a feature that allowed devices to connect to a wireless network without having to enter a security key. It was designed for cheaper devices such as printers (that often didn't have a keypad/touchscreen interface to enter the key). A user could connect their printer to the network by pressing the "WPS" button on their access point and then waiting for it to pair with their wireless device.
- WPS exchanges an 8-digit code with the wireless device, which can be easily detected through brute force. The eighth digit of the code is a checksum, and the first four digits are evaluated separately from the next three. WPS therefore requires a maximum of 11,000 attempts to brute force it.
- WPS is available on residential-grade equipment

Captive Portals

- A Captive Portal is a website that shows up when an unauthorized user connects to a Wi-Fi network

- Typically, a captive portal is installed on an open "guest" network such as at a hotel, airport, shopping mall, or library
- The user is required to authenticate using a username/password or just a password
- The captive portal may require the user to pay to access the internet (or to access the internet at a faster speed)
- The user will need to agree to an Acceptable Use Policy agreement; the vendor may be able to monitor the type and amount of traffic generated by the user
- The captive portal is a web page that would be hosted on an internal server or firewall.
- Essentially, http (port 80) and https (port 445) traffic is redirected to the captive portal. The firewall may also redirect all DNS traffic to send the user to the captive portal page.
- While the user is unauthenticated, the firewall should be configured to block any traffic outside of port 80 and port 445, and block any traffic external to the captive portal.
- If external traffic/ports are open, the user could circumvent the captive portal by establishing a VPN tunnel

6.4 Given a scenario, implement public key infrastructure

- *Components*
  - *CA*
  - *Intermediate CA*
  - *CRL*
  - *OCSP*
  - *CSR*
  - *Certificate*
  - *Public Key*
  - *Private Key*
  - *Object Identifiers (OID)*
- *Concepts*
  - *Online vs. Offline CA*
  - *Stapling*
  - *Pinning*
  - *Trust Model*
  - *Key Escrow*
  - *Certificate Chaining*
- *Types of Certificates*
  - *Wildcard*
  - *SAN*
  - *Code Signing*
  - *Self-Signed*
  - *Machine/Computer*
  - *Email*
  - *User*
  - *Root*
  - *Domain Validation*
  - *Extended Validation*
- *Certificate Formats*
  - *DER*
  - *PEM*
  - *PFX*
  - *CER*
  - *P12*
  - *P7B*

Components

A Public Key Infrastructure has several important components, which work together.

- **CA. The CA is the Certification Authority**. The CA is responsible for issuing certificates. The CA is trusted to issue a certificate.
    - The CA will have a certificate of its own. It uses its certificate to digitally sign certificates that it issues.
    - A web browser or computer will automatically trust the certification authority. It will be equipped with the certificates of the most common authorities. A user choose to trust additional CAs by installing their certificates.
    - When a user attempts to visit a secure website, the website's server will present a certificate. The certificate proves the identity of the website. The certificate will be signed by a certifying authority.
    - The user's computer verifies the signature on the certificate.
    - The CA's certificate is also known as a root certificate.
    - The most popular CAs are
        - Comodo
        - Symantec
        - GoDaddy
        - GlobalSign

- **Intermediate CA**
    - Instead of signing a certificate with the root certificate, a CA can create a certificate known as the intermediate certificate. The CA signs the intermediate certificate with its root certificate.
    - The CA then uses the intermediate certificate to sign the certificates that it issues.
    - Why? If the root certificate is compromised, a hacker could create fake certificates and sign them. The CA would need to revoke every certificate that it signed with that root certificate. A large CA could have issued millions of certificates.
    - The CA could create a tree of certificates. It could create multiple intermediate certificates (signed by the root certificate), and then create multiple additional intermediate certificates, signed by the intermediate certificates.
    - When a user installs a certificate, they may need to also install and trust the intermediate certificates. If an intermediate certificate is compromised, fewer certificates are vulnerable, then if a root certificate was compromised.

- **CRL**
    - **A CRL is a Certificate Revocation List**
    - Each CA maintains a list of certificates that it has revoked prior to their expiry dates (certificates automatically expire after a specific period)

578

- A certificate can be revoked
  - If it was improperly issued
  - Its private key was compromised
  - If the user violated the terms of use of the certificate issuer
- The CRL is digitally signed by the CA.
- Only the CA can modify an entry on the CRL.
- Each time a certificate is presented, its validity should be checked against the CRL. For example, each time you visit a website, your web browser will check that website's certificate's validity against the CRL.
- The main problem with the CRL is that it requires a certificate checker to have an online connection to the CRL. If the CRL is unavailable or unreachable, then the user will not be able to complete the operation requiring the certificate.
- A user can make an offline copy of the CRL and validate certificates against the offline copy. The disadvantage is that the offline copy may not be updated, which would allow a user to accept certificates that have been revoked.
- A certificate can be suspended (put on hold). A suspended certificate is effectively revoked but can be returned to active status.

- **OCSP**
  - CRLs are being replaced with the Online Certificate Status Protocol
  - An OCSP request contains less data than a CRL
  - An OCSP responder is a server that receives requests to determine whether a certificate is valid. The responder returns a yes/no response, which is digitally signed by the CA's certificate.

- **CSR**
  - **Certificate Signing Request**
  - An applicant (a user/server that requires a certificate) creates a CSR and sends it to the CA to obtain the certificate
  - The applicant creates a private key and uses it to generate a public key
  - The applicant generates a CSR, which contains
    - Certification Request Information (the name of the applicant, the website/server that needs to be secured, etc.). This information also includes the applicant's public key.
    - Signature Algorithm Information
    - Digital Signature
  - The CA receives the CSR and verifies that the information inside it is accurate
  - The CA creates a certificate using the information provided by the CSR, and signs it with its root or intermediate certificate
  - The CA encrypts the signed certificate with the applicant's public key. Remember that the CA must send the applicant a certificate with a private key, which cannot be

disclosed. Only the applicant can decrypt the signed certificate. That is the reason for having the applicant create a public/private key pair.

- **Certificate**
  - A certificate is a file that proves the identity of a computer or person
  - The X.509 standard governs the format of each certificate
  - The certificate contains
    - The identity of its owner
    - An expiry date
    - An issue date
    - A digital signature of the CA that issued it
    - The name of the CA that issued it
    - A serial number
    - The permitted uses of the certificate
    - Additional information as required

- **Public Key**
  - In public key cryptography, a public key is a key that is used to encrypt messages or verify digital signatures
  - The public key is generally publicly available so that others can use it to validate signatures and so that they can encrypt messages
  - It is important that a user relying on a public key can verify that a specific public key belongs to the user that it claims to belong to

- **Private Key**
  - The private key is secret
  - A private key is issued to a user or server
  - The private key is used to generate the public key
  - The private key is used to digitally sign documents and to decrypt messages that were encrypted with the corresponding public key

- **Object Identifiers (OID)**
  - An object identifier is a unique number
  - Each item in the certificate is labeled with an object identifier

Concepts

Some concepts for Public Key Cryptography

- **Online vs. Offline CA**
  - An offline certificate authority is one that does not access the internet
  - Recall that the certificates are trusted from the root certificate to the intermediate certificate to the local certificate
  - The root certificate is precious. If the root certificate is compromised, then all the certificates that it signed are also compromised. There could be millions of certificates.
  - To keep it safe, the root certificate can be kept offline. It can be brought online only when it is needed, such as when an intermediate certificate must be signed.
  - The root CA cannot host a CRL when it is offline. That is not an issue if the root is used to verify multiple intermediate CRLs.
  - A Validation Authority is another server that can verify if a certificate is valid or not, on behalf of an offline root CA. The validation authority will not be able to revoke a certificate, only verify its status. The validation authority will receive updates from the CA when additional certificates must be revoked.

- **Stapling**
  - The formal name of stapling is Online Certificate Status Protocol (OCSP) stapling
  - It is a process for checking if a certificate has been revoked
  - The CA may receive billions of requests regarding the validity of a certificate
    - Each time a web page secured by a certificate is loaded, the user's web browser asks the CA to validate the certificate. Consider a website like Amazon.com, where billions of requests are made every day
    - The requests could burden the CA
  - The solution is
    - The web server holding the certificate queries the CA at regular intervals
    - The CA responds with a proof of the server certificate's validity, which is signed by the CA
    - When a user visits the website, the web server "staples" the signed response to its certificate, and sends the entire package to the user's web browser
    - The web browser will only accept a stapled response that is signed by the CA; if the server is unable to provide a valid response, then the web browser will query the CA directly
  - If the certificate is revoked, but the stapled response is still valid, then it is possible for the user's web browser to accept a revoked certificate
  - Not all web browsers support stapling, and not all web servers support stapling

- **Pinning**
  - Key Pinning is a system where a certificate or key is associated with a host

- Consider that a user needs to connect to a host (a server of some kind).
- A hacker could spoof a DNS record and present a fake host, with a fake certificate. How does the user know that it should trust this host? How does the user know that this host is legitimate?
- How does pinning work?
  - The first time that a device connects to a host, and the host presents a certificate, the device pins the certificate to the host
  - The device expects to see the same certificate on subsequent connections
  - A hacker would need to hijack this connection the first time that a host connects (which is unlikely)
  - The certificate can be pinned to an application during development. This happens offline (before the application ever connects to the internet). A hacker would not be able to pin a fake certificate unless he gained access to the development environment.
- What can be pinned?
  - The certificate
    - Some web servers rotate their certificates (but the public key remains the same)
    - If an application pins a certificate that connects to a web server, then the application must be updated each time the certificate changes
    - Each time the application runs, it checks that the certificate it received from the host is the same one as the certificate that is pinned
  - The certificate's public key – subjectpublickeyinfo
    - The key is pinned
    - It might be difficult to extract a public key from a certificate
    - The application verifies that the pinned key is the same as the key that is received

- **Trust Model**
  - The trust model tells us how and when to trust a certificate. There are several different trust models.
  - **Direct Trust**
    - Every certificate is trusted directly
    - The user who receives the certificate verifies its validity with the CA
    - Direct trust is difficult because if a CA issues millions of certificates, it may not be able to verify all of them
  - **Hierarchical Trust**
    - Each certificate is signed by CA
    - The user trusts the CA

- If the user trusts the CA, then anything that the CA has signed is also trusted; therefore, intermediate certificates are also trusted
- The certificates form a tree of trust
- If a certificate is signed by something that the CA has indirectly signed, then it is trusted
- The hierarchical trust only operates in one direction; the CA would never trust something signed by a user
- If two users share a common trusted CA, they will trust each other provided they can verify the entire chain of certificates from each user to the CA

  o **Indirect Trust**
  - Certificates can be self signed, and self issued
  - A user or server can issue its own certificate. An organization may issue certificates for its internal use because certificates signed by a public CA will be more expensive.
  - A self-signed certificate is not signed by a CA but must still be trusted.
  - The user marks the certificate in his computer as trusted if the user can verify its source
  - Users or organizations that self-sign certificates may not maintain a CRL to notify stakeholders of the certificate revocation status

  o **Peer-to-Peer Trust**
  - When users do not share a common CA but must find a way to trust each other, they can use a Peer-to-Peer Trust
  - The participating CAs issue bidirectional certificates indicating that they trust each other
  - Since each user trusts everything that their CA trusts, then each user trusts the users belonging to the other CA
  - A Peer-to-Peer trust can function across multiple CAs, but then each CA must issue certificates for each of the other CAs in the group

- **Key Escrow**
  o The idea is that the government should be able to decrypt any form of encrypted communication, if it has a valid court order
  o Each person who uses encryption must deposit their private key in an escrow
  o If an encrypted communication is used to commit a crime, the government can go to a court and obtain an order allowing it to obtain a key from the escrow and decrypt the data.
  o The government may also be able to obtain the key from the escrow without a court order in the event of a threat to national security or to the life of an individual
  o A key escrow is bad because a corrupt individual in the government could use the escrow to unlock encrypted communications without any court order

- A key escrow could be hacked by a rogue third party or a foreign government. If the government has access to private keys, then anybody could have access to private keys.
- No key escrow exists in the United States or Canada, although the government has attempted to introduce one in the past
- There are many key disclosure laws which require persons to disclose their private keys in response to a court order
  - In Canada, a court will not compel key disclosure because people have the right to not self-incriminate themselves
  - In the United States, courts have ruled in favor of key disclosure and against key disclosure. It is difficult to predict how a court will rule.
  - In the UK, The Regulation of Investigatory Powers Act requires an individual to disclose keys even without a court order

- **Certificate Chaining**
  - A certificate chain is an order of certificates beginning at the root and continuing through the intermediate certificates and then to the final user certificate
  - Each certificate is signed by the certificate above it (the intermediate certificate is signed by the root certificate and the user certificate is signed by an intermediate certificate)
  - The root certificate is not signed
  - If a user trusts the root certificate then the user will trust any certificate in the chain

Types of Certificates

There are many types/features of certificates. A certificate can contain more than one feature.

- **Wildcard**. A wildcard certificate is one that can be used with multiple subdomains
  - Consider that amazon.com is a domain
  - If the amazon.com domain is secured by a wildcard certificate, then www.amazon.com, books.amazon.com, aws.amazon.com, and any other subdomain is also protected by the same certificate. The wildcard certificate would be called *.amazon.com
  - Typically, a certificate will protect the root domain (amazon.com) and the www subdomain (www.amazon.com) at no additional cost. A wildcard certificate that protects all subdomains is more expensive.
  - A wildcard certificate may not secure the second level subdomain such as fiction.books.amazon.com, unless the certificate is issued as a wildcard for books.amazon.com. The wildcard certificate would be called *.books.amazon.com
  - The following are not allowed
    - * (this would secure every possible domain)
    - *.com (this would secure every possible .com domain)
    - *.*.domain.com (this is a certificate with multiple wildcards in the same domain)
    - books.*.domain.com (this is not allowed because the wildcard is in the middle of the domain)
    - abcd*.domain.com (this is a partial wildcard; it would allow domains like abcdefgh.domain.com; it is allowed, but not accepted by major web browsers)

- **SAN**
  - A Subject Alternative Name certificate allows a user to host multiple SSL websites on the same IP address (typically an IP address must be bound to a certificate). IPv4 addresses are limited and a company may choose to host multiple websites on the same web server/IPv4 address
  - A SAN also allows a user to secure multiple domain names on the same certificate

- **Code Signing**
  - A code signing certificate allows a software developer to digitally sign their application
  - The users can verify that the software they are running is the legitimate version
  - Windows by default will not allow a non-digitally signed driver to be installed
  - Windows by default will not trust a software application that is not signed. Windows will display an alert saying that the publisher is unknown.

- o An application will also verify that software updates are signed by the legitimate developer

- **Self-Signed**
  - o A self-signed certificate is one that is signed by the user that issued it
  - o A self-signed certificate does not cost a user anything (as opposed to a CA-signed certificate which could cost thousands of dollars)
  - o The entity that signed a self-signed certificate could always generate a new certificate and sign it. Therefore, the values of the certificate should be manually validated before it is trusted

- **Machine/Computer**
  - o A machine/computer certificate secures a physical computer. It verifies the identity of the computer.

- **Email**
  - o An email certificate allows a user to secure and digitally sign an e-mail
  - o It is installed inside an e-mail application, such as Outlook

- **User**
  - o A user certificate verifies the identity of a user. It is not attached to any computer. The user certificate may be attached to a smart card

- **Root.**
  - o The root certificate is issued by the CA and is used to sign its intermediate certificates and any other certificates issued by the CA

- **Domain Validation**
  - o A domain validation certificate verifies the identity of a server
  - o The CA verifies that the person requesting a domain validation certificate is the owner of the domain (through whois records)
  - o www.example.com has a domain validation certificate, then users can be assured that they have accessed a web server that belongs to that domain (as opposed to having arrived at a rogue server because of DNS hijacking)

- **Extended Validation**
  - o An extended validation certificate verifies the identity of a server
  - o It also validates the legal entity that owns the domain/server
  - o The CA verifies that the person requesting a domain validation certificate is the owner of the domain. The CA also verifies the telephone number and physical address of the owner of the domain

- An extended validation certificate is more expensive than a regular domain validation certificate
- Web browsers previously displayed extended validation certificates with a green address bar, which also showed the name of the company to whom the certificate was issued
- EV certificates are no longer popular
- For example, if a rogue individual purchased www.amaz0n.com and attempted to secure it
  - The rogue individual would be able to obtain a domain validation certificate (since he is the owner of the domain)
  - The individual would not be able to obtain an extended validation certificate (at least not in the name of Amazon.com Inc., but possibly in the name of their own company); unless the individual managed to register a business entity with the same name but a different state. For example, Amazon.com is incorporated in Delaware; if an individual registered the company name in Texas, he could obtain a certificate. Amazon would need to be vigilant and protect their name.
- It is not possible to obtain a wildcard extended validation certificate
- The maximum duration is 397 days

Certificate Formats

X.509 is a standard that defines the public key certificate format.

The structure of the certificate

- Certificate
    - Version Number
    - Serial Number
    - Signature Algorithm ID
    - Issuer Name
    - Validity period
        - Not Before
        - Not After
    - Subject name
    - Subject Public Key Info
        - Public Key Algorithm
        - Subject Public Key
    - Issuer Unique Identifier (optional)
    - Subject Unique Identifier (optional)
    - Extensions (optional)
        - ...
- Certificate Signature Algorithm
- Certificate Signature

There are several file formats for storing a certificate. A certificate can be transformed from one format to another.

- **DER**
    - **Distinguished Encoding Rules**
    - Stored in binary format
- **PEM**
    - Container that could contain a single certificate or multiple certificate chains
    - A PEM file is a DER file that is base64 encoded
- **PFX**
    - **Encrypted PEM file**
    - The PFX file contains the public and private certificates
    - The PFX file can be decrypted into public and private certificates
    - A user can export the public and private certificates into a PFX file, which can then be transferred to another server
- **CER**

- - Canonical Encoding Rules
  - Stored in ASCII format
  - Recognized as a certificate by Windows (PEM is not)
- **P12**
  - **Encrypted PEM file**
  - The P12 file contains the public and private certificates
  - The P12 file can be decrypted into public and private certificates
- **P7B**
  - **PKCS number 7**
  - Certificate format used by Windows for key interchange